Live and Let Live

EVELYN M. PERRY

Live and Let Live

Diversity, Conflict, and Community in an Integrated Neighborhood

The University of North Carolina Press *Chapel Hill*

This book was published with the assistance of the Authors Fund of
the University of North Carolina Press.

Set in Arno Pro by Westchester Publishing Services
Manufactured in the United States of America

The University of North Carolina Press has been a member
of the Green Press Initiative since 2003.

Library of Congress Cataloging-in-Publication Data
Names: Perry, Evelyn M., author.
Title: Live and let live : diversity, conflict, and community in an integrated
    neighborhood / Evelyn M. Perry.
Description: Chapel Hill : University of North Carolina Press, [2017] | Includes
    bibliographical references and index.
Identifiers: LCCN 2016038685 | ISBN 9781469631370 (cloth : alk. paper) |
    ISBN 9781469631387 (pbk   ) | ISBN 9781469631394 (ebook)
Subjects: LCSH: Cultural pluralism—Wisconsin—Milwaukee. | Riverwest
    (Milwaukee, Wis.)—Social conditions. | Riverwest (Milwaukee, Wis.)—
    Ethnic relations. | Minorities—Wisconsin—Milwaukee—Social conditions. |
    Community life—Wisconsin—Milwaukee. | Neighborhoods—Wisconsin—Milwaukee.
Classification: LCC HN80.M58 P47 2017 | DDC 305.8009775/95—dc23 LC record
    available at https://lccn.loc.gov/2016038685

Cover illustration: *Falcon Bowl* by Mike Fredrickson. Used courtesy of the artist.

For my parents,

Kathryn Senn Perry and Wilson David Perry

Contents

Illustrations

Acknowledgments

This book has been a community project in many ways. It is about community life, and it is the product of communal efforts. I want to acknowledge the significant contributions of those who supported the project.

First, I want to give special thanks to the generous people of Riverwest for welcoming me to the neighborhood and helping me learn about this unique spot in the world. All of those who sat down to chat with me about their experiences in Riverwest or invited me to share a slice of their daily life in the neighborhood have been invaluable teachers. I am deeply grateful for my Pierce Street neighbors, who made life on the block comfortable, colorful, and certainly captivating.

This project began in the Indiana University Department of Sociology, where my mentors and colleagues provided the perfect mix of challenge and support. I am grateful to Tom Gieryn for taking the Perry-Mata team under his wing and preaching the power of place. Tom's courage to write in his own voice inspired me to find my own. It has been a pleasure and an honor to work with Gerry Suttles, someone who gracefully combines a sharp, critical mind with enthusiasm, humor, and humility. I benefited tremendously from his fieldwork expertise and vast knowledge of all things urban. Rob Robinson is an excellent sociologist, an outstanding editor, and a trustworthy guide. His encouragement and unwavering support have been true gifts (and at a few key moments, they made all the difference). Elizabeth Armstrong helped me develop essential tools for the craft of qualitative research, a cultural lens, and an appreciation for the art of theory drawing. I am grateful to Bernice Pescosolido for meaningful and useful professional and intellectual guidance. She is an inspiring model for those who wish to employ the tools of our discipline for research, innovative pedagogy, institutional change, and social justice. I am indebted to my Colorado College mentors—Jeff Livesay, Margi Duncombe, and Kathy Giuffre—for starting me on this sociological journey. I strive to inspire my students as they inspired me.

Scholarship is a collective endeavor. I am incredibly lucky to have found so many smart colleagues/beautiful friends at Indiana University and Rhodes College, who feed my brain and my heart. Jason Beckfield, Gordon Bigelow, David Blouin, Katie Bolzendahl, Elizabeth Bridges, Kara Cebulko, Suzanna

Crage, Anita Davis, Kyle Dodson, Lindsay Ems, Judson Everitt, Emily Fairchild, Angela Frederick and Daniel Frederick, Ron Garcia, Claudia Geist, Kristin Geraty, Ernest Gibson, Kyle Grady, Judy Haas, Laura Hamilton, Julia Hanebrink, Sarah Hansen, Niki Hotchkiss, Charles Hughes, Rachel Jabaily, Heather "Shared Brain" Jamerson, Kimberly Kasper, Susan Kus, Jeanne "NeeNee" Lopiparo, Laura Loth, Geoff Maddox, Doris Maldonado, Joey Mata, Janice McCabe, Ann McCranie, Tom McGowan, Charles McKinney, Milton Moreland, Shelley Nelson, Shiri Noy, Brea Perry, Natalie Person, Nate Plageman, Melissa Quintela, Rashawn Ray, Ashanté Reese, Jason Richards and Rashna Richards, Zandria Robinson (connector extraordinaire), Michael Rosenbaum, Patrick Sachweh, Reinhard Schunck, Abigail Sewell, Christi Smith, Jessica Sprague-Jones, Robert Strandburg, Jenny Stuber, Brian Sweeney, Amanda Tanner, Walt Tennyson, Elizabeth Thomas, Francesca Tronchin, Jocelyn Viterna, Marsha Walton, Lisa Weber-Raley, Katie White, Chris Whitsel, and Adrianne Williams have, each in his or her own way, contributed to the completion of this project.

I am fortunate to have learned from and studied with assorted superheroes along this journey, including Sonali Balajee, Mark Behr, Emily Bowman, Joey Feinstein, Teya Gamble, Kim Jenkins, Bart Mallard, Hilary Povec, Josh Povec, and Cheryl Roorda. I thank Shelby Haschker and Sigrun Olafsdottir for being the biggest and best cheerleaders in the history of the universe.

I am grateful for the financial support of the United States Department of Housing and Urban Development and the National Science Foundation. The research grants awarded by these institutions supported this project in many ways, including making it possible for me to hire Jenny Urbanek, a brilliant undergraduate research assistant. I am grateful for Jenny's contributions of time, effort, creativity, spirit, and insight.

I feel so fortunate to have worked with the University of North Carolina Press. Joe Parsons, an enthusiastic and engaging editor and true advocate, expertly guided my project from a pile of words to a book. Allie Shay and the rest of the UNC Press team provided exceptional support. I want to thank Japonica Brown-Saracino and Sarah Mayorga-Gallo for providing encouraging, critical, and constructive feedback, which undoubtedly helped me improve the book.

I am indebted to my Mosaic Milwaukee family—Genyne Edwards, John Fitzgerald, Ossie Kendrix, and June Perry—for their friendship and for being models of living with integrity, empathy, and purpose. This book would not have been possible without the support of my Maxie's Southern Comfort family, who provided both rent money and much-needed fun. Thank you mighty Weeds and pickup soccer stars, for delivering a steady dose of joy and turf burn.

I am incredibly grateful to Wilson David Perry and Kathryn Senn Perry—to whom I dedicate this book—for teaching me about compassion and justice; for their encouragement; and for their generous material, moral, intellectual, and emotional support. My Milwaukee family—including Mom, Dad, Lizzy Perry, Danny Poppert, Maureen O'Grady, Patrick O'Grady, Megan O'Grady, Derek Jorgensen, Jackson, Theo, Augie, Finley, Lulu, and Ruby—provided me with enough love, wisdom, hugs, food, beers, soccer games, laughter, dance parties, and laundry detergent to see this project through. I thank my sister, Lizzy, for setting a good example from day one. She is (and always has been) an inspiration to me.

I thank Daniel O'Grady for making this book possible. You have met the challenges of being an academic's partner with humor and grace. I recall countless times that you helped me work through intellectual puzzles (usually while walking our dog, Vision). Your keen observations of people and places and your unique storytelling gifts have shaped how I see and show my work. Thank you for throwing epic block parties, waiting by the fire in the backyard, and making every day of my life better. Finally, I am grateful to Olivia Perry O'Grady for showing up and turning everything beautifully upside down.

Live and Let Live

CHAPTER ONE

Interrogating Integration

Diversity can work, but making it work is a messy, contentious business.
—Peter Skerry, "Beyond Sushiology: Does Diversity Work?"

We are in a bind. On the one hand, the common and sociological wisdom is that residential racial and economic integration holds great promise for bridging social divides and reducing inequality in the United States. On the other hand, it seems we're not very good at living with difference. Researchers have found that the tensions and conflicts associated with heterogeneity pose significant challenges to community engagement, order, and stability. When it proves too difficult to fashion harmony out of dissonance, certain groups are pushed out or flee. The concentration on integration's potential or its expected failure has left us with little understanding of how residents of stably mixed neighborhoods manage to live with diversity.

In July 2007, I returned to my native Milwaukee, Wisconsin, and moved into a rented flat in the racially and economically mixed Riverwest neighborhood.[1] A student of cities and inequality, I was intrigued by this unusual place, which had managed to remain integrated for over three decades. Throughout that time, residents and onlookers had warned of impending sweeping changes. They had predicted that the neighborhood would be swallowed by the ghetto one day, and forecasted the arrival of the gentry the next. Yet Riverwest has neither tipped nor flipped. Somehow, neighborhood residents have figured out how to live with difference. Don Sitko, a police officer who works in the neighborhood, puzzles over this pluralistic place: "I think just any way you could possibly put it, that has to be the most diverse area I have ever seen. I would have to believe that if you wanted to build a sod hut, you could. And if you wanted to paint your house deer hunter's orange, you could do it. . . . I think everybody is striving to be something different, but you know what, they are all together. And they all seem, no matter who it is, to survive. . . . And I bet you if they had a block party, they would all come out and all hoist a beer, and do whatever they wanted to do. And nobody would think anything of it because that's the way Riverwest is. It's just unique." Although Riverwest may seem unique, particularly in a hyper-segregated city like Milwaukee, an increasing share of metropolitan neighborhoods are integrated.[2] Since cities in the United States are becoming more diverse, and heterogeneous communities more common, neighborhoods like Riverwest warrant attention.

Segregation's Harms

"Segregation is benign." "People just prefer neighbors who are like them." These everyday understandings of residential segregation align with the comforting myth of a postracial, equal opportunity United States. Yet segregation is, in fact, an engine of inequality. Neighborhoods bundle different combinations of resources and troubles. There is considerable variation in the quality of public schools and neighborhood services; the responsiveness of public servants; levels of crime and violence; exposure to environmental hazards; access to transportation, health care, and nutritious food; and local connections to helpful social networks. A particular address, then, is linked to a set of assets and obstacles that influence one's choices and perspective. Residential segregation concentrates advantages and disadvantages in ways that constrain the social mobility of large segments of minority populations, heighten tensions in interracial and interclass relations, and maintain a profoundly uneven geography of opportunity.[3]

Though we have substantially deepened our understanding of racial segregation over the last century, we know relatively little about residential *integration*. Diverse communities have typically received scholarly attention as places in transition—sites of neighborhood racial change. From Schelling's influential model of racial "tipping," in which whites flee neighborhoods once a nonwhite threshold is reached, to William Julius Wilson and Richard Taub's recent exploration of racial dynamics in four Chicago neighborhoods, racially diverse communities are characterized as fragile, unstable, and vulnerable to resegregation.[4]

However, recent research indicates that not only are many integrated neighborhoods stable over time, but the number of racially mixed neighborhoods is on the rise.[5] The broad demographic changes driving the growing diversification of urban areas (e.g., globalization and immigration), coupled with the slow but steady declines in housing discrimination and black–white segregation, suggest that the diverse neighborhood is an expanding urban form.[6] Because the growth of racially mixed communities is relatively recent, however, the processes contributing to the *durability* of neighborhood heterogeneity have received little scholarly attention.[7]

Economic segregation also shapes the geographic dimension of inequality in the United States. Although the majority of its neighborhoods are middle class or mixed income, the United States has increasingly become residentially segregated by class over the last few decades.[8] US2010 Project researchers find that "the share of the population in large and moderate-sized metropolitan areas who live in the poorest and most affluent neighborhoods has more than doubled since 1970."[9] We are witnessing an intensification of class-based community divides within metropolitan areas, marked by the growing residential isolation of poor and affluent households and a shrinking share of neighborhoods that are middle class or economically mixed.[10] This spatial manifestation of growing income inequality in the United States restricts opportunities for economic mobility.[11] It exacerbates inequalities in labor market and educational success, as well as access to public goods and services, quality health care, and a healthy and safe neighborhood environment.[12]

Living in enclaves of sameness also limits opportunities for meaningful interclass and interracial interactions, and restricts the development of relationships across social divides. For example, whites who grow up in racially isolated environments tend to maintain segregated social lives, even in more integrated work and school settings.[13] These experiences of isolation, in turn, shape racial attitudes and understandings. Segregation fosters a sense of white racial solidarity and superiority and bolsters negative views of racial others.[14] The growth of islands of affluence and poverty may similarly thwart the cultivation of empathy. It is not difficult to imagine how the concentration of those with considerable power and influence in elite enclaves might support the adoption of divisive understandings of social problems and hamper the development of a sense of common fate and shared responsibility. Such perspectives, formed and fueled in economic isolation, may be funneled into policies and practices that have a huge impact on the lives of poor, working-class, and middle-class people.[15] When we bridge social distances, however, assigning blame and responsibility becomes far more complicated.

Integration: Potential, Pitfalls, and Paradoxes

There are those who believe that the very existence of Riverwest, a diverse neighborhood in the heart of hypersegregated Milwaukee, is reason for celebration. In the midst of racial tensions, the widening gap between rich and poor, and an intractable and often poisonous urban–suburban divide, coexistence is possible. When race and class inequalities persist despite remarkable gains associated with the integration of once segregated or exclusive social spheres (e.g., education, work, and politics), some pin their hopes of progress on residential integration: if we can figure out how to live together in shared neighborhoods, maybe we can create a more just society.

Public policy makers incorporate such thinking into strategies to decon-
centrate poverty and expand access to opportunity-rich communities. These
integration initiatives take a variety of forms. People-focused residential mobility programs like Gautreaux and Moving to Opportunity provide poor
families with housing vouchers to relocate to lower-poverty (and, at times,
more racially diverse) neighborhoods. The Department of Housing and Urban Development (HUD) combined relocation voucher provision with a
place-focused program, HOPE VI, which supported the replacement of distressed public housing with mixed-income housing. HUD's Choice Neighborhoods program embeds a similar strategy in a more comprehensive
approach to revitalizing communities with distressed public or subsidized
housing. The rationales for all these programs are rooted in the belief that
positive residential changes—moves to higher-resource neighborhoods, substantial local investment, income mixing—will generate positive changes
for individuals and families. However, evidence about the success of top-
down, policy-driven integration efforts is decidedly mixed.[16]

Social scientists with a range of research interests also endorse the integration "solution." They argue that socially mixed neighborhoods have the
potential to improve race relations, build coalitions across class divides, reduce prejudice and discrimination, enrich civil society, strengthen democracy, drive innovation, and more evenly distribute opportunities in ways that
challenge existing class- and race-based inequalities.

How might diverse communities work such magic? There are a number
of core assumptions underlying arguments about integration's powerful
potential. The first assumption is that diverse neighborhoods foster meaningful and useful relationships across social differences. Such connections
might change attitudes about stigmatized "others," link people to previously
inaccessible resources (e.g., information about jobs), or create a broader "we"
identity. The second assumption is that the right mix of people has a positive impact on community life. Those who are privileged by virtue of class or
race (i.e., those who are white) can leverage that advantage to benefit the
neighborhood—for example, by attracting private amenities or exerting
political pressure to improve local public services. Although rarely explicitly
stated, some believe that the presence of relatively advantaged residents will
encourage community members to adopt "mainstream" goals and enforce
"mainstream" standards of behavior. Such assimilationist shifts theoretically support individuals and families in upward social mobility as well as
collaborative efforts to improve local livability (reducing crime, developing
amenities). Difference-bridging social ties and an advantageous mix of residents,

then, are key mechanisms that theoretically link heterogeneous neighborhoods to an array of expected benefits.

But not everyone embraces such a rosy view of socially mixed places. Many approach diversity as a problem, arguing that heterogeneity breeds conflict, tension, and antipathy. Diversity poses persistent challenges. City politicians and planners struggle to manage competing interests in the multicultural metropolis. Community organizations develop all manner of programs to fashion harmony out of urban social dissonance. Social theorists continue to ponder how to create order in diverse—and therefore disorderly—cities.

Does the research on heterogeneous communities settle this debate? There is some evidence that suggests that socially mixed neighborhoods can positively impact intercultural relations by supporting the development of cross-race social ties and improving attitudes about racial others.[17] However, contrary to the expectations of champions of social diversity, socially mixed communities are often discordant places. Neighborhood diversity hampers cooperation and interaction with neighbors; reduces mutual trust, social cohesion, and civic engagement; makes it difficult for residents to achieve shared goals; and is associated with increased crime, instability, and social exclusion.[18] It appears that what is good for transcending social divides is bad for community.

Many observers of social life have contemplated the multiple paradoxes of integration.[19] As they struggle to make sense of this contradictory urban form that improves race and class relations while undermining local quality of life, they unearth fundamental tensions between diversity and community. Iris Marion Young argues that the goals of unity and shared values built into the community ideal require denial or even erasure of social differences. "The most serious political consequence of the desire for community . . . is that it often operates to exclude or oppress those experienced as different."[20] These tensions are also expressed in popular discourse. When idealistic celebrations of multiculturalism run up against the messy complexities of dealing with difference, diversity talk often devolves into calls for cultural assimilation.[21] This begs the question: assimilation into what—whiteness? the middle-class mainstream?

For Mary Pattillo, these tensions are at the heart of a central "conundrum of integration politics": "Promoting integration as the means to improve the lives of Blacks stigmatizes Black people and Black spaces and valorizes Whiteness as both the symbol of opportunity and the measuring stick for equality. In turn, such stigmatization of Blacks and Black spaces is precisely what foils efforts toward integration. After all, why would anyone *else* want to live around or interact with a group that is discouraged from being around itself? . . . Poverty is a highly stigmatized condition. Working to get poor people away from other poor people, and around nonpoor people, reaffirms the stigma of poverty, and affirms the decisions of nonpoor people to move 'up and out.'"[22] It seems we have few readily available models for creating solidarity in socially mixed groups without enforcing sameness or denigrating difference.

What has been lost in all this talk of integration's promise, pitfalls, and paradoxes is an understanding of how integration is *lived*. The overwhelming attention to products (What can integration do?) has eclipsed process (How is integration done?).[23] Might an examination of the everyday "doing" of diversity shed some light on its inherent contradictions? J. Eric Oliver calls for such an examination in the conclusion of his empirical investigation of the multiple paradoxes of residential racial integration: "The most important problem with our romantic notions about integration is that we have little understanding of how it works in practice, particularly for people's feelings of community and belonging. If our primary concern is building a sense of connection and shared purpose among America's different racial groups, then one of our crucial points of attention should be on how people in integrated settings experience community life."[24] Investigating on-the-ground integration practices may also shed light on critical questions about the potential for integration to disrupt powerful and entrenched place-based processes that reproduce economic and racial inequalities.

This book begins to fill these gaps in our understanding of integration through an exploration of how residents of a diverse neighborhood make sense of their local experiences. How do Riverwest residents negotiate difference in everyday community life? What kinds of challenges and opportunities are presented to those living in diverse communities, and how do they respond? Do residents perceive their neighborhoods as positive, problem-filled, or promising places? How do residents manage the tensions between diversity and community? Can socially mixed neighborhoods redress the cumulative harms of residential economic and racial segregation?

Emplacing Meaning and Action: The Role of Culture

One analytic approach to neighborhoods is to treat them as containers of descriptive statistics: poverty rate, percent of population that is white, proportion of houses that are owner occupied, average educational attainment level, and so on. Taken together, these different features of a particular place form an approximation of the local social context. Approaching neighborhoods in this way facilitates useful comparisons between places. Such comparisons have convincingly demonstrated that where you live influences what you do, what you get, and how well your neighborhood is able to solve shared problems.[25] Yet we still know relatively little about *how* neighborhoods influence our individual and communal lives. How do neighborhoods shape the perceptions, behaviors, and opportunities of those who live in them?

To better understand these social processes, I approach Riverwest not as a bundle of variables or backdrops but as a *place*. This requires, according to Thomas Gieryn, attention to three key elements of place: geographic location, material form, and investment with meaning (i.e., culture).[26] A central strength of a place-sensitive approach is that it allows for a more expansive assessment of what is *shared* by residents, enhancing the set of tools we employ to understand how and why neighborhoods matter. This book sheds light on the paradoxes of diversity by demonstrating how the demographic mix in Riverwest together with key place features—its location as a buffer neighborhood, the design of its housing stock and division into residential blocks, and residents' interpretations of the neighborhood—affect intergroup relations and the coordination of daily local life.

I put particular emphasis on Gieryn's third element of place: culture—that is, shared ways of perceiving and doing. "The very idea of 'neighborhood' is not inherent in any arrangement of streets and houses, but is rather an ongoing practical and discursive production/imagining of a people."[27] The stories people tell about a particular place (its identity, residents, history, and imagined future) contain and transmit ideas about local values, standards, social boundaries, and practices. Analysis of local culture reveals how a place is collectively constructed through investments of meaning that, in turn, influence the ways in which people act in and toward that place.[28] For example, in a study of a Latino housing project in Boston, Mario Small finds that residents' neighborhood frames—the sets of cultural categories through which they make sense of their neighborhood and define its role in their lives—affect their levels of local civic participation. Those whose frames are embedded in the neighborhood's history of powerful political engagement are much more likely to participate in local efforts than are those who view their neighborhood as the "projects."[29]

In another study of neighborhood framing, Japonica Brown-Saracino looks at how those who move to new communities seeking "authentic" community work to preserve the character of their new neighborhood. These people enact strategies to protect what they see as the neighborhood's authenticity, including organizing efforts to prevent the displacement of longtime residents.[30] Their actions, then, are linked to their understandings of where they live. In her study of a working-class Chicago neighborhood, Maria Kefalas demonstrates how a shared sense of place shapes local responses to perceived threats and the maintenance of symbolic boundaries between the neighborhood and the encroaching ghetto.[31] In all of these studies, local culture provides a guidebook for neighborhood navigation. Through regular interactions in a shared place, residents learn how to read local cues and act in accordance with local rules.

All neighborhoods, be they bastions of sameness or social bricolage, transmit lessons about difference, belonging, and worth. Residents' evaluations of their neighborhood environment inevitably entail boundary drawing. Urban ethnographers routinely identify patterns in cultural classification, including determining who is and who is not a "real" community member, a threat, or an acceptable neighbor; separating people into status groups; distinguishing between codes of conduct; or demarcating between safe and unsafe places.[32] These symbolic categorization schemes can have very real consequences for how people treat one another and how resources and opportunities are distributed. Residents draw on shared notions of who belongs, what it means to be a good neighbor, and what constitutes a problem to guide everyday encounters. In the aggregate, these encounters constitute patterns of inclusion and exclusion. Of course, local interpretations do not exist in a vacuum; they are influenced by broader social, economic, and political forces. Places filter, mold, and rework prevailing cultural frames in ways that can maintain or challenge dominant understandings of difference and, by extension, maintain or challenge existing inequalities.[33]

This book examines how Riverwest residents construct their neighborhood and carve out their place in it. I focus primarily on block-level social processes, which illuminate patterns in the day-to-day use of local culture and demonstrate how neighborhood frames offer distinct organizing principles for dealing with difference.

Difference Negotiation

The residents of heterogeneous neighborhoods regularly confront practices (leisure activities, economic activities, property maintenance, communication styles, the use of public space, consumption practices, parenting approaches) that differ from their own. These differences may be embraced, tolerated, romanticized, ignored, challenged, condemned, or even criminalized. Indeed, Riverwest residents deal with difference differently.

Keith Bennett's Take

One of the things we need to do with the diversity in this neighborhood is to stop being so forgiving. I don't care whether you are black, white, or Hispanic. When you are a bum, you're a bum and you are outta here. I think they cut them too much slack. I think everybody is so afraid of stepping in and saying, "This has got to stop." "Oh, you're a racist." "No, this has got to stop." But the moment they use that, everybody backs off. "Oooo, maybe we just don't understand their culture." What? The woman is yelling, "Get in here you little motherfucker!" to a two-year-old child in the street. I'm not going to put up with that!

Tamika Evans's Take

A really attractive gentleman and his friend—two guys in this really nice car—they got the top down, you know, they're stylin'. They're in front of my house. And they throw—the car is immaculately clean—they throw a piece of paper out of the car. And I'm working in my garden. . . . That crossed the line. So I walked over, picked it up, and I said, "Honey, you're way too handsome to be throwing garbage out of a car. Now, this neighborhood may not be pristine, but you look like you've got too much going on to throw garbage out of a car. Not cool." He was like, "Aw, ma'am, I'm sorry, I'm sorry, I'm sorry, I'm sorry, sorry sorry sorry." Done. It's an easy place to live. The world is an easy place to live if you just let it be. So there's another neighbor that I have—I believe this gentleman and his wife are renting the house—and it's . . . kitty-corner across the alley from me. And they've got a fire pit outside. Once in a while they have a party. And like, at two o'clock in the morning, the music is still "dun dun dun dun dun a dun dun dun dun dun," and they're not even outside. And if I look out—if it wakes me up, and I look out, and I still see people? I leave it. Because part of living in my neighborhood is that, if my windows are open—'cause I don't have air conditioning—somebody might be partying on the weekend at two in the morning, and I need to get over it. 'Cause, it's not like they do this every night. And you know what? I could close the window, crank up the fan, and I'll be fine. So that's what I did. . . . The guys in the car were black. The guy and his wife who have the parties, they're white. The people directly behind me are Hispanic. And the son used to come in, like Friday night, and he'd have rap music really loud, and his windows down, pulling into the garage. And what can I say? Nothing! This is my hood! This is the way some people roll! It's five minutes. I'll go back to sleep if I'm really tired. 'Cause my bedroom is right at the back of the house, on the alley. And anytime that I'm gardening and have NPR blasting, I've never heard anyone complain. You know?[34]

In this book, I argue that neighborhoods play a significant role in shaping how residents make sense of and manage difference. Local culture provides a shared rubric for neighborhood navigation that influences residents' everyday practices: their social control strategies, interactions with neighbors, and interpretations of their proximate environment. For example, while some residents, like Keith, attempt to enforce strict conformity to mainstream norms of neighborly conduct, most, like Tamika, use flexible, contextualized, and often personalized definitions of transgressions. *Different*, then, isn't necessarily *wrong*. While some sets of local understandings and practices reproduce, legitimate, or obscure existing inequalities, others unsettle relations of power and privilege. Living in Riverwest shapes how residents read and respond to disorder, deviance, and difference in ways that, at times, refashion notions of value and belonging as well as challenge classed and raced stereotypes.

The tensions and conflicts in diverse neighborhoods that have so troubled urban researchers are, in fact, central to the production of social order and contribute to the durability of neighborhood diversity. In Riverwest, stability is produced through the constant negotiation of small instabilities. Life on the block is an endless stream of confrontations, resolutions, accommodations, and collaborations. Along the way, people develop multifaceted understandings of their neighbors that enable the contextualization of their conduct. When problems arise, local cultural codes encourage residents to employ informal strategies (e.g., talking with nuisance neighbors) before calling city authorities or the police. As a result, Riverwest residents produce a tentative social order without sacrificing their neighborhood's distinct social diversity. The tensions produced by Riverwest's location as a buffer between concentrated disadvantage and concentrated privilege also contribute to neighborhood stability. Through managing the perceived threats of the ghetto (e.g., crime) and the gentry (e.g., displacement), residents reproduce Riverwest as a distinct place.

Living to Learn: Studying the Neighborhood

Extending from W. E. B. Du Bois's foundational work *The Philadelphia Negro* and the distinguished tradition of the Chicago School of the 1920s, urban ethnography has offered a strong model for investigating the relationship between the local conditions in which people live and how they make sense of their experience and arrive at shared understandings. I employed the tools of urban ethnography to explore the lived experience of integration. The arguments in the following pages are based on over three years of ethnographic fieldwork and sixty in-depth, open-ended interviews with a wide range of people who were knowledgeable about and actively engaged in the neighborhood. To flesh out interpretive constructions of the neighborhood, I also collected and analyzed a range of local media accounts of Riverwest. Although there is a detailed description of research methods in the appendix, I think it is important to introduce my approach to fieldwork.

Move-In Day: July 14, 2007 (reconstructed from field notes)

Daniel and I pulled up to our new home on a hot July afternoon. Daniel had found our rented, upper-level duplex while I was away, so this was my first introduction to the block. Some houses were in need of serious repair (rotting woodwork, deteriorating roofs), and one was boarded up. Others, with elaborate gardens and new siding, looked well maintained. The block was buzzing with activity. People were hanging out on their front porches. Others gathered on the sidewalk, chatting and watching people pass by. It took us a few hours to unload the rented moving truck. During that time, no fewer than ten of our new neighbors came over to introduce themselves and welcome us to the block. This crew of white and Latino/a greeters, ranging in age from two to seventy, included other recent arrivals, a man who had lived on the block for thirty years, members of a family with three generations living on the same block, and an alternately affectionate and aggressive pit bull. In those few hours, we were told that everybody on the block is up in everybody else's business, neighbors help each other out, everyone looks out for one another, things are much better since they got rid of the crack houses, and we had moved onto the best block in Riverwest. One neighbor, Gordon, offered to help us unload. He had long, curly hair and smelled strongly of patchouli. As we climbed the stairs with boxes in our arms, he told me he was a currently unemployed, honorably discharged veteran who liked to make jewelry. He seemed pretty tired after a few trips, so I encouraged him to take a break. When I thanked him for his help, he asked me for a ride to a fast-food restaurant so he could use a gift certificate. After we finished unloading, we slumped down on the floor of the empty truck, sweaty and exhausted. We were startled out of our brief repose by a thunderous "Welcome to the neighborhood!" Bob, a man in his thirties who is built like a truck, has a Mr. Clean-esque shaved head and is covered in tattoos, poked his head inside the truck. Bob had heard from our landlord that Daniel was a woodworker and said the neighbors had all kinds of projects lined up, including building an elaborate cage for his neighbor's pet dragon. With a wry smile, he offered to pay Daniel for his labor in beer.

I approached my initial, informal interactions in Riverwest as a curious newcomer, interested in learning more about my new home. Entrance into the field required ongoing negotiation as I investigated multiple contexts, each with its own set of gatekeepers (be they people or rules of the game). I identified and created relationships with a range of key informants who helped me gain access to a variety of settings, introduced me to people in their neighborhood networks, and occasionally allowed me to accompany them as they went about their daily routines. My relationship with these key informants gave me a level of credibility that facilitated building rapport with their friends and associates.

I began my observations in more public settings—my block and neighboring blocks, public parks, streets with considerable pedestrian traffic, neighborhood gatherings (e.g., local festivals and block parties), and public meetings (e.g., Riverwest Neighborhood Association meetings and Milwaukee Police District Five crime-trend meetings). Over time, I expanded my participation in the daily life of the neighborhood. I shopped and socialized locally. I drank coffee and worked on my laptop at local cafés; drank beer in neighborhood bars; ate at local restaurants; and patronized local convenience stores, grocery stores and co-ops, liquor stores, variety stores, and retail shops. I attended church services, fund-raisers, music shows, block-watch meetings, art openings, and school events. I visited, received services from, and occasionally volunteered for local organizations. I took Spanish lessons from the local Catholic priest with several of his parishioners. I sat on my porch or the steps in front of my house. I worked my way onto other blocks and took in the scene from other porches. I accepted invitations to residents' backyard gatherings and into their homes. I walked my dog. For the most part, I traveled within the neighborhood on foot.

I generally find it very easy to talk to strangers and to make people feel comfortable. I employ a variety of conversation starters—asking a question, offering a sincere compliment, taking a photograph—and then quickly find my way to some sort of common ground. In the neighborhood, my interactions were guided by the goal of understanding local meanings and concerns.[35] To this end, I encouraged residents to share stories, make comparisons, and explain why things are the way they are. At other times, I found it more effective to simply listen and observe situated interactions. I would, for example, slowly sip a beer at a corner pub and take in the argument on my left and the flirtations on my right. Or I would join a group of people in their pajamas gathered at midnight on the sidewalk and listen to their colorful commentary as they watched a scene unfold involving a hollering neighbor, two fire trucks, and several police officers.

Who I am influences what I see, how I see, and how I'm seen. Being a white, highly educated, liberal, gregarious, quirky, inquisitive, bourbon-drinking, shit-talking woman who grew up in an affluent, white Milwaukee suburb and worked as a restaurant server and teacher while cohabitating with a male partner affected my interactions with residents. In any given interaction in this diverse neighborhood, I was both insider and outsider, usually sharing a few but rarely many social and cultural characteristics with those whom I encountered. That some of what was or wasn't shared became apparent only through multiple interactions or changed over time added layers of complexity to my status. Yet my insider/outsider status was hardly unique in Riverwest; it is the norm for residents of a socially mixed community. My social negotiations, then, helped generate useful data. As I documented the development of my relationship-management strategies, I became increasingly sensitive to the differences between residents' approaches to neighborhood navigation—differences regarding which markers of distinction (from beer preferences to snow-shoveling habits) they deem significant, how they read those differences, and how they respond to them.

The Path Ahead

This book explores the everyday "doing" of difference in a diverse neighborhood. Chapters 2 and 3 provide an introduction to the Riverwest neighborhood. I use Gieryn's three-pronged definition of place to guide my analysis, focusing on Riverwest's geographic location, material form, and cultural construction.[36] I identify the face block—the two sides of one street between intersecting streets—as a key site of difference negotiation. I then describe two dominant neighborhood frames that represent different interpretations of what Riverwest is (full of potential vs. strong and diverse) and how it should be (improved vs. protected).

The prevailing view among urban researchers is that diversity impacts local social organization by posing challenges to social control: the regulation of residents' behavior according to collective ends. In chapter 4, I unpack the diversity problem for neighborhood regulation by exploring the links between neighborhood frames and residents' strategies for reading and responding to difference. Mainstream notions of what constitutes crime (that which is illegal) and how to address it (call the police) run up against flexible conduct norms and a preference for informal, direct strategies of social control. I identify local socialization mechanisms that teach residents about neighborhood cultural codes and examine the impact they have on policing in Riverwest. In the end, residents can contain but not eliminate crime.

Those who share a social context also share a way of seeing—of reading and responding to their environment. In chapters 5 and 6, I examine the social bases for shared perceptions of specific features of the neighborhood. I find that the meanings of environmental cues of disorder (e.g., graffiti, groups of young black and brown men hanging out, public drinking, and the presence of bars) are contested in Riverwest. Local cultural frames offer distinct approaches to social differentiation. Repeated block-level interactions that contextualize neighbors' behavior further complicate interpretations of the social surround. I find that through these definitional conflicts, broad social categorization schemes and racialized notions of criminality—though sometimes reinforced—are often challenged.

An individual's residential mobility trajectory not only tells us a great deal about that person but also tells us about place. Where someone has lived, the changes he or she has witnessed, and where he or she hopes to be all affect how that person thinks about place. In chapter 7, I share five Riverwesterners' residential mobility narratives. Their stories bring together key themes from preceding chapters to illustrate place effects, showing how features of the neighborhood interact with individual preferences and skills to jointly affect understandings and experiences of place. I consider how these narratives help us identify mechanisms that mediate the effects of neighborhood diversity.

In the closing chapter, I present an explanation for the durability of Riverwest's social diversity, which centers on everyday processes of difference negotiation. I discuss the implications of my findings for inequality, power relations, and our understanding of the "good" community. I then return to a discussion of the paradoxes of integration and explore the productive possibilities of conflict.

CHAPTER TWO

Locating Riverwest

If you look at this neighborhood with an eye to notice boundaries and edges, the whole place can be seen as one big meandering borderline between different races, classes, ages, lifestyles, education levels, and political preferences. If you look without that kind of discernment, the way the old eyesight gets after a couple of beers, everything kind of mushes together. I guess you call that diversity. The charm and potential of Riverwest, however, exists in those liminal spaces. In those uncertain, dangerous places where you step just outside your comfort zone and try something new. Those situations when there is no easy answer. Those moments when your internal dialogue shuts down, just for a second, and you get a chance to really listen to something completely unexpected that has a chance to slip into your worldview. Something you never would have thought of on your own.

—Jan Christensen, "Liminal Spaces"

The idea that neighborhoods matter is fundamentally rooted in an appreciation of the situated nature of social life. Neighborhoods are places. They are located within the broader structure of the city. They run up against and interact with other neighborhoods. They contain boundaries, buildings, and routes. They structure practices and patterns of activity. They bring people together and keep people apart. They are invested in and attached to and made sense with. They are constructed by and carry meanings.

This is not a pitch for making the neighborhood *the* determining factor in structuring the opportunities and social practices of its residents.[1] Rather, attention to place as more than backdrop provides a rich set of tools for understanding how the local physical, social, and cultural environment interacts with social processes. In a review of the role of place in sociology, Thomas Gieryn argues that conducting place-sensitive analyses requires attention to three key features of place: geographic location, material form, and investment with meaning.[2] In this chapter and the next, I address these features of place to introduce Riverwest and establish the framework for a *situated* neighborhood study.

Milwaukee: Segregated Metropolis

Milwaukee, like many metropolitan areas in the United States, is highly segregated by race. According to U.S. 2010 project analyses of census data, the

Milwaukee metropolitan area ranks first in the nation in black–white segregation, second in black–Hispanic segregation, and thirteenth in white–Hispanic segregation.[3] This is not news. Milwaukee has remained one of the top five most black–white segregated metropolitan areas for over thirty years. This persistence of segregation in Milwaukee is characteristic of Rust Belt cities in the midwestern and northeastern United States.[4] However, while most of those cities experienced modest black–white desegregation between 1980 and 2010, Milwaukee's segregation rates barely budged.[5] There are only a few communities in the city that are racially integrated.

The pattern of residential segregation in the city of Milwaukee maps onto concentrations of disadvantage and advantage. For example, neighborhoods that are predominantly black (80 percent or higher) have poverty rates four times higher than neighborhoods that are predominantly white (80 percent or higher).[6] In 2010, 33 percent of African Americans, 14 percent of Hispanics, and 2 percent of whites in the city were living in extreme-poverty neighborhoods.[7] Only 9 percent of blacks in the metropolitan area live in the suburbs, making Milwaukee's black suburbanization rate the lowest in the country. Though a larger share of the area's Hispanic population lives in the suburbs (30 percent), Milwaukee's Hispanic suburbanization rate still falls far below that of other comparable cities.[8]

An Urban Institute research team recently assigned metropolitan areas racial-equity grades based on residential segregation, neighborhood affluence (for the average black, Latino, and non-Hispanic white resident), public school quality (for the average black, Latino, and non-Hispanic white student), employment (among working-age adults), and homeownership. Milwaukee received Fs for black–white equality and Hispanic–white equality, highlighting the area's considerable opportunity gaps.[9]

Milwaukee residents are aware of their "race problem"—what one city planner I interviewed referred to as the city's "badge of dishonor." The *Milwaukee Journal Sentinel* regularly runs stories pointing to problems associated with racial tension and segregation. Although they sometimes refer to the city's growing Hispanic population or, more rarely, its Southeast Asian population, these stories overwhelmingly focus on black–white divisions and disparities. *Milwaukee Journal Sentinel* columnist Eugene Kane puts race front and center in many of his editorials, which invariably generate a slew of racist comments (and heated responses to those comments) by readers. Popular local narratives about the inner city pathologize poor black families or conflate race and class in monolithic representations of Milwaukee's black and Hispanic populations. In public forums related to the city's crime problem or the struggling Milwaukee Public School system, some residents place blame on "culture," while others raise concerns about institutional discrimination. There have been a variety of programmatic responses to racial tensions designed to build cross-race relationships and facilitate productive conversations about race. Milwaukee has not received the same level of national attention for segregation as, say, Detroit, but locals have a strong sense that their city is sharply divided along racial lines.

Though less discussed, the Milwaukee area also has high levels of economic segregation. The suburban affluent and the central-city poor live in disconnected and dissimilar worlds. In 2000, Milwaukee ranked third nationally in terms of a central city–suburb income gap.[10] The rate of concentrated poverty in Milwaukee (the share of people living in census tracts in which 40 percent or more of residents are living in poverty) decreased considerably during the 1990s (from 48 percent to 24 percent) and plateaued in the 2000s (23 percent), but the current rate is still more than double the 1979 rate.[11] The Milwaukee metropolitan area's poor face the highest level of economic isolation in the nation.[12] Moreover, the city's class clustering reflects national trends. Rising income inequality in the United States is related to an increase in enclaves of affluence and poverty and a shrinking proportion of neighborhoods that are predominantly middle class or mixed income.[13]

The Construction of Division

How did a city once characterized by a diversity of ethnic neighborhoods become a hypersegregated place divided into three worlds—a poor, black inner core; a Latino south side; and an outer ring of affluent white suburbs? Historian John Gurda characterizes the period from the late 1880s through 1900 as "the triumph of the workingman."[14] During this time, local industry thrived, employing increasing numbers of people (many of them foreign born) in milling, brewing, tanning, iron production, and metal fabrication. Germans were the largest group in the city, but the Polish community was growing rapidly. The city's booming economy also drew Irish, Italians, Greeks, Serbs, Slovenes, Croats, Eastern European Jews, Hungarians, Norwegians, Ukranians, and others in search of work. Although some ethnic enclaves developed, many neighborhoods were ethnically mixed. Industry continued to boom during and after World War I. Faced with a shortage of unskilled laborers, manufacturers began recruiting African American and Mexican workers in the 1920s, who then settled into communities on the north side and south side of the city, respectively. Milwaukee's rapid population growth pushed the geographic expansion of the city, and the growing white middle class began moving to the suburbs.

After World War II, the city and suburbs engaged in turf wars and annexation battles, which resulted in a fractured metropolis. The demand for wartime labor sparked rapid growth in Milwaukee's African American population. These newcomers met aggressive resistance from many white ethnic communities and were funneled into the "inner core." Many black veterans entitled to home mortgage assistance were unable to take advantage of the GI Bill housing provisions because banks denied their loan applications. A host of other discriminatory practices—including blockbusting, restrictive covenants, and redlining—relegated blacks to overcrowded, neglected, and substandard housing in neighborhoods with deteriorating public services.[15] Housing shortages, the construction of an expressway system through the heart of the inner core, and the incorporation of an "iron ring" of suburbs exacerbated the intense residential divisions in Milwaukee by facilitating white flight to the flourishing suburbs and disinvestment from the inner core.

Historian John Gurda argues that these shifts in the city's racial and economic geography had serious social and political consequences: "Like most American cities, Milwaukee had always been a stratified community. . . . Some neighborhoods housed the movers and shakers, while others housed the moved and shaken. But social distance had been leavened by physical proximity; Milwaukeeans of all stations tended to know the lives of their neighbors, great and small, in general outline if not detail. That familiarity vanished with the suburban exodus following World War II. . . . What was lost in the process was a certain urban fluency, a working knowledge of the conditions of other ethnic and economic groups. It tended to shape public perceptions of the metropolis and ultimately public policy."[16]

In the 1960s, a group of citizens began an organized fight against housing discrimination, demanding that the city council pass fair-housing legislation. The NAACP Youth Council regularly staged marches in support of open housing. Racial tensions exploded into riots in late July 1967. After the violence subsided, the marchers continued their efforts until an open-housing ordinance passed in Milwaukee in 1968. During this dynamic era, Milwaukee's black and Hispanic civil rights movements also challenged racist practices and policies in education, policing, welfare rights, and employment.[17] In *The Selma of the North*—an analysis of this tumultuous era in the city's history—Patrick D. Jones concludes: "What unified the struggle for racial justice during the 1960s was an underlying effort to convince white Milwaukeeans and the existing power structure that the problems of the inner core were legitimate, that they emanated chiefly from racial discrimination and systemic inequality and that they required significant and sustained action by the entire community."[18] Although there have been some important gains, Milwaukeeans continue to labor at this monumental task.

Growing Hispanic and Hmong communities are contributing to the racial/ethnic mix in the city. Between 2000 and 2010, the Hmong population grew 25 percent to nearly 10,000. During the same period, the Hispanic population surged to over 100,000—a remarkable 43 percent increase. Most are Mexican or Puerto Rican, although this broad category of new Milwaukee residents includes numerous ethnic and national identities. Most of these new arrivals, like waves of Hispanic people before them, have settled in the historic south side.[19] This is a result of both pull factors and barriers to accessing housing in other parts of the city.

Milwaukee's economic story during the last four decades mirrors that of other Rust Belt cities. Deindustrialization spurred dramatic economic decline and a sharp reduction in manufacturing jobs. During this time, concentrated poverty, economic disinvestment, and unemployment in the inner city rose dramatically as its population declined. The continued exodus of the affluent drained the city's economic resources by weakening the tax base and consumer markets.[20] While the suburbs benefited tremendously from the economic boom of the 1990s, its effects were muted in Milwaukee's inner-city neighborhoods.[21] The recent recession has also disproportionately affected central-city economies. Between 2000 and 2010, the median household income in the city of Milwaukee dropped 22 percent, falling from $42,166 to $32,911.[22]

The city's African Americans have been hit particularly hard by economic transitions. Economist Marc Levine reports that "no metro area has witnessed more precipitous erosion in the labor market for black males over the past 40 years than has Milwaukee. . . . By 2010, barely more than half of African American males in their prime working years were employed, compared to 85 percent almost forty years ago."[23] Racial disparities in male employment and college degree attainment are wider in Milwaukee than in almost every other metropolitan area.[24] Racial residential segregation contributed to and is exacerbated by the disproportionate effects of deindustrialization on Milwaukee's black population.

The economic state of Milwaukee is profoundly affected by epidemic-level incarceration rates for black males in the city. In 2010, roughly one in eight African American working-age men were behind bars—the highest percentage of incarcerated black men in the country.[25] This means that a significant portion of city residents face substantial barriers to employment and securing affordable housing. The negative impacts of racialized mass incarceration on family and community stability are geographically concentrated. Two-thirds of black men who served time between 1990 and 2012 came from six zip codes in the poorest Milwaukee neighborhoods.[26] The clustering of economic disadvantage and correctional supervision in black communities is created by and reinforces long-standing geographic divisions in the city.

Persistent segregation also shapes politics and race relations in the region. The metropolitan area's stark and deepening political divisions fall along the fault lines of race, class, and place. Rival definitions of local problems spur markedly different approaches to regional governance. Many Milwaukee-area residents believe that the concentration of disadvantage and crime in some African American and Hispanic communities reflects the moral failings of their residents rather than being the result of a complex interplay of political, economic, and social structural forces. Many city dwellers view the suburbs as racist and exclusionary. *Milwaukee Journal Sentinel* reporter Craig Gilbert describes the city's pronounced urban–suburban divide: "Democrats and Republicans aren't just strangers to each other in their politics—they increasingly live in separate worlds. In its ultrapartisan geography, this is arguably the most polarized place in swing-state America."[27] The division of residents into distinct residential spheres limits perspective-widening opportunities and exacerbates race and class tensions. In 2006, the Public Policy Forum, a nonpartisan public policy research organization in southeastern Wisconsin, conducted a race relations survey in the region. The report concludes that although many see improving race relations as very important for the region, most perceive the current state of these relations as "not good" and "not improving."[28]

Milwaukee is a city of neighborhoods, which contributes to the parochial feel of daily life in the city. As Gurda observes, "Milwaukee is built at the human scale. It has all the resources of a much larger city, but it has preserved the easy pace and even the intimacy of a much smaller community."[29] Yet this segmentation of Milwaukee into a mosaic of little worlds can also sharpen existing divides by shielding neighbors from alternative views. However, when a neighborhood pulls together a mix of people, the parochial spirit can have uniting potential.

Riverwest

The history of the area now known as Riverwest, as documented by Tom Tolan, is one of ethnic transition.[30] This area was likely first a mixed settlement of Potawatomi, Sauk, Ottawa, Chippewa, and Menominee tribes, and later

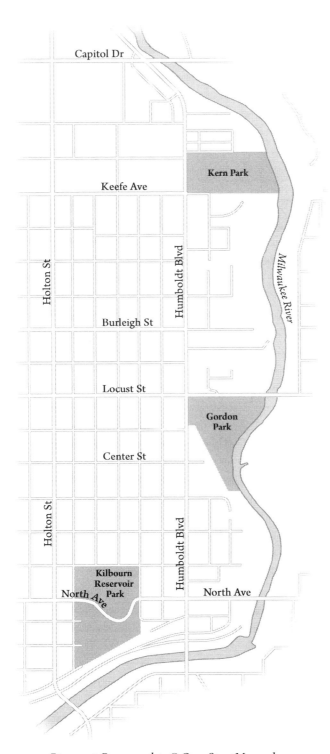

MAP 1 Riverwest. Base map data © OpenStreetMap and
Milwaukee Department of City Development.

became home to French missionaries and traders. By the 1840s, the Native American population had drastically declined due to disease, land dispossession, and forced displacement.[31] In the 1880s, Milwaukee's German aristocrats, drawn by the quiet, green landscape and the choice swimming areas along the Milwaukee River, built their summer estates in the area. As working-class Germans and Poles began building permanent residences west of the river, the wealthier families moved east of the river toward Lake Michigan. The growing, largely poor, and working-class Polish population established themselves as a community with the construction of St. Casimir Church in 1894. In 1908, they completed construction on another church, St. Mary of Czestochowa, to accommodate their rapidly expanding parish. These Catholic churches, which also housed schools, were the anchoring community institutions for the neighborhood's Poles. In the 1930s, a number of Italian families joined the Germans and Poles in the area now known as Riverwest.

From the 1940s to the 1960s, Milwaukee's African American population grew rapidly, as many people migrated from the south in search of work. As the community to the west of Holton Street quickly transitioned from largely white ethnic to majority black, the future Riverwest remained almost exclusively white. According to Tolan, fewer white residents in the community were willing or able to join the flight to the suburbs. Some of those who stayed actively prevented African Americans from moving in. They created informal restrictive covenants, refused to serve African Americans at commercial establishments, and denied black children access to parish schools. Holton Street, the boundary between the two neighborhoods at that time, remains an important neighborhood and racial boundary today. In the 1960s, urban renewal destroyed a thriving Puerto Rican neighborhood on the east side. Many of the Puerto Rican families who had been displaced resettled along Holton Street and, over time, re-created a vibrant, tight-knit community.

In the late 1960s and 1970s, there was a slow but steady increase in the African American and Hispanic presence in the neighborhood. This period was also characterized by local expressions of broad cultural and social movements. Homegrown activists and the various counterculturalists who were beginning to migrate to the area formed a number of organizations with diverse missions, including Puerto Rican mutual assistance; social, economic, and racial justice; youth empowerment; poverty alleviation; the creation of a socialist democracy; civil rights promotion; and renters' rights advocacy. One organization, the East Side Housing Action Committee (ESHAC), was founded in 1972 by antiwar and civil rights activists at the University of Wisconsin–Milwaukee. Its goal was to create a working-people's movement.

TABLE 1   Racial mix in Riverwest, 1970–2010

Year	% White	% Black	% Hispanic
1970	93	5	5
1980	75	11	12
1990	64	20	13
2000	53	27	17
2010	63	20	12

Source: United States Census, 1970–2010.

Notes: 1970–90 percentages based on five census tracts; 2000 and 2010 percentages based on five tracts and one block group. The numbers in 1970 add up to more than 100 percent of the population because Hispanic people were counted as either blacks or whites, and many Hispanic respondents who identified their race as "other" in 1970 were counted as white.

ESHAC focused early local efforts on organizing tenants and holding slumlords accountable for their misdeeds. Over time, the mission shifted to unifying the neighborhood across race, class, and religion through efforts to address shared neighborhood concerns. ESHAC took the lead in battles against the city and helped launch a cooperative grocery store, a local credit union, a neighborhood employment service, an industrial development agency, and a community business association.[32] ESHAC functioned as one of the central community-based organizations in the neighborhood for over twenty-five years.[33] The organization was instrumental in fashioning (although some argue *imposing*) a new coherent neighborhood identity, including naming the area Riverwest.[34]

By the early 1980s, this community was home to substantial black, white, and Latino (largely Puerto Rican) populations and had become known for being racially diverse. Though this troubled a number of long-standing residents, it made the neighborhood attractive to newcomers. The 2010 census shows that approximately 62 percent of Riverwest's 12,500 residents are white, 20 percent are black, 12 percent are Hispanic, 2 percent are Asian, and 3 percent are multiracial.[35] The nonwhite population in the neighborhood increased in the 1970s, 80s, and 90s, but decreased in the last decade. Riverwest has never experienced dramatic racial turnover (see table 1); it is among the most stably integrated communities in Milwaukee.

The neighborhood was hit hard by the economic challenges associated with deindustrialization.[36] Declining homeownership, housing values, and property upkeep in the 1970s and 1980s reflected climbing poverty and unemployment.[37] In the 1990s, Riverwest battled gangs, crime, and violence.

TABLE 2   Economic mix in Riverwest, 2010

Household-Income Quintile	% Riverwest Households
Lowest fifth (less than $25,000)	34
Second fifth ($25,000–$50,000)	31
Middle fifth ($50,000–$75,000)	20
Fourth fifth ($75,000–$125,000)	10
Highest fifth (more than $125,000)	5

Source: American Community Survey, 2006–10.
   Note: Income ranges based on 2010 household-income quintiles. Range ceilings adjusted to align with ranges reported at the tract level.

Neighbors organized to shut down dozens of drug houses responsible for deteriorating conditions on their blocks. Despite these challenges, the relative affordability and location of Riverwest attracted renters and first-time home buyers. From the late 1990s until today, recurrent development interest in the neighborhood has sparked waves of gentrification worries.

In media accounts and local chatter, Riverwest is regularly identified as a working-class neighborhood. In 2010, the median household income was $37,098, and 24 percent of families were below the poverty level. These statistics mask the socioeconomic diversity in the neighborhood (see table 2). Another indicator of the community's social-class mix is educational attainment; in 2010, 15 percent of residents over the age of twenty-five did not complete high school, 18 percent earned high school degrees, 27 percent completed some college, 29 percent earned bachelor's degrees, and 11 percent earned graduate degrees.[38]

In the 1980s, the city of Milwaukee commissioned artist Jan Kotowicz to design a neighborhood poster series. Her Riverwest poster features what is known locally as a "Polish flat"—a story-and-a-half workers' cottage made of wood and brick (see figure 1). Milwaukee's early Polish communities had unusually high rates of homeownership for a financially limited immigrant group. Polish building and loan associations helped families purchase and incrementally develop properties. They built simple, one-story cottages that, when additional capital was available, could be moved to the back of the property (alley house), added on to, or raised up on posts to construct an additional semibasement unit underneath (the Polish flat).[39] The workers' cottage (in its various iterations) is a common housing type in Riverwest. There are many lots with three living units—an upper flat and a lower flat in the front house, and a back cottage.

FIGURE 1 Riverwest neighborhood poster. Jan Kotowicz, Historic Milwaukee, Inc.

A typical block in the heart of the neighborhood is lined with a variety of two-story, two-family duplexes, single-family houses, and an occasional small apartment building in the mix. Most lots in the neighborhood are narrow, so blocks are densely packed, with enough room for just a narrow walkway between houses. The area of the neighborhood closest to the river, however, is less dense, has fewer nonwhite residents, and has more single-family homes than other parts of the neighborhood.[40] Storefront houses are sprinkled throughout the neighborhood, vestiges of a vibrant and diverse neighborhood microeconomy. There is one public-housing high-rise in the neighborhood, with 230 one-bedroom units designated for elderly, disabled, or near elderly persons. Only 36 percent of the housing units in Riverwest were owner occupied in 2010, so the majority of the residents are renters. This statistic provides a somewhat skewed picture of residential stability, as there are many long-term renters and even a small share of lifetime Riverwest renters. In 2010, 69 percent of renters lived in the same house as in the previous year.[41]

Riverwest's social mix extends beyond race and class to include diversity in sexual orientation, gender identity, ability, age, political ideology, religion, family form, lifestyle, and scene. In Riverwest, you will find working-class blacks, Latinos, and whites; aging hippies; artists; musicians; Polish and Puerto Rican families who have lived in the neighborhood for many generations; college students; entrepreneurs; alternative professional anti-yuppies;

poor households struggling to make ends meet; people with disabilities; anarchists; hipsters; punks; producers and consumers of hip-hop culture; lesbian, gay, bisexual, and transgender people; formerly incarcerated women and men; retired or laid-off factory workers; mechanics; craftspeople; alternative health-care providers; teachers; service industry workers; lawyers; and the occasional professor. The multiple axes of social differentiation in the neighborhood do not map neatly onto a set of distinct groups, orientations, or cultural dispositions. As David Harding finds in his study of culturally heterogeneous neighborhoods, residents rarely wholly identify or act in accordance with discrete subcultures.[42]

Boundaries

The neighborhood is long and thin, roughly thirteen blocks by seven blocks. It is bordered by Capitol Drive to the north, by the Milwaukee River to the east and south, and by Holton Street to the west (see map 2). Residents are in agreement about the eastern and western boundaries, but the northern and southern boundaries are debatable. Some consider Keefe Avenue to be the northern border because it marks a transition from residential to largely industrial use. Because the residences along Humboldt Boulevard continue all the way to Capitol Drive, many include those additional blocks in their definition of Riverwest. The southern part of the neighborhood includes the area now officially known as Beerline B (or, unofficially, "Condoland"). This narrow corridor, which runs along the riverbank, was named for the railroad line that used to service a number of industries (including the Blatz, Schlitz, and Pabst breweries) located near the river. In the 1990s, the Department of City Development spearheaded the redevelopment of the industrial skeletons and brownfields into a residential and recreational area. The mostly upscale condominiums and apartments are at river level, physically separated from the Riverwest neighborhood by a steep bluff. The area's tenants, assumed to be wealthier than most Riverwesterners, are sometimes cast as consumerist yuppies uninterested in connecting with the community behind them. The vast majority of Riverwest residents, citing the physical and social separation of Beerline B, do not include this strip along the river in their definition of the neighborhood.[43] Some consider North Avenue the southern boundary of Riverwest.

Geographic Location: Riverwest as Buffer

> It's like Holton is the Mason-Dixon line. And it's like it's funny because you have a strong African American base on the other side of Holton, and then you got Holton, which is Latino, and then you got this mixing

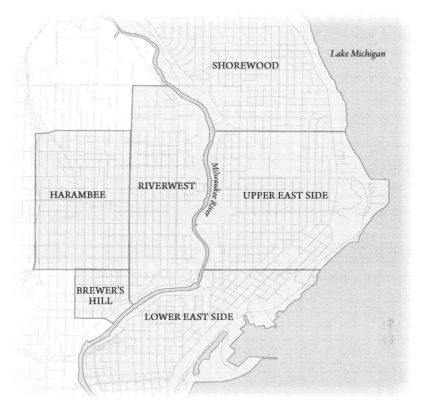

MAP 2 Riverwest and surrounding neighborhoods. Base map data © OpenStreetMap and Milwaukee Department of City Development.

pot Riverwest, and then if you go this way [*points to the east*], it's all white. Whiiiite! And it's funny because Riverwest is weird, but it's great! (Jelani Harris, Riverwest business owner)

Riverwest is an in-between place. The neighborhood's ongoing struggle to manage the countervailing pressures of gentrification and decline is expressed in its geographic location. Riverwest is sandwiched between a much more affluent, predominantly white, university neighborhood, which is considered part of the east side, and Harambee, a lower-income, predominantly African American, higher-crime neighborhood, which is considered part of the north side (see map 2 and table 3). Holton Street has long served as the border between Riverwest and Harambee, symbolizing for many the line between Riverwest and the "ghetto."[44] According to historian John Gurda, the neighborhood's location has shaped its spirit: "For well over a century . . . the neighborhood's character has been determined by the mingling of currents

TABLE 3   Characteristics of Harambee, Riverwest, and Upper East Side, 2010

Characteristic	Harambee	Riverwest	East Side
% White	8	63	88
% Black	79	20	3
% Hispanic	9	12	3
Median Family Income	$25,200	$38,000	$79,500
% Families Below Poverty Level	42	24	9
Median House Value	$111,100	$158,400	$286,288

Source: United States Census, 2010; American Community Survey, 2006–10.

from the North and East Sides. It might be said, in fact, that Riverwest is the east side of the North Side and the north side of the East Side."[45]

Brewers Hill, the neighborhood to the southwest of Riverwest, has experienced gentrification and related displacement of lower-income residents—processes that began in the mid-1970s.[46] Although property values and rents in Riverwest have increased since the early 1990s, this has not produced dramatic demographic change in terms of the socioeconomic makeup of neighborhood residents. Many fear that the neighborhood is vulnerable to gentrification and its attendant erosion of economic and racial diversity. There have been multiple waves of concern (or celebration) about gentrification in the neighborhood's recent history. There was a significant uptick in home renovations in the late 1970s. Researchers studying the neighborhood in the early 1980s identified Riverwest as an "ethnically heterogeneous, working-class, revitalized neighborhood."[47] In the late 1990s, the construction of condominiums along the river in Beerline B triggered anxieties about neighborhood transition. Property values in several parts of the neighborhood jumped in the early 2000s. Hazel Carver—a young white woman who was born and raised in Riverwest—worries about how gentrification will change the character of the community: "I hate the condos. I don't like it because it makes the neighborhood feel a lot more yuppier than before, and fancier, and east side. It's like—Riverwest is not a fancy neighborhood. It's just a chill neighborhood with lots of kinds of people, and now it's like we face rising property values and that kind of thing." Some residents, however, hope that gentrification will stimulate economic development and substantially lift property values in the neighborhood.

Clearly there are competing narratives about revitalization and upscaling in Riverwest. There are those who would welcome increasing home values and an influx of higher-income residents. Some residents claim the neighborhood is already gentrified. Others consider gentrification to be in process. Still others identify existing gentrification pressures and claim that residents have worked and can continue to work against unwanted changes. Despite divergent assessments of the neighborhood's real or potential transformation, the concept of gentrification is woven into residents' understandings of Riverwest.[48]

If the east represents the threat of gentrification, the west represents the threat of crime and decline.[49] Most Riverwesterners believe that the majority of the reported crime in their neighborhood comes from the west—if not from Harambee then from other proximal, higher-crime areas of the north side urban core.[50] This aligns with a common Milwaukee perception of crime as a black, inner-city problem. Keith Bennett, a white homeowner who has lived in the neighborhood for over twenty years, believes that his neighborhood absorbs the shock of troubles from the west in ways that benefit those living east of the Milwaukee River. "Did you know that the people over on the east side consider us as their buffer zone and the river as their moat? That's what maintains the integrity and value of their east side property. They know they aren't going to have a problem with that crime because they have Riverwest to act as a buffer." Robin Lund's assessment of the neighborhood's in-between location is colored with her characteristic humor: "There's anger from people who don't have the privilege—the underclass. . . . And we're the buffer. So we feel it more than the east side. I keep saying, we should have classes for these people. Don't steal from the people in Riverwest. They don't have anything. Go to the east side."

The threat of crime is central to Riverwest's social organization and figures prominently in many outsiders' views of the neighborhood. Riverwesterners are aware that many consider their neighborhood to be "sketchy" or "shady." The Milwaukee edition of the *Onion*'s now defunct city guide website, the Decider, offered this description of the neighborhood: "It might be a little rough around the edges, but there's no Milwaukee neighborhood as cool, colorful or iconoclastic as Riverwest. A haven for artists, writers, musicians, and other assorted weirdos, Riverwest is imbued with a special energy that's irresistible to locals who don't mind the occasional car break-in or nonlethal gunshot wound. Still, it can be a somewhat intimidating place if you've never been there before."[51]

I often heard Riverwest residents complain that the neighborhood's reputation as unsafe is undeserved. Several residents remarked that crime in Riverwest is inaccurately portrayed in the local media. Crimes that happen on the city's west side, outside the neighborhood's boundaries, are frequently reported as happening in Riverwest. Residents find that they have to regularly challenge others' negative assumptions about the neighborhood. "Isn't it dangerous?" "That's the ghetto, right?" "You are crazy to be living there." When people question Miguel Acosta's choice to stay in Riverwest, he insists that crime is ubiquitous and he prefers the Riverwest variety: "People talk about, you know, it's dangerous. . . . But there's dangerous parts everywhere, you know what I mean? You can live in the suburbs. I'd rather live, you know, over here and know what's going on than live in the suburbs and not know what's going on in my neighbor's basement." Despite these concerns about outsiders' misperceptions, when asked about the downsides of living in the neighborhood, almost every community member I encountered brought up the issue of crime.

Although most residents note that crime was, is, or can be an issue, I found widely disparate assessments of neighborhood safety. When my partner, Daniel, and I agreed to help a local community organizer by going door-to-door to conduct a brief survey with residents, we were struck by the variation in responses to questions about safety. We worked our way down a block where there had been a shooting the previous month. At the first house, an elderly African American woman said that community safety wasn't a priority because the neighborhood was "safe and wonderful." Her next-door neighbor, a middle-aged white woman, said that safety should be a top priority. She had "had enough" and was moving out of the neighborhood because of the crime. In the next house, an elderly white woman noted how much safer the neighborhood had become and praised Riverwest's "community values."

According to Milwaukee Police Department officers in District Five and longtime residents, crime rates in Riverwest have remained relatively stable for the last ten years. These residents embed the recent stability in two different narratives about the neighborhood's crime trends. Some argue that criminal activity in the neighborhood cycles through periods of high intensity and periods of low intensity. Others believe that Riverwest's crime issues have consistently improved over time. Compared to the heightened gang, drug, and violence problems in the late 1980s and 1990s, the neighborhood now seems relatively calm. The vast majority of reported crimes in Riverwest are property crimes, including thefts, vehicle thefts, locked vehicle entries (auto break-ins), and burglaries. There are also violent crimes, including robberies, assaults, and occasional homicides (see chart 1).

Riverwest, a buffer neighborhood, exists in a state of tension with its surroundings. As I will demonstrate, this tension is part of what fuels the ongoing production and reproduction of the neighborhood as a distinctly diverse place, as neither homogenized east nor homogenized west. Journalist and

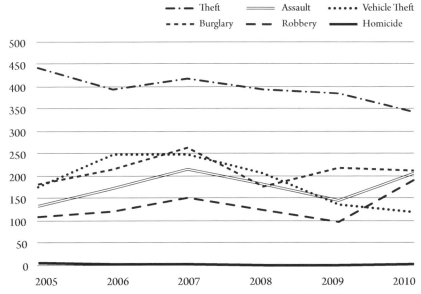

CHART 1 Reported crime in Riverwest, 2005–10. Source: Milwaukee Police Department: Wisconsin Based Incident Report, Group A Offenses.

former Riverwest resident Eugene Kane observes that the neighborhood is perpetually on the edge:

> Riverwest is an area of the city that seeks to defy stereotypes about urban living. It has long been populated by an eclectic group that often seems torn between the urge to publicize all the good things about the neighborhood while also hoping to keep the place to themselves. Tucked between the east side of Milwaukee and a central-city area known for economic and social upheavals, the neighborhood is one of those hidden treasures for the kind of people who don't believe you have to flee to the suburbs to raise a family, own a business or just live a comfortable life. . . . I used to live in Riverwest about 15 years ago. Even then, it had the reputation as a "changing neighborhood" always on the verge of becoming something else. Most times, the good people in Riverwest manage to hold firm to their special piece of Milwaukee and maintain it as a close-knit area with a strong sense of community.[52]

Play, Consume, and Organize

For a dense urban neighborhood, Riverwest has a surprisingly rich supply of green space. There are wooded trails that run along the river, two large county parks, a handful of city parks, and an increasing amount of community gardens springing up each summer. Riverwesterners are, as evidenced by the name of a Riverwest Neighborhood Association committee, "Guardians of Green Space." Groups of committed residents have organized to create or revive parks, protect the river from new development, and plant gardens on plots of land owned by the city (with or without permission). One group has taken the lead in the city's Victory Gardens Initiative, encouraging people to grow vegetables in their yards, on their patios and rooftops, and in communal spaces. Its motto is: "This is a grassroots movement. Move grass. Grow food." In 2009, the group created a seventy-six-bed victory garden in the neighborhood's Kilbourn Reservoir Park and, thanks to growing interest, added beds the following two summers. Local families, organizations, and high-school interns tend the 133 raised beds.[53] The building and planting of the victory gardens is just the most recent stage in the transformation of an overgrown, trash-strewn, run-down park into a vibrant play and garden area. It's also just the beginning of what one resident organizer sees as a major transformation of the neighborhood's food supply. "Urban agriculture is the next thing for Riverwest. What is our goal? 50 percent of our fruits and vegetables grown within the neighborhood limits within five years."

Riverwest prides itself on having a range of independent small businesses, including child-care centers, barber shops, a beauty salon, convenience stores, art galleries, a variety store, a scooter shop, a fish and aquarium supply store, a bike shop, liquor stores, an independent fashion boutique, an eyeglass store, a glass pipe store, an oriental medicine practice, a vintage clothing store, a "Las Vegas–style" intimate apparel boutique, a video-rental store, a brewery, a hardware store, a coffee roaster, and a Puerto Rican deli and grocery. The neighborhood is dotted with coffee shops, restaurants, and many corner bars, catering to a variety of subcultural scenes. Although most of these establishments are located along one of the commercial strips in the neighborhood (Center Street, Locust Street, and Holton Street), some are sprinkled throughout the residential blocks. Riverwest's creative, do-it-yourself (DIY) spirit is also expressed in cottage and other small industries that produce an interesting assortment of goods, including natural pet food, oil-waxed garments, rustic furniture, and packed herring. The cooperative business model has a long history in the neighborhood and finds its current expression in a housing co-op, the Riverwest Investment Cooperative (focused on housing rehabilitation and small business loans through resident investments in development), the Riverwest Co-Op Grocery and Café, and the Riverwest Public House Cooperative—a bar dedicated to "building community one drink at a time!" Some Riverwesterners make a concerted effort to buy local in order to support homegrown cooperatives and entrepreneurs.

Like most small businesses in the United States, many small businesses that are launched in Riverwest have a short life span. There are several storefronts that cycle through new ventures every few years. A number of the more established businesses, like Fuel Café, have become woven into the fabric of Riverwest's identity. Fuel Café was born on Center Street in 1993, long before the coffee-shop craze hit the Midwest. Among the sea of posters on the café's front windows advertising upcoming concerts, art shows, motorbike races, and other events, there are two neon signs boasting "Killer Coffee" and "Lousy Service." From its beginnings, this smoky hangout was a magnet for punks, alternative kids, and misfits of various stripes. In the past few years, the owners have renovated the space, expanded the menu, and made Fuel's interior smoke-free. These changes have softened Fuel's edge somewhat. There are a number of former regulars who see this as representative of the gradual erosion of Riverwest's rebellious spirit. They lament that the pirate radio stations are long gone and that there are fewer basement shows (underground, DIY, punk concerts held in residences). Still, there are many longtime Fuel patrons who remain faithful, and the recent changes seem to have diversified the clientele. Since I occasionally worked or had meetings at Fuel, I documented café happenings in my field notes. The following is one snapshot of morning clientele: "Just another work day at Fuel. On my way in, I nodded to the housepainter and his assorted crew sitting outside having their morning coffee, cigarette, and bull session. As I headed to the counter, I passed a white guy with facial piercings and tattoos with his head buried in a book, two older black men deep in discussion over partially eaten pastries, two hipster kids—one light skinned and fauxhawked—tapping on their laptop keyboards. In front of me in line, a young white hippie couple showed off their newborn to the barista. The group of black and white city firefighters that seems to drop into Fuel almost every morniɴg came in a few minutes after me, suspenders and all."

Although there are several minority-owned businesses in the neighborhood, the majority of businesses are white owned. This reflects the staggering underrepresentation of black and Hispanic entrepreneurs in the city. In 2007, Milwaukee ranked last out of thirty-six metropolitan areas in both the number of black-owned businesses and the number of Hispanic-owned businesses relative to the size of those respective populations in the region.[54] Segregation continues to stifle Milwaukee's minority business development. Black entrepreneur Jelani Harris's decision to locate his business in Riverwest was driven, in part, by a desire to diversify his clientele. "Well, I started a new business and I want to make money. How do I grow my business? I asked myself some hard-hitting questions. How can I grow this business? Let's broaden that base. But these are things that I just never, never chose to use because of my environment where I was in. So once I took myself out of that environment [and] I put myself into a multicultural environment, I was able to do more.... [Now] I have a very eclectic client base from young to old, from black to white to Hispanic, you name it, I have it." Jelani goes on to explain how the neighborhood has nurtured his professional life in ways that he hadn't anticipated: "Riverwest has allowed me to be more creative. They can appreciate my creativity.... I think that being here has made me a more complete businessman. Just from the reaction from the community because you get back what you put out."

Riverwest has a rich organizational life. What follows is a selection of civic institutions, religious congregations, and local organizations. There are three neighborhood public elementary schools (two of which have Spanish-English bilingual or dual-language programming, one of which is designed to serve students with disabilities), two parochial (parish-affiliated) schools, and one Christian middle school. Although all these schools serve at least some neighborhood kids, none are considered exclusively neighborhood schools. Riverwest is home to a number of religious congregations, including a Quaker meetinghouse, Iglesia Genesis (Assembly of God), storefront Baptist and Pentecostal churches, a Lutheran church, and a Catholic parish (when the congregations of St. Casimir and St. Mary of Czestochowa shrunk, the two churches merged into one parish) that now holds both English and Spanish masses. A yoga school and tai chi ch'uan center share a building in the center of the neighborhood. There are several local massage practices and a massage school. The COA Youth and Family Center is the largest and most long-standing social service agency in the neighborhood. The Meta House campus in Riverwest includes a women's residential substance abuse treatment center, outpatient clinic, and administrative center. There are also two Head Start centers in Riverwest, one of which serves Spanish-speaking families. After ESHAC dissolved in 1998, residents formed the still-active Riverwest Neighborhood Association (RNA) to collectively address local issues. The Peace Action Center hosts Peace Action Wisconsin—a peace and social justice organization—and several other environmental and social change organizations. Woodland Pattern—a nonprofit contemporary-literature bookstore, art gallery, and culture center—is a neighborhood institution, having served Riverwest for over thirty years.

During my time in the neighborhood, there were some significant new-comers, as well. The Cream City Collectives (CCC) opened its doors in fall of 2006. The CCC was home to an infoshop, art gallery, screen-printing collective, and lending library, and offered its space for music, lectures, theater, and other gatherings. There was a range of anarchist literature available at the CCC. The intensity of its anarchist connections and the value or threat of those connections were topics of debate among a set of Riverwest's more engaged residents. On its website, the CCC described itself as "a bunch of people who can't wait—not for politicians, not for 'the economy,' and especially not for technological developments to provide for our needs."[55]

The places of commerce, consumption, entertainment, and engagement vary in the social diversity of their clientele or participant base. The membership and volunteers at the Riverwest Co-Op are predominantly white, while most of those who shop at Lena's grocery store are black. The Art Bar, though known as a gay bar, attracts gay and straight, old and young, alike. If you spend an afternoon at Sunrise Foods, a convenience store on a major street, you'll likely see the full range of Riverwest diversity represented in the endless stream of locals stopping in to buy cigarettes, lottery tickets, snacks, kitchen staples, and alcohol (from cheap hooch to pricey microbrews). Some spots, even those that attract a mix of people, become identified with a certain social group and are referred to simply as the Puerto Rican deli, the gay bar, the old man bar, or the black barbershop. For example, during my time in the neighborhood I met a handful of people who consider the Fuel Café to be a "white" place. These labels can act as barriers by making certain residents suspect that they aren't welcome, will be closely watched, or simply won't fit in. Other places have more flexible reputations; the character of the crowd changes with each event theme or live music lineup.

Local businesses and organizations are not the only social gathering places in the neighborhood. Many residents, including those who participate only minimally in local commercial consumption, socialize on the block (see figure 2).

Spatial Organization: The Face Block

At every RNA meeting, the board sets aside time for introductions. All those present are asked to share their name and where they live. Although individuals occasionally give their full addresses, they typically identify their face block. "I'm Elizabeth Karpniak, and I live on 2700 Booth Street." Several scholars have identified the face block as a significant sociocultural unit in dense urban communities, including heterogeneous neighborhoods.[56] In

FIGURE 2 Typical block in Riverwest.

Riverwest, the face block (the two sides of one street between intersecting streets) matters a great deal. The face block includes all dwellings and businesses that face the same block-length section of a street, the public sidewalks that run along both sides of the street, and the street itself. It is the principal geographic component of neighborhood social organization in Riverwest.

Sociologist Ralph Taylor applies an ecological-psychological framework to local social organization, defining face blocks as behavior settings. These are "freestanding natural units of the everyday environment with a recurring pattern of behavior . . . and a surrounding and supporting physical milieu. These units organize community life."[57] These behavior settings are also cultural settings. As ethnographer Gary Alan Fine observes, situated contexts like the face block shape "the evaluation and interpretation of action. Put another way, the local provides a stage for action and creates a lens by which participants typify groups or gatherings, establishing boundaries. As a result, the local is both a material reality and a form of collective representation. Action is always generated in response to other actions within a local scene as well as to the local meaning of that scene."[58] In this proposed framework, the face block mediates the relationship between neighborhood structural conditions and residents' responses to those conditions and is integral in the production of the local social order.

Those on the same block share the conditions of their immediate environment. They are given ample opportunity to interact with or at least observe one another. In Riverwest, face blocks are also key sites of difference negotiation. Most blocks in the neighborhood are diverse in multiple ways. They house various combinations of renters and homeowners; poor, working-class, and middle-class families; young and old; white, black, and Latino; gay and straight couples; college students and retirees; activists and artists; and longtime residents and new arrivals. The large number of duplexes and properties with additional living units in the back of the house (instead of garages) forces many residents to park on the street rather than in the alley. The abundance of multifamily dwellings creates a level of population density that necessitates the management of shared spaces and relationships with near neighbors. Yet density is low enough to make the face block knowable. The majority of houses have porches facing the street, and in the warmer months, many people hang out on their front porches and stoops. The nature of the housing stock in the neighborhood thus facilitates monitoring of neighbors' activities and opportunities for social interaction.

Block Bonding

> Just be out on your porch! You know, that's all you have to do if you wanna enjoy Riverwest, you know. People walking by will say, "Hi." You will spark a conversation. Just be out on your porch. (Heriberto "Eddie" Cardenales, Riverwest native)

In the warmer months, residents tend to socialize on sidewalks, some of the most neutral spaces in the neighborhood. Face-block neighbors feel a sense of collective ownership of their shared sidewalks, corners, and streets. An individual resident may make additional claims to the stretch of sidewalk directly in front of his or her home, but the prevalence of multiunit dwellings and the frequent use of the sidewalks as gathering spots attenuate such notions of proprietorship. The broadly accessible and widely shared sidewalk is where one meets neighbors as neighbors. The lack of barriers to entry and the separation (often by just a few feet) from class- and culture-marking possessions and practices of the domestic sphere make this a relatively inclusive and leveling space. This separation from the home allows neighbors to maintain a boundary between public and private.

The invitation to visit with a neighbor on his or her porch, then, is a significant step, one that signals a modest deepening of trust and acceptance. There are even more fine-grained distinctions between sitting together on the porch steps and mounting the steps to join a neighbor on the porch proper. Many Riverwest houses have a gate separating the front of the house from the back, so an invitation to enjoy beers around the fire pit or grilled bratwurst in the backyard marks another meaningful transition to deepened intimacy. The final step is inviting a neighbor into one's home. This adds another layer of complexity and nuance to observations of block life. One can watch relationships develop and shift. When someone transgresses place norms by, for example, entering a more intimate space without invitation, it can feel like a violation and is often perceptible to sympathetic onlookers.

These emplaced transitions are sorting mechanisms. Although inclusion and exclusion are often influenced by perceived social similarities (e.g., a recent college graduate is more likely to invite those similar in age or education to a backyard gathering), the existence of multiple steps provides many low-stakes opportunities to safely engage with neighbors and facilitates the creation of a range of connections. This staged progression also enables residents to find a workable, neighborly balance between closeness and separateness—one that can be tailored to uniquely fit each relationship.[59] This is particularly important in a socially mixed neighborhood. Without these relatively neutral associational spaces, assumed differences might more powerfully demarcate local ties.

When I ask residents about what (if anything) makes them feel like part of the community, they talk about neighborhood events, specific hangout spots, local organizations, a general feeling of acceptance, rallying around a fellow resident in crisis, the community's response to challenges, and evidence of shared values. They also talk about their block. Lucy Pallotta, a white homeowner who works for a nonprofit organization, reflects on the multiple ways that her block connections influence her experiences and perspective:

LUCY: I have to say I don't know if our block club has made a difference, but it certainly makes a difference in my perception.
EVIE: When you say it's made a difference in your perception, what do you mean?
LUCY: Just one, knowing my frustrations are not mine alone and knowing that there are ten other households that would gladly help me out with the same thing that I would want to call the police about. Or when we are doing something fun like a block party or working in [the community] garden, just kind of knowing that that community—not to overuse that word—exists. I am not one of those people who feels like I can do everything alone. I definitely need people to pat me

on the back. I need engagement. I would like to—my daughter is already getting at it. She's like, "Mommy, I think we have the best block in the world!" And I said, "Really, why?" And she said, "Think of how many people we know and how fun they all are!" And I was like, "Wow! [*laughs*] Alright."

Face blocks also produce a meta-level of neighborhood leadership. In some cases, neighbors consider an official block-watch leader to be head of the block. Other blocks have "mayors," "mothers," "mamas," or "captains" who have been given their titles by virtue of their tenure on the block, their extensive knowledge of local gossip, their connections to organizational resources, or their abundance of proximate social ties. Recognizing these block-level figures and their influence provides a fuller and more complex picture of neighborhood leadership than would a more traditional survey of organization and business leaders.

Keeping an Eye on Things

Riverwesterners develop a sense of the rhythm of block-level activity.[60] They observe their neighbors' routine movements in, out of, and around the block: people going to and from work, taking bundled kids to day care, walking the dog, and holding court on the porch. They become familiar with the local soundscape: Fred's Friday night band practice, Linecia calling her dog to come inside, the pack of youngsters teasing each other as they walk home from school, Carlos's need for a new motorcycle muffler (made evident by every departure and arrival), the occasional yelling match between the young couple down the street, Tara's backyard gatherings (more boisterous by the hour). They mark the season's changes based on the level of sidewalk and porch chatter and property maintenance projects (those tackled and those ignored). These recognizable patterns contribute to residents' sense of control by making the proximate environment predictable and helping residents identify atypical activity.

The threat of crime, coupled with residential instability, provides additional incentive to get to know one's most proximate neighbors. The definition of "getting to know" encompasses a broad spectrum of interaction, from simple physical recognition to the development of deep, intimate ties. Weak ties need not develop into strong ties to contribute to the maintenance of proximal order. These social connections, coupled with block-level observations, provide residents with information to determine who belongs on the block, who is safe, and what they should expect from their neighbors. After over a decade in Riverwest, black renter-turned-homeowner June Jones has learned the value of block awareness: "You have to keep a close watch of who's going in and who's coming out. If you don't know, that will hurt you. But the more you know, the more you have power to control what goes on." Leon Wade, a black teacher who lives in the neighborhood, describes how those on his block look out for one another:

> I love my block. I have, like, my neighbors to the north of me? Great guys. I know every person down my side of my block. I know the person to the other side of me. I know my people across the street. I know my people. I love my block because when we're outside, we're waving to each other. You know? It's stuff like that. If [Franny] goes out of town, she'll call me and tell me she's going out of town. If [Corey's] going out of town, he'll call [Franny] and she'll tell me, you know, boom boom boom. And if [Kyle and Erica] are doing their thing, they'll let us know. And [Luisa] who lives next door to me, the little Puerto Rican lady, all their kids—her kids pretty much watch my house like a hawk. "Who are you? What are you doing at [Leon's] house?" They're like little watchdogs. They're crazy. She'll call me at work, "[Leon], are you at home? Because someone was by your house." I'm like, "Nice."

Riverwest is described, at least internally, as being "block by block" (i.e., varying in quality from one block to the next), which underscores the important influence proximate neighbors have on one's quality of life. The standard advice residents offer to those looking for housing in the neighborhood is, "Find out about the block." Neighbors may have very different ideas about appropriate noise levels, property maintenance, child-rearing practices, leisure activities, economic activity, and so on. When residents share stories about confronting nonnormative behavior, these encounters have typically taken place on their block.

The socially diverse face block is where residents make sense of difference. They sometimes discover commonalities that erode previously perceived differences and forge a sense of belonging. They figure out how to distinguish between the dissimilar and the deviant. They wrestle with the appropriate steps to take with a problematic neighbor. They learn how to determine when others find their behavior unacceptable. In uniting against a common threat, face-block neighbors may also develop a sense of collective self, a meaningful "we" identity.[61] The block is, for these reasons, a key site of difference negotiation and social control.

Some face blocks are more tightly knit than others. Shorter blocks, those with less residential stability (i.e., high renter turnover), and those lacking a central figure tend to be less interconnected. Also, levels of engagement fluctuate over time. The emergence of a problem or the arrival of a gregarious neighbor can spark associations or revitalize face-block collaboration. Block reputations can also rise and fall with changes in property ownership, rental occupants, and the effectiveness of neighbor alliances.

Although there are variations in social organization from block to block, face blocks are not islands. There is, as I will demonstrate, a rough coherence to neighborhood life. The face block functions as a filter of collective understandings and shared standards by stressing certain elements more than others. To make block life predictable, residents develop an alternative, flexible, and revisable set of guidelines for navigating daily life. The utility of this bundle of understandings and street literacy skills is not confined to the block. Residents apply the strategies they develop on the block to assist them in negotiating interactions throughout the neighborhood.

Emplacing integration makes the shared conditions of everyday life in a diverse neighborhood accessible. As Gieryn asserts, it opens "place effects" to examination, allowing us to consider how "the tight coupling of geography, built-form, and subjective topological understanding mediates the effects of size, demographic patterns, and values on the possibility or achievement of community."[62] The anomalous diversity of Riverwest in a divided and divisive city, the neighborhood's positioning between relatively advantaged and disadvantaged places, and the arrangement of streets and dwellings that subdivides the neighborhood into intense interactional worlds together influence how social heterogeneity is lived and understood in this Milwaukee community.

CHAPTER THREE

Placemaking
Culture and Neighborhood Frames

Some people value diversity. Some people don't. I guess that's what
diversity looks like [*bursts out laughing*].
—Robin Lund, Riverwest resident

People make and remake places through the stories they tell, the descriptions
they fashion, and the working theories they develop about a particular place.
"I got pistol-whipped in Riverwest. Twice!" "I can't imagine living anywhere in
this city other than Riverwest. I don't care if I had a billion dollars. I wanna live
here." "Riverwest is trying to save the whole damn world. I think it's working."
Placemaking is not a solitary endeavor; it is a social enterprise. Collectively
constructed perceptions and interpretations are as important as the objective
facts of places in shaping how insiders and outsiders act on and within places.
These shared understandings are central to creating an ongoing social order.
Culture is, in the words of sociologist Gary Alan Fine, an "organizing force."[1]
Attention to neighborhoods as cultural contexts, then, can reveal mechanisms
linking neighborhood conditions to residents' daily decisions and interactions.[2]

Mario Small calls attention to the importance of being sensitive to *variation* in the ways in which people respond to neighborhood conditions: different cultural frames are linked to different ways of navigating a particular
place.[3] It is unlikely that residents of socially mixed communities have uniform interpretations of (or responses to) diversity.[4] During my years of fieldwork, I encountered quite an assortment of Riverwests, from "just plain
shitty" to "deserving of a Nobel Peace Prize!" But some clear patterns emerged
out of the cacophony of resident voices. Here, I introduce the two prevailing frames that residents use to make sense of Riverwest. In later chapters, I
demonstrate how residents' understandings of what their neighborhood *is*
and *should be* are linked to the strategies they adopt for neighborhood negotiation and dealing with difference.

Diversity Talk and Diversity Work

Recent studies of contemporary meanings and uses of diversity reveal that
diversity-affirming initiatives rarely produce significant challenges to existing

social inequalities.[5] While mayors, college presidents, CEOs, and ministers trumpet the value of diversity, their efforts tend to maintain the status quo. When they celebrate social differences in ways that abstract those differences from broader relations of power, they miss or avoid opportunities to draw attention to unjust group privileges (e.g., white privilege, heterosexual privilege, able-bodied privilege). In her investigation of racial diversity discourse in university, corporate, and neighborhood settings, sociologist Ellen Berrey finds that decision makers employ definitions of racial progress that largely reflect the interests of whites and other dominant groups. For example, when white neighborhood leaders' embrace of diversity does not extend beyond the *selective* inclusion of only those nonwhite residents who conform to their notions of appropriate behavior and civic orientation, they shore up rather than challenge the presumed (and unstated) superiority of white, middle-class norms.[6] Racial diversity projects that "welcome" nonwhites to support existing organizational objectives have limited transformative potential.

These findings underscore the importance of assessing the links or disconnects between how people talk about diversity and how they negotiate difference. Berrey argues that understanding culture is essential for exploring these connections. "Integration is not simply a demographic or political process. It is a cultural one—a meaning-making process produced through human agency and shaped by social relations, power dynamics, competitive markets, institutional interests and other forces. Diversity discourses and initiatives serve as organizing principles from which organizations and people improvise as they engage in and make sense of integration."[7] The following three chapters explore different facets of the relationship between framing and doing difference in Riverwest and consider their complex interactions with local dynamics of social stratification. While qualitative researchers who study diverse communities often focus on organizational-level processes, I concentrate on microlevel processes, examining the daily encounters with difference in which neighbors respond to and shape their environment.

Diversity Is Our Strength

In July 2003, a racial separatist group calling themselves the Riverwest Anti-Nigger Movement distributed hate flyers encouraging "good, moral white people" to "take back the neighborhood. . . . Do not befriend the blacks." They demanded that African American residents leave Riverwest: "Go West of Holton St. and don't come back."[8] The accompanying literature included anti-Arab, anti-Semitic, and anti-black messages. The next day, nearly three hundred people gathered at Gordon Park to demonstrate their outrage at the flyer's message and their support for an integrated Riverwest. The neighborhood's Peace Action Center collected donations to support the production of hundreds of "Diversity Is Our Strength" yard signs that soon dotted the neighborhood. A few of these signs remained staked in the front yards of Riverwest homes in 2010.

Eugene Kane, a black *Milwaukee Journal Sentinel* columnist who often writes about race, was puzzled by the hate group's targeting of Riverwest: "It seems particularly stupid that fliers were passed out in Riverwest, a diverse neighborhood of homeowners and renters with children who play together and connect along cultural lines better than in most parts in the city. I lived in Riverwest for six years; it was a place where coffee shops, art galleries and community organizations co-existed with drug dealers and rowdy taverns. The people in Riverwest handle the racial dynamics in their area as well or better than anybody else in town."[9] This key event threatened and thus served to bolster the neighborhood's identity as a community that prizes its diversity.

In his history of the neighborhood, Tom Tolan describes Riverwest as "distinctly bohemian and proudly diverse, a neighborhood that any number of groups can claim as their own."[10] Residents are aware of their exceptional status as a racially diverse neighborhood in a hypersegregated city. Riverwest's unique status strengthens the perception of diversity as a significant community asset and a source of local pride. The "diversity is our strength" frame almost always refers to the neighborhood's racial and ethnic mix, but is usually expanded to include diversity in class and subculture. Some residents add diversity in age, sexual orientation, gender identity, political ideology, beliefs, ability, and the catchall "background." Dora Ramos, a bicultural Latina, moved to Riverwest in the mid-1980s and has worked in the neighborhood's public schools for over thirty years. She describes her take on the local social mix: "It is a community that is so rich with culture and experience and oh! the arts! . . . Riverwest is a place that people of all different perspectives can live, not just backgrounds but perspectives. You know, one house on a block can have the McCain [Republican presidential candidate in 2008] bumper stickers and be very clear—the red white and blue and all this stuff. They have that and their neighbor next door can have the rainbow flags and gay lesbian stuff right there. And people can live on the same block, in the same neighborhood, and people respect that. It's kind of a place where I feel people can believe what they want to believe and it's tolerated." Many residents, like Dora, cite visible markers of diversity in politics and identity, although some argue that the local political spectrum ranges from communist to centrist.

In addition to the coexistence of various categories of people (classes, races, subcultures, etc.), residents' diversity talk references what they perceive to be conditions or products of that coexistence: tolerance, inclusion, freedom of expression, creativity, innovation, and intrigue. The semantic flexibility of the word *diversity* lends this frame strength in terms of numbers. Many Riverwest residents can claim to value something shared and widely seen as positive. However, residents' use of this broad, elastic, and often celebratory definition of diversity can also obscure or ignore issues of inequality.

Outsiders In

Unlike other areas or in other cities where you might walk down the street and people will be like, "Oh, an outsider," there is so many different people here that you will never have the feeling of being an outsider. (Hazel Carver, second-generation Riverwest resident)

Those who feel outside the mainstream are drawn to and are generally welcome in this neighborhood. The prevalence of nonconventional appearance is symbolic testament to the broad embrace of diversity. Body adornment (from piercings to tattoos), hairstyles (from dreadlocks to mohawks), and styles of dress (from rockabilly to the latest hip-hop fashion trends) signal "outsiders in." Tamika Evans, a black resident in her thirties, values the local offbeat parade: "It's awesome. I mean, you see the people in this neighborhood? Like, I was sitting out here . . . three weeks ago maybe with a few friends: two business owners, one very, very conservative woman, who was interesting. But anyway, this guy walks by, and he's got on a kilt. No shoes. He's pushing a baby. He's got a baby on his back. He's got both nipples pierced, he—and I didn't flinch, 'cause it's like, that's my neighborhood. This is my neighborhood. This is how we roll." Numerous local businesses are run by or employ people with unorthodox appearances. Several residents remarked on how this sanctioning of things nontraditional in the typically more formal and rule-bound world of business amplifies the community's embrace of diversity.

Marcus Zwic, a biracial artist, did not feel at home in the predominantly white or predominantly black communities he lived in. His comfort in Riverwest is related to its racial and ethnic diversity but also to what he sees as a broad acceptance of differences deemed problematic elsewhere. For Marcus, the neighborhood is "a literal circus of culture. I love it. I like being a part of it. I am a freak, too. It's where the freaks live, and we are all happy. We can go anyplace else in town, either they look down their nose at you, or you are a target, or you are something *else*. But here, all that stuff is cool." He sees Riverwest as not only appreciative of difference but also inclusive. This is why so many fellow artists have found their way to the neighborhood. "It's eclectic, bohemian, artsy, and multicultural. Different ages . . . there are rich people, poor people—there are all kinds. There is every type of faith and denomination. It's all mixed up. . . . It's also gay and lesbian friendly, too; there is a lot of alternative lifestyle intermingling. So it's like, shit, come on! And ain't nobody really saying anything. It's like everyone is just like, 'yeah cool.'" One of Marcus's friends offered a bumper-sticker summary: "Outsiders in!"

In Riverwest, there is support for an alternative prestige hierarchy in which wealth accumulation, material consumption, and degrees are less likely to garner reputational reward than creative expression, community engagement, meaningful vocation, or thrift. Robin Lund, a resident community organizer, believes that this different approach to evaluating success is contributing to neighborhood stability. She has noticed that the young people who used to spend a few years in the neighborhood and move on are now settling in Riverwest: "I think they're taking responsibility and feel like they have an investment in this neighborhood and they're making it their own. They're making it the way they want it to be even though they fight all the time about what they want it to be. Their idealism isn't being crushed. They aren't being asked, 'When are you going to get a real job?' They're figuring out that they don't have to go to work for big corporations. There's no stigma in not being able to afford real, you know, new cars. In fact, there's kind of a stigma associated with buying anything new. The culture is about thrift shops and alley shopping. There's too much stuff in this culture, so let's just redistribute what people are throwing away." Tamika Evans left a corporate-track job with high earning potential to do something she enjoys for far less financial reward. She believes that those who are baffled by her decision would likely struggle with the neighborhood's culture:

> I really appreciate people who are motivated by money. I think that's great if that's your thing. If that's what makes you happy, then go for it! I will respect whatever it is that moves you. It'd be nice if you had some level of respect or could assign some level of value to what moves me, but if you don't and money moves you, it tells me something about you. I don't wanna make a judgment about it, but that is what it is, too. I mean, democracy and diversity cost. And there are going to be people in this beautifully diverse neighborhood who are diverse and say, "You fucking poor people! [*laughs*] Do something better! This neighborhood

could be the East Side! [*laughs*] It could be Tosa![11] Why are you fucking it up?" 'Cause it's Riverwest, and Riverwest is Riverwest.

Tamika went on to explain that living in this class-mixed neighborhood is "just easier" for residents who accept that people have varying attitudes about and opportunities for economic mobility.

For Lucy Pallotta, a white homeowner, local definitions of success that privilege collective well-being over individual gain are at the core of the neighborhood's collaborative culture. "You are either a 'me' person or a 'we' person. The 'we' people tend to get along a lot better in Riverwest. Because the 'me' people I think are usually—they are going to be swimming upstream." Lucy believes that this particular aspect of Riverwest culture is strong enough to shape residents' experiences of belonging or fit.

Don't Mess with Us

The neighborhood's activist orientation contributes to its reputed strength. The official designation during the 1970s of the neighborhood as "faltering" and subsequent battles with the city over plans for proposed neighborhood improvements helped shape the neighborhood's identity as inclusive, engaged, and fiercely self-determining.[12] A significant subset of residents take an active interest in shaping Riverwest and are quick to respond to perceived threats. Robin Lund puts it bluntly: "This is who we are. Don't mess with us."

For John Bauer, a white homeowner who has lived in the neighborhood since the early 1970s, Riverwest's diversity, strength, and resilience are its defining characteristics. When I asked him what he meant by strength and resilience, he said, "People who have put up against crime, people that have put up against government ignoring them, people that have been able to withstand predatory lenders, people that have put up with the constant negative image that people have about the neighborhood and still haven't allowed it to bother them. This isn't anything recent. This is decades where this has been going on. People have been able to put up with problem houses on their blocks and still not run, and have allowed the neighborhood to continue as it is. They figure there's enough evidence to say it's improving." Residents combat crime, neglect, and neighborhood stigma. As I will discuss, they also combat development proposals that they perceive as threatening the character or integrity of Riverwest.

Local activists direct their efforts toward not only resistance but also creation. The neighborhood houses several justice-promoting organizations, including Peace Action Wisconsin and Rethinking Schools, an organization that seeks to improve public education through teaching social justice. During my time in Riverwest, there was a steady stream of resident-initiated movements and projects flowing through the neighborhood, such as creating alternative local or time-based currencies; launching all manner of cooperatives; instituting an annual Power Down week, which focuses on creative strategies for reducing energy consumption; freecycling (giving away or obtaining goods that might otherwise be thrown away); reclaiming and repurposing neglected public spaces; developing urban farms; restoring and protecting the riverfront; advocating for economic justice and nonviolence; promoting youth empowerment and community engagement; and creating public art projects.

For Jess Durand, a white local entrepreneur who is raising her family in the neighborhood, Riverwest's innovative spirit is a point of pride: "Riverwest can be—it can be glorious. It can be a community that's talked about elsewhere in the country and used as a model for other areas. You know? I really feel like the public schools, the private schools, the arts and the education, all of the amenities, whether it be access to cultural things in the city, that kinda stuff? Our neighborhood fuels it. A lot of people in Riverwest are fueling that—are helping to create it. That's what Riverwest is about to me. It's about people taking initiative to create projects."

Resident Scott Farago is often teased by fellow civil servants about the seemingly endless change initiatives and radical ideas championed by his neighborhood's busy activists. "I'll get a lot of, 'You still saving the world over there? How's that socialism thing working out in Riverwest?' . . . It's fun to make fun of Riverwest for taking itself too seriously or being a little too idealistic, which is all valid criticism, but I think you'd much rather live in a place where there's people taking a few risks to make fun of than living in a place where everyone is just trying to fit in." Although residents like Scott observe that neighborhood crusades often fall short of their ambitious goals, they see their community as a place that cultivates imaginative alternatives to the status quo and allows people enough latitude to try them out. Leon Wade, a black teacher and local homeowner, believes that idealism is part of what connects the assortment of residents:

Everything under the sun lives here. A description of them? Just different. Different. We're all different but we're all the same because we all have that commonality. Something drew us here. You know, it's just like, we all have that "save the world" mentality to some degree. It hasn't been engineered out of us. There's that common "I want to make the world a better place" thread. To some degree, we're kinda pompous about it. We're like, "Yeah, I live in Riverwest." You never hear anybody say, "Yeah, I live in Riverwest" [*mumbles, head hanging*]. No one holds their heads down when they talk about Riverwest. We could all get fuckin' tattoos on our arms or wear big belts that say "Riverwest!" We're like a little gang, but we're a positive gang.

Leon is proud to be part of a neighborhood that he views as committed to positive social change.

Frame Supports

There are a range of organizational supports for the diversity frame. The East Side Housing Action Committee—the neighborhood organization credited with giving Riverwest its name—also helped shape its identity. ESHAC's efforts to bridge differences and build a coalition for neighborhood empowerment and change contributed to Riverwest's reputation as a place of diversity and activism.[13] In 1999, the YMCA Housing Initiative facilitated a neighborhood planning process. In community meetings, focus groups, and neighborhood assessment surveys, the importance of maintaining Riverwest's socioeconomic and racial-ethnic diversity emerged as a central theme and therefore figures prominently in the goals and objectives of the Riverwest Neighborhood Strategic Plan.[14] The plan recommended, among other things, creating a neighborhood newspaper and a neighborhood association.

Riverwest Currents began as a local newsletter in 1999 and became a monthly newspaper in 2002. It is now published in print and online. The mission description on the newspaper's website incorporates the diversity frame: "The *Riverwest Currents* is dedicated to writing about issues and events important to those who live, work, and play in and around the Riverwest neighborhood. We believe Riverwest is a good place to make a home or set up a shop. We want to help promote a safe and affordable neighborhood, to embrace urban aesthetics, to respect diversity, and to make Riverwest residents aware of the opportunities available to them. . . . Our mission has always been to promote fair housing and to encourage the preservation of diversified home ownership in Riverwest."[15] *Riverwest Currents* highlights the positive aspects of diversity in neighbor profiles and coverage of neighborhood events, organizations, and businesses. Even in the newspaper's occasional discussions of Riverwest's divisions and challenges, diversity is overwhelmingly portrayed as an asset worthy of attention and protection. The vast majority of contributors—writers, cartoonists, illustrators, and photographers—are locals. The paper's editor, Jan Christensen, believes that the paper has helped shape and broadcast the neighborhood's identity: "It's good for the neighborhood for people to look at themselves and write about themselves. It helps them define their identity. . . . We have a documented history that's accessible now, so that really, really feeds into the character of the neighborhood. I think there's a lot of pride in our neighborhood. The *Riverwest Currents* has helped to put the definition of our neighborhood out there. I think it is more respected in the city as a whole. You know, people still say 'Riverwest,' but instead of saying 'Riverwest' with fear, they say it with intrigue or affection, you know, for a mischievous, slightly misbehaving, red-headed stepchild."

Diversity maintenance is also central to the stated mission of the Riverwest Neighborhood Association (RNA). The organization's bylaws state that the RNA "exists to empower, educate and advocate for the residents of the Riverwest neighborhood" and to "promote and uphold the unique identity of our neighborhood, including our history, our traditions of cooperation, our support for locally-owned businesses, our social and civic engagement, and the diversity of race, economics, culture, family and lifestyle found in Riverwest."[16]

The neighborhood's identity is discursively constructed and maintained through comparisons to other places.[17] Many Riverwesterners are protective of their uniqueness and resist being clumped with other areas in the city. They reject outsiders' characterizations of their community as "ghetto." While some shun comparisons to Brady Street—a trendy district that has been revitalized and gentrified—others see Brady Street as a model of neighborhood development. Some residents claim that their neighborhood is the antithesis of the homogeneous, conformist, mainstream suburbs. Residents also compare Riverwest to Bay View, an urban neighborhood that has started to attract some of the same types of people as Riverwest. Some of those who share the widely held belief that Bay View is less racially and economically diverse and has far less crime than Riverwest brand Bay View the "Riverwest retirement community" or "where hipsters go to die." They suggest that it is a neighborhood for white people who are too soft to handle urban living (which variously refers to living with crime, living with difference, or living with non-white people). One of my Riverwest neighbors described Bay View as "Riverwest without ethnic people." The prevalence of this biting and often judgment-laden comparison can make the decision to move particularly loaded. As Jeff Reimer, a white renter-turned-homeowner, observes, "There's a lot of Riverwest-rooted people who have moved to Bay View, and they are always trying to justify it and it's a big trauma for them and they feel guilty or conflicted about it. A lot of people try to sneak away and don't want people to know." Jeff finds that those who have incorporated the "diversity is our strength" frame into their identity anticipate negative criticism when moving to places deemed inferior by Riverwest standards.

A handful of annual events accentuate features of the local character. During my time in Riverwest, I attended all the local festivals—many of them more than once. The Locust Street Festival is the largest Riverwest function. The festival was launched to commemorate the success of local efforts to block the proposed widening of Locust Street in the mid-1970s. Although some residents approved of the plan to improve traffic flow between the interstate and the East Side, ESHAC-linked activists organized to prevent the razing of properties and the associated displacement of residents and local businesses. After the throughway in the heart of the neighborhood was fixed up (rather than expanded), the neighborhood threw a party on Locust Street, and a tradition was born.[18] Because it draws tens of thousands of people from all over the city, many residents tout the festival as an opportunity to show Milwaukee what the neighborhood is all about. One Milwaukee weekly paper highlighting the 2010 event noted, "From its modest beginnings as a neighborhood festival with an understated bohemian streak, the annual Locust Street Festival, now in its 34th year, has blossomed into one of the city's most crowded outdoor gatherings, without losing the friendly, oversized-block-party feel that made it so charming."[19] The festival begins with the Beer Run: hundreds of participants, some donning outrageous costumes, run a 1.8 mile course that includes four mandatory stops for hydration (i.e., beer drinking). Bands perform throughout the day on one of a handful of music stages. There are art, craft, food, and beer vendors; street theater performances; and activities for children. Since entrance to the festival is free, most Riverwest residents who want to attend do so. People wander up and down the lively, loud, packed street to people-watch and take in the scene.

Center Street Daze is the quirkier, more local little sister to the Locust Street Festival. This early fall street festival kicks off with the Riverwest Artist Association's art-cart race at the east end of the blocked-off street. Riverwesterners construct assorted human-powered wheeled carts—from spaceships to president-ridiculing thrones—to race on a course in the middle of the street. One resident affectionately refers to Center Street Daze as "our freak pageant." The small businesses, restaurants, and bars on Center Street open their doors. A string of local characters endure a shift in the RNA's dunk tank. Children play games and have their faces painted. A notable addition to the live music, food, and art typical of Milwaukee street parties is the car show. The proud owners of custom rides, dream cars, and classic autos drive down Center Street in a slow, colorful parade and then park their cars for display at the west end of the street.

The first time I attended Center Street Daze, I took note of the racial geography of the festival. Although there was some mixing, white festivalgoers clustered at the east end of the street, and black attendees clustered at the west end of the street. There were relatively few Latino/a attendees at either end of the street. This mapped onto both the location and the racial composition of key festival activities, as the vast majority of art-cart race participants were white, and the vast majority of car-show participants were black. This also mapped onto the racial geography of the bordering communities: the majority-white East Side and the majority-black Harambee to the west. In the two subsequent Center Street Daze festivals, I observed less stark divisions but was still struck by the diverse yet largely racially segregated space.

Another annual fall event, the Riverwest Art Walk, was started in 1979 to showcase the abundance of local artists. Attendees are given a map that guides them through a walking tour of artists' studios, local galleries, and other assorted art spaces. At Rockerbox, the annual motorcycle show–street party, café racers, choppers, scooters, and sidecars line Center Street for all to admire.

The newest addition to the lineup of neighborhood events is the Riverwest 24 (RW24), a twenty-four-hour bike race through the neighborhood. RW24 organizers launched the race in 2009 as a celebration of urban biking and to promote community connection and a positive image of the neighborhood. One of the event creators, Jeremy Prach, is a special education teacher who came to Riverwest in search of fellow punk rockers and ended up settling in the neighborhood with his wife and children.[20] On the event website, there is a picture of Prach beaming as he pedals across a neighborhood bridge. The accompanying text reads: "The RW24 was born through community block watches throughout Riverwest. It is a way for our neighborhood to welcome new people, strengthen relationships within the community (and beyond), and show everyone why Riverwest is amazing. From riders to volunteers, organizers to community sponsors, everyone brings a different talent and interest to the table. There is no way a few people talking about a bike race in their back yards could have come up with something like this. A whole neighborhood made this. I'm sure I speak for everyone when I say, VIVA LA RIVERWEST!"[21]

Those living on streets along the race route organize block parties and gather to cheer on the riders. Locals volunteer staff bonus checkpoints where participants have their tarot cards read, haul buckets of compost up to a rooftop garden, or get a RW24 tattoo for extra points. One local paper provided a short event description: "Just as irreverent as the neighborhood it calls home, the RW24 is less a race than a day-long block party on wheels."²² Resident Paul Kelley believes that it takes a particular kind of neighborhood to host such an event: "You have to have a place like this where people care enough to let it happen, but don't care about it enough to get pissed about it. And there is a unique thing about Riverwest." Many residents describe the RW24 as an event that embodies the "anything goes" spirit of the neighborhood. Although the race draws a mix of neighbors to their porches and front sidewalks to support or shake their heads at the racers, the official participants (cyclists and volunteers) are mostly young (twenty to fifty years old) and overwhelmingly white.

Residents variously draw on these neighborhood organizations and events in framing Riverwest as proudly diverse and decidedly offbeat.

Maintaining the Mix

This neighborhood frame defines what Riverwest *is* and is linked to a vision of what it *should be*. Riverwest's diversity, culture, inclusiveness, and right to self-determination need to be nurtured and protected. Many view gentrification—the influx of wealthier residents and displacement of lower-income residents—as a real threat to the neighborhood's economic, racial, and cultural diversity. For Robin Lund, a white renter, gentrification means homogenization: "The thing that makes Riverwest so desirable is the fact that it's diverse. And if it stopped being diverse, it's going to look like Brookfield or Whitefish Bay [two predominantly white, upper-class suburbs,] and it's going to be a boring place to live."

Many proudly diverse Riverwesterners do not see positive neighborhood change as a linear process in which upscale growth and economic development are "natural" occurrences. They tend to resist top-down plans for progress while enthusiastically endorsing grassroots innovations that fit or augment their sense of the neighborhood. Any proposal for residential or commercial development is met with suspicion by one group of civically engaged Riverwesterners. However, this small but vocal collage of residents often disagree on tactics and goals. While some adamantly oppose almost every large-scale development proposition, others work to ensure that locals have a role in shaping the planning process. Many engaged Riverwest residents expect their public representatives and service providers to be responsive, although that alternately means intensified intervention and staying out of local affairs. Maliha Noor, an Arab American resident and vocal neighborhood advocate, believes that the city government and developers see Riverwest as a force to be reckoned with: "I think there is some sense, a sense here of, 'This is our neighborhood, these are our streets, these are our buildings, this is our property.' I think there is a recognition among development people among the city and people who might want to come in and change things that there's going to be trouble. . . . So I think there is a sense that—that we have made this neighborhood ours. The legitimacy comes because we are recognized for it." A Milwaukee Department of City Development planner confirmed that Riverwest has earned the reputation of being "hostile to development."

"Diversity is our strength" is the dominant framing of the neighborhood. When asked to describe their neighborhood, the majority of Riverwest residents bring up diversity as a defining, positive feature of the community. The use of this frame cuts across race and ethnicity, class, age, tenure in the neighborhood, subculture, and homeowner and renter status. Diversity is part of what pulled some of these residents to the neighborhood in the first place. Others developed an appreciation for the unique mix of residents after moving to Riverwest and being exposed to local place narratives. Some native Riverwesterners have adopted "diversity is our strength" but remember a time before their community celebrated its assortment of people and practices.

There is considerable variation in their residential mobility trajectories, as well. Residents who embrace the social mix come from affluent suburbs, poor urban communities, and rural towns, and some were born and raised in Riverwest. I found more concentrated use of this frame among the more formal leadership in the neighborhood, including neighborhood association members, organization leaders, community organizers, and local business owners. This very loosely affiliated group of engaged residents is whiter and more highly educated than is the neighborhood as a whole.

Is this difference touting merely "happy talk"? In an analysis of everyday discourse in the United States, Joyce Bell and Douglas Hartmann find that conversations about diversity tend to celebrate difference in the abstract while ignoring the realities of related inequalities.[23] Although social differences like race, gender, class, and sexual orientation are ranked and embedded in power relationships of domination and oppression, discussions about the value of diversity rarely include acknowledgment of racism, sexism, classism, or heterosexism. In Riverwest, context influences how residents talk about the neighborhood's social mix. When residents employ "Diversity is our strength" to promote or defend their community, they rarely pair this frame with analyses of power and privilege. They tend to extol the virtues of neighborhood integration by projecting an image of an intriguing and vibrant mosaic.

In spaces more conducive to reflection and critique (e.g., casual gatherings or insider meetings for community members), however, some residents offer understandings of the neighborhood that include recognition that differences are not neutral and that discrimination and inequality are part of the local story. For example, they question the legitimacy of predominantly white or majority-homeowner groups that claim to represent the neighborhood or challenge their neighbors' assumptions about "suspicious" black men. As the following chapters will demonstrate, examining diversity discourse *and* practice reveals a more nuanced account of Riverwesterners' everyday navigation of integration.

The Neighborhood Has Potential

In Riverwest, the embrace of the neighborhood's multifaceted heterogeneity is widespread though hardly universal. Some residents long for the tight-knit Polish or Puerto Rican communities of their youth; others link racial and economic diversity to crime. Some see heterogeneity as a demographic fact instead of a valued asset. The alternative neighborhood framing I heard most from those engaged in the community, however, was "the neighborhood has potential." For this relatively small group of residents, many of whom have moved to the neighborhood in the last decade, Riverwest has enormous promise. The combination of natural resources (multiple parks, the riverfront); proximity to downtown and other desirable destinations; access to public transportation; eclectic collection of bars, restaurants, and boutiques; and comparatively low housing prices makes Riverwest a good choice for investment.

According to this frame, such investment, in the form of increased homeownership and responsible economic development, will bring much-needed stability to the neighborhood. These residents feel a deep sense of ownership of the neighborhood and see themselves as responsible for protecting and improving it. They demonstrate this ownership through language (e.g., "This is MY neighborhood") and acts of stewardship (e.g., pressuring their alderperson to make specific improvements). For some, this feeling of ownership is connected to a sense of neighborhood belonging. For others, it is an extension of the entitlements associated with property ownership. These

residents see Riverwest's rebellious and fiercely antidevelopment reputation as a considerable obstacle to neighborhood improvement. They would
like to redirect local civic engagement toward addressing ongoing crime
problems, attracting "successful" people to the neighborhood, and pressuring
the owners of dilapidated and neglected properties to maintain their homes.

George Morris, a black, retired civil servant who has lived in Riverwest
for decades, is tired of irresponsible resistance to neighborhood development
opportunities:

> Diversity and all that craziness? I could care less about it. Each to
> his own. You have yours I have mine, you don't mess with me I don't
> mess with you, but the development? Gentrification? I am sorry. Time
> moves on. If something has to be remodeled it has to be remodeled.
> There is nothing cheap about it. The Unconventional Thought and
> Action Coalition [George's name for diversity defenders]—they think
> that people have a right to live in this neighborhood, and we argued
> about this. "Oh, they have a right to live here but who are you to come
> in and fix your house up and whatever, I can't live here I can't afford it."
> "Oh I am sorry. Get a better job. Make more money. I can't help that.
> I have a right because I am putting my right and my effort into it and
> you are saying you have more right than me? Who are you to say what
> I can and cannot do just so you can live here?"

While George is clearly upset by what he sees as empty entitlement claims,
he is equally frustrated by middle-class residents who are apathetic and assume others will take care of their community. For George, the right to live
in the neighborhood is connected not only to having enough resources to
withstand property value increases but also to being responsible for maintaining and improving Riverwest.

Adrian Romero, a Latino Riverwest business owner who has invested his
energy in neighborhood improvement for decades, acknowledges the concerns of those opposed to development but sees projects like condominium
construction as broadly beneficial. "Some people will be unhappy about it
that the property values are increasing. In my point of view those are all really
good things, and I know that's always a concern about—well, what happens
to those people and the little old ladies who live in their houses who have a
hard time paying their property taxes because the value of their property went
up? But all in all I would say that I am in favor of this kind of development—
because the alternative is going in the other direction and then that's much,
much worse." The neighborhood's buffer location makes it vulnerable to

crime and decline. Adrian has witnessed the destruction and demoralization caused by periods of heightened gang and drug activity. For him, the potential of intelligent commercial and housing investments to secure the neighborhood far outweighs their costs.

Megan and James Chapman, a young interracial couple, bought a condo in Riverwest in 2004. They are both professionals, and the neighborhood is conveniently close to their workplaces. They appreciate the neighborhood parks and the friendliness of the neighborhood. Despite the fact that their politics rarely align with the majority opinion among Riverwest's grassroots leaders, the Chapmans view the neighborhood's sense of ownership and sense of community as assets. Megan has been disappointed, however, to find that the supposed valuing of diversity and open-mindedness does not extend to condo owners or those perceived as having less modest means:

> It's not like we all have to get along and hug and love is in the air, but if there is some way to be different but move things forward, I think that that would be good. I think that it's unfortunate that a lot of people in the neighborhood in Riverwest have been so angry about condo development, because I think it's prevented a lot of people from getting to know us—us being condo owners. What is so ironic about it—and I would also call it hypocritical—is that Riverwesterners claim to be very open-minded, very liberal, very welcoming, yet I would say that just the opposite happened to us. People approaching us when we're coming out of our own house saying that we shouldn't live there. "Rich people." And you know? Not really.

For some time, Megan felt rather isolated in terms of her views on development and positive growth. Eventually, she connected with residents who shared her vision for the neighborhood. Like many of these like-minded residents, her husband, James, sees the diversity rhetoric as a red flag: "Well I think because a lot of people, they don't really understand or want true diversity. What they want is a representative group of people of different races, colors, and genders all thinking the exact same way. To me, that's not diversity. In fact, it's the exact opposite. It perpetuates the problem because what you've got here are a lot of mini social engineers. They've committed themselves to enforcing a vision of diversity that can't really work over time, and the unintended consequences of that leave the neighborhood not recognizing its potential."

A few clever residents invested in Riverwest's potential proposed a new motto for those who trumpet diversity rhetoric: "Diversity is our alibi." Like

James, they believe that some residents use the diversity discourse in ways that mask their privilege or obscure how their interests and tastes—rather than true representations of diverse interests—drive their agenda.[24] They describe several pockets of vocal leadership in the neighborhood (like the core of the RNA) as predominantly white and politically homogeneous. The neighborhood advocacy claims of what one resident termed the "self-appointed ruling class" ring hollow when those advocates fail to acknowledge that their stances on local issues are not developed through an inclusive process. Championing diversity provides cover.

Riverwest residents who are invested in the neighborhood's potential are also acutely aware of and frustrated by lifestyle clashes (e.g., inappropriate use of public space, permissive parenting practices, loud neighbors, and disruptive leisure activities) and what they see as broad tolerance for bad behavior. They are not opposed to living in a diverse neighborhood but don't see diversity as worthy of special protection. As some predict, future changes in neighborhood demographics will likely be a consequence of neutral market forces at work rather than malevolence.

White homeowners Joanne and Mark Jansen, though disappointed in the slow pace of change, believe Riverwest is headed in the right direction. They are invested in building a network of residents who share their vision of neighborhood development and progress. The Jansens think that the housing market is trending in their favor:

MARK: The neighborhood is vastly blue collar, poor people who are struggling and aren't involved. And a lot of them have been here for a long time. I can tell you when a house goes on the market, if it sells, this is not who buys it. . . . The people we grump about aren't buying because they can't.

JOANNE: So as these people retire, leave, die, . . . these houses get sold if [the] kids don't move into it and run it into the ground for you. If they change ownership, it changes to people who are home-buying people, who tend to be people with careers.

MARK: But they're not blue-collar factory workers with an eighth-grade education who worked at the plant. They're not buying into the neighborhood.

JOANNE: 'Cause you can't buy a house on that anymore. That doesn't exist.

MARK: This is my one big chunk of hope that I hang on to, big time. 'Cause they're not buying in. They're leaving. That run for the neighborhood is done. It ain't happening fast enough. We're trying to encourage anybody we know to move in who represents what we think is a better stabilizing force.

The Jensens are confident that neighborhood succession will drive neighborhood uplift.

To reduce this frame to support for gentrification driven by economic self-interest would be a distorting simplification. As Japonica Brown-Saracino finds in her study of gentrifiers, the desire to work for neighborhood revitalization and upscaling is often more complex than a personal investment strategy. Like the group Brown-Saracino identifies as "social homesteaders," these residents feel that neighborhood improvements (progress toward a good, stable, middle-class community) will uplift all residents.[25] They view the neighborhood's future as uncertain, and they want to steer Riverwest in a positive direction. They see the "diversity is our strength" residents as fearful of change and invested in efforts to preserve the neighborhood that will, instead, precipitate its decline.

James Chapman believes that more black professionals like him would be willing to move to the neighborhood if "they felt certain things were not tolerated." He argues that increases in property values, decreases in crime, and related improvements will help Riverwest and neighboring Harambee: "You've got inner city basically infiltrating every now and again. I would love to get some development to push that away so you can get in the inner city, start to see some development there, and work its way out rather than working its way in. Culture constantly changes. People have to make a decision when it changes. You can either assimilate or leave." James warns that the inner city's "ghetto culture" is working its way east. If Riverwest is truly invested in supporting its poor residents and neighbors, it needs to push back with mainstream, middle-class values and spread what works. When diversity-championing residents advocate preserving their island, they are being naive and selfish.

Who are these residents? The "neighborhood has potential" frame cuts across some social divisions, including race and ethnicity, political ideology, and, to a limited extent, subculture and age. However, almost all of these residents are homeowners, many of whom have moved into Riverwest in the last decade. They are more privileged—in terms of education or profession—than the average neighborhood resident. Although some grew up in more affluent, suburban communities, a few view their residence in Riverwest as a "step up" in their individual mobility trajectory.

For a short time, a subset of these residents had an online presence as the Riverwesters for Progressive Growth. They described themselves as "a friendly, loose affiliation among neighbors in Riverwest and the surrounding neighborhoods who have a pragmatic interest in keeping their blocks clean, safe, peaceful and enjoyable." In an open letter to the candidates running for alderperson in 2008, they outlined their shared beliefs:

- We support home ownership in all of its forms.
- We support the development of retail and commercial spaces in the neighborhood. These jobs will employ our neighbors.
- We desire a safe, clean and enjoyable neighborhood and will work with the police and public officials to help achieve that.
- We support responsible landlords who take care of their properties and their tenants, and will not tolerate irresponsible landlords.
- We support sustainable development in the neighborhood.[26]

At first glance, this list may seem indisputable. Who doesn't want to live in a safe, clean, and enjoyable neighborhood with responsible property owners and good development? And yet in Riverwest, as we will see, the definitions of *safe, clean, enjoyable, responsible,* and *good* are contested.

Residents of Riverwest share a place, and they interact with common features of this place: its geography, spatial configurations, architecture, boundaries, businesses, blocks, reputations, residents, and routines. However, the two predominant neighborhood frames provide distinct lenses through which residents view Riverwest and interpret these place features. As I will demonstrate, these shared lenses also shape how residents respond to their social surround. Navigating a heterogeneous neighborhood involves interpreting the world around you and deciding what to do in it and about it. Residents of Riverwest do manage to construct some order in the chaos by either enforcing rigid standards or relying on rough guidelines to muddle through.

CHAPTER FOUR

Regulating Difference
Local Social Control

The juxtaposition of divergent personalities and modes of life tends to produce a relativistic perspective and a sense of toleration of differences.

—Louis Wirth, "Urbanism as a Way of Life"

Hey, you know what? As long as whatever you do doesn't really fuck with me too much, go ahead and do it. See if I care.

—Paul Kelley, Riverwest resident

Social Organization in Heterogeneous Neighborhoods

The production and maintenance of order in the midst of diversity is an enduring topic of concern for social scientists. Classical theorists including Ferdinand Tönnies, Émile Durkheim, Georg Simmel, and Max Weber wrestled with the problems and potential of the heterogeneous metropolis.[1] How does social life work in cities packed with countless different ways of being? The Chicago School urbanists took up these questions of order in their investigations of American cities. Their focus on neighborhood-level dynamics set the stage for decades of research on the impact of various neighborhood conditions on a range of individual and communal outcomes.[2] One significant tradition in neighborhood effects research examines the relationship between neighborhood context and social organization—a community's capacity to realize shared goals and solve shared problems.

In an early articulation of social organization theory, Clifford Shaw and Henry McKay proposed that key neighborhood conditions—ethnic heterogeneity, poverty, and residential instability (high rate of population turnover)—undermine social organization by negatively impacting local social control (i.e., the regulation of residents' behavior according to collective ends).[3] The basic theoretical framework is supported by mounting empirical evidence.[4] Quantitative studies in the social organization tradition link heterogeneity to a range of indicators of neighborhood tension and disadvantage: neighborhood diversity hampers cooperation and interaction with neighbors; reduces mutual trust, social cohesion, and civic engagement; and is associated with increased crime, instability, and social exclusion.[5]

Although these studies establish connections between neighborhood heterogeneity and aspects of local social organization, the social processes that explain these relationships remain unclear.[6] This reflects an ongoing challenge in neighborhood research: the identification of mechanisms that explain *how* neighborhoods shape the perceptions, opportunities, and behaviors of those who live in them. In a review of the neighborhood effects literature, Robert Sampson and colleagues suggest examining culture to shed light on these social processes: "Although much effort has been put into understanding the structural backdrop to neighborhood social organization, we need a deeper focus on cultural, normative, and collective-action perspectives that attach meaning to how residents frame their commitment to places."[7]

Shaw and McKay advanced a cultural explanation for the relationship between ethnic heterogeneity and social control. They argued that because ethnically heterogeneous neighborhoods contain multiple subcultures with different and often conflicting values, it is challenging for residents to come to agreement about guidelines for behavior. In other words, heterogeneity is problematic because it produces friction and conflict and makes it difficult for residents to achieve the consensus and collaboration necessary for effectively addressing neighborhood concerns.[8] To assess this assertion and unpack the diversity "problem" for communities, we need a better understanding of the nature of the challenges presented to those living in a socially mixed neighborhood and the ways in which residents make sense of and respond to them.[9]

Organized for What?

Because social control is goal oriented, studies of social organization cannot be divorced from the objectives of collective efforts. As sociologist Robert Sampson has argued, instead of asking how socially organized a neighborhood is, we should be asking, Organized for what?[10] The overwhelming emphasis on the goal of keeping a neighborhood free of crime is often coupled with two problematic assumptions. First, researchers tend to assume that there are universal definitions of what constitutes unacceptable behavior. This assumption is supported by the general lack of evidence for race or class variation in attitudes toward criminal behavior.[11] Sociological definitions of deviance, however, emphasize that it is socially constructed and therefore context dependent: "Social groups create deviance by making the rules whose infraction constitutes deviance, and by applying those rules to particular people and labeling them as outsiders."[12] Although it seems that people universally want safe neighborhoods, there may not be a uniform definition across or even within communities of what constitutes a "safe" or "good" neighborhood. If definitions of unacceptable behavior or a livable community vary from one neighborhood to the next in subtle but significant ways, then the goals of social organization should be a topic of investigation in their own right. When researchers and policy makers operate on the assumption that their definitions of a good community are universal, they might mistake a community's successful efforts toward an alternative set of common ends for a community with a limited capacity for self-regulation.[13]

I emphasize *set* of common ends to highlight the second problematic assumption in social organization research: that the goal of neighborhood safety is in harmony with other, rarely considered collective goals. Though maintaining safe streets is an important and often immediate priority, it is only one of a range of social goods potentially provided by neighborhoods.[14] To better understand the production of local social order, then, it is important to examine not only the content of multiple collective goals but also the relationships among them. A neighborhood's shared goals may exist in tension with one another, or there may be disagreement about the appropriate means to collective ends.

Negotiating Difference in Riverwest

Everyday conversations about diversity in the United States often touch on the challenges associated with diversity: disunity, fragmentation, conflict, misunderstanding, intolerance, and inequality.[15] Perhaps most people would not be surprised to learn that members of diverse communities face obstacles to achieving shared goals. What is interesting, then, is exploring the content of these challenges and how neighborhoods deal with them.

In chapter 3, I introduced two competing neighborhood frames. In this chapter, I examine how neighborhood frames are connected to practices for dealing with difference. Table 4 provides an overview of the chapter. It indicates key differences between neighborhood navigation rubrics—cultural packages of neighborhood frames and associated conduct codes and social control strategies.

Diversity Is Our Strength: Live and Let Live

> There are no conformists in this neighborhood. There is nothing to conform to. And that is sort of ideal for me. It's not ideal for everyone. I recognize that, but it's ideal for me. (Paul Kelley, Riverwest resident)

The framing of Riverwest that celebrates neighborhood diversity is often linked to a widespread local mantra, "live and let live," that functions as a

TABLE 4 Neighborhood navigation rubrics

Neighborhood Frame	Riverwest Needs...	Difference-Negotiation Code	Problem Definition	Social Control Strategies
Diversity is our strength	to be protected	Live and let live	Flexible, contextualized, loosely connected to illegality	Informal and direct
The neighborhood has potential	to improve	Hold to a higher standard	Fixed, "mainstream," anything that is illegal	Formal and indirect

prescriptive cultural code for evaluating and responding to difference. "I recognize that we are quite different," so the logic goes, "but I won't interfere with your ability to live your life the way you want to. And I expect the same from you." "Live and let live" is an alternative to the enforcement of rigid conformity. Conformity requires a hierarchical ordering of difference in which certain lifestyles, tastes, and ways of being are deemed superior. Expecting adherence to a strict set of standards is viewed by some residents as oppressive, creativity constraining, or simply impractical in a diverse neighborhood. On the surface, this might seem like an individualistic, even libertarian principle (i.e., maximize individual freedom, limit external constraints). In practice, however, it serves as a guide for communal relations and social responsibility—a code of conduct in service of shared goals.[16]

Paul and Karen Kelley, a white couple in their thirties, bought their home in Riverwest nearly ten years ago. Although it took them some time to figure out the neighborhood, Paul says that they now embrace local conventions:

> The atmosphere of the "live and let live" condition is very appreciated. People recognize that every once in a while a loud party is going to bring about a visit from the police, or a knock on the door from a neighbor saying, "Can you knock it off?" I think people tend to keep to themselves as far as—I shouldn't say they keep to themselves because it's not like people are avoiding or ignoring each other, but people are just relaxed about what others are up to. . . . I would say there is a lot of people who really care about what's going on in the neighborhood, but they aren't Nazis about it. They care about the quality of life but not

necessarily about if your grass is mowed or if you are working on your house and it's taking too long. The appearance of the neighborhood is still a little bit more free form. And I think there is overall a kind of openness towards difference in attitude in, you know, lifestyles.

For the Kelleys, "live and let live" is about not withdrawal from community life but a moderate, elastic engagement. This type of tolerance requires a degree of normative flexibility, a willingness to contextualize evaluations of others' behaviors rather than impose one fixed set of standards.

When I'd been in the neighborhood for only a short time, I went to visit with Charlie Mason, a white artist with a flexible union job who has lived in the neighborhood for over thirty years. He gave me his address and told me to look for the "jungle" house on his block. It was easy to identify his home. The entire property was a sprawling garden, blanketed in dense green vegetation. Charlie greeted me at his front gate with a large bowl in one hand and garden shears in the other. As we made our way to the back entrance, he snipped leaves and stalks off various plants in our path until he filled the bowl. He explained that it was for a new batch of his elixir. I sipped a sample of already-prepared Charlie Mason elixir, an emerald green potion, as we sat on his sun porch and talked about Riverwest. Early in our conversation, I asked him to describe the neighborhood. In response, he expressed his deep appreciation for the neighborhood's normative flexibility:

> I would say that it's an area that allows for more individual expression than a lot of communities where you're sort of like, "OK, well, this is the way things are supposed to be on this block." You know, what I've got going here is a bit rambunctious by a lot of lawn standards. This is like, "Oh man, you're running my property values down." Around here, it's "live and let live" kinda rules. . . . I've got my hands full living my life and doing my own creative work and stuff, and it's not for me to be wagging my finger in someone else's face and telling them how they should be living. But I appreciate being cut some slack in some basic ways. I don't feel like I've got to live up to somebody else's expectations of the way things are supposed to be on this block.

Charlie recognizes that in some neighborhoods, his take on appropriate property maintenance and decoration would have neighbors complaining about its effect on property values. In Riverwest, he benefits from a more relaxed set of standards that allows him creative freedom. In other words, there is enough normative wiggle room to accommodate his unique expression of home.

"Live and let live" does require compromise. Though a resident may not like her neighbor's car tinkering because of loud engine revving, peel outs, and auto parts strewn in the alley, she accepts that it brings her neighbor pleasure, appreciates that someone is monitoring activity in the alley, and ignores the noise and traffic violations. In exchange, when she decides to paint her house bright purple and landscape her front lawn with tall prairie grass and bicycle wheels, the car tinkerer, though he may grumble under his breath, doesn't protest or call the Department of Neighborhood Services about lawn code violations.

The reach of neighborly tolerance in Riverwest occasionally extends to accepting behaviors that are illegal. For example, there are a number of people (some of whom live in Riverwest) who go through the recycling and trash bins in neighborhood alleys to collect materials that can be recycled for money. Some residents view "canning," though illegal, as environmentally friendly, honest work. Maliha Noor, a longtime resident, shared her reaction to seeing police officers stop a man canning in the alley. She asked them why they were writing him a ticket. "'Well, he was going through people's recycling.' And I said, 'But surely he can't pay a $180 ticket if he is picking up recycling to feed himself.' [One of the officers responded,] 'Well, you can get a permit for that, and if you have a permit you can do it, but you still can't pick it out of people's bins.' And I said, 'You are telling me this guy who is picking up recycling, picking up garbage off the street, has to go and get a permit to do it? I think we should give him an award for doing it!'" Maliha reasons that this man's conduct is not causing harm. Legality, in this case, is too restrictive a guideline for what constitutes acceptable behavior. Residents routinely tie their judgments of behavior to the extent to which the neighbor's actions affect others' quality of life. That an act is illegal is often of less importance than if the act is perceived as harmful to others.

John Bauer, a successful white local entrepreneur who has lived in the area for decades, shares his take on the reach of neighborhood tolerance: "If it is a drug house, it affects you. If vermin live in the house, it affects you. If it's a matter of broken windows and peeling paint, if that's the way the person chooses to live—especially around here where people have more tolerance and kind of look the other way, and understand that someone might not have the means—they might not do anything about it and just tolerate it." John sees Riverwesterners' tolerance as embedded in their recognition of socioeconomic diversity and empathy for those who may be facing financial hardship. These examples suggest that "live and let live" shapes the way residents interpret their surroundings. What looks like disorder in many communities may not be viewed as out of place in Riverwest. Because they view diversity as an asset and resist uniform visual standards, these residents interpret some forms of disorder (e.g., Charlie Mason's jungle house) as expressions of neighborhood character or representations of collective strength.

The Limits of Live and Let Live

Residents who are willing to tolerate (and even appreciate) behaviors that are not in line with their personal code of conduct occasionally encounter situations that they believe merit a response. They make distinctions between lifestyle differences and flagrant standards violations.

Leon Wade, a young black homeowner and landlord, describes where and why he draws the line: "If a guy wants to smoke a joint on his porch—dude, go nuts, smoke a joint all day. Smoke ten joints all day. Because you're not gonna do anything. You are gonna sit there, smoke your joint, drink your beer, that's OK, man. But if you're selling rock out of the back of your house? Negative. That's not gonna happen. I'm not going for that. I live here. This is *my* place, and you can't drive me out of my place or make me feel unsafe in my place." To Leon, smoking marijuana and drinking beer are nonthreatening personal recreational activities, but dealing crack is an affront. He explains that this distinction is rooted in an assessment of the activity's impact on the block. Crack addicts are, in Leon's experience, disorderly, unpredictable, and difficult to manage. Dealing attracts theft and violence. Participation in the illegal drug trade of crack cocaine may be a personal business decision, but it has ramifications for the neighborhood that Leon is unwilling to tolerate.

How, then, do they respond to conduct that they view as not simply non-normative but problematic? Almost every block in Riverwest has a story about how neighbors came together to deal with a problematic neighbor (e.g., a disorderly bar, a chronically bad neighbor, or a drug house), and these narratives unfold in a remarkably similar way. When faced with a problematic neighbor, residents generally begin with informal, direct methods of addressing the problem (e.g., talking to the neighbor or a member of the neighbor's friendship or kinship network). Only if such measures fail do they employ increasingly indirect and formal strategies (e.g., contacting the landlord, collaborating with near neighbors, alerting city authorities, or reporting to the police).

For example, several residents of what I will call the Sparrow block described their response to the Romano family, who were the problematic white tenants of a property owned by an absentee landlord.[17] Near neighbors observed alcohol and drug abuse linked to disruptive behavior; loud fights late at night, which occasionally escalated into violence; and little monitoring of the children's activities. Several Sparrow block residents attempted to create relationships with the Romanos. Some tried to connect the tenants with resources available at a local family center. Others confronted them about how their conduct was affecting the neighbors. A block matriarch reached out to the children and invited them to participate in organized activities. These attempts at connection and confrontation ultimately failed to significantly alter the Romanos' behavior.

Over time, the problems escalated. There were more violent fights in and around the home. The Romanos and their visitors became increasingly belligerent in their interactions with neighbors, and their young children damaged and even stole some neighbors' property. The increase in activity intensified the buzz on the block. In casual interactions, residents exchanged information about what was going on and how they were addressing the situation. They reassembled the club they had formed several years before to rid the block of drug houses, and they made collective decisions about how to proceed. Every time there was an incident, they called the landlord. They even offered to connect the landlord with a person interested in buying the property. When the landlord failed to respond, they reported code violations to the Department of Neighborhood Services, which, in turn, issued fines to the landlord. Eventually, as a last resort, they started reporting incidents to the police.

In the midst of this protracted battle, I met a group of five Sparrow block members at a town hall meeting in the basement cafeteria at St. Casimir Church. Nik Kovac, one of the alderpersons serving Riverwest, had invited residents to attend an open forum to discuss any neighborhood or city issues. As usual, residents had myriad concerns about proposed development projects, poverty, hunger, job growth, and crime. At the tail end of the meeting, one of the Sparrow block residents, Paul Kelley, said he wanted to talk about "neighborhood quality of life." He described his neighbors' considerable efforts to deal with a "serious problem property" and expressed their mounting frustration. He reported that in the last few days, someone had thrown a brick through the Romanos' window, the couple had gotten into a physical fight, and the property's power had been turned off. "What will it take to get rid of these people?" Several community members responded, eager to share their experiences dealing with their block's problem houses. The seasoned veterans offered strategic advice on pressuring the landlord, getting an official nuisance property designation, and making the case a priority with the district attorney. They emphasized the importance of staying vigilant and warned that getting rid of problem neighbors often takes a great deal of time and effort.

After months of pressure, the landlord decided to evict the tenants. Though they welcomed the restoration of peace on the block, several neighbors expressed ambivalence about the final outcome. The problem was not really solved, only moved (to, as it turns out, a house several blocks away and still in Riverwest). Paul Kelley described how difficult it was for him to make the shift to more formal social control efforts: "It took a really long time for me to get to the point with them to be like, there is nothing any of us can do . . . to make their condition better for them—and, as an extension of that, better for us. I think if you can somehow figure out a way to not have to resort to the police or have someone thrown in jail for the night—I don't think that gets very far." Other Sparrow block residents articulated similar concerns about the effectiveness of the criminal justice system, the legitimacy of police authority, and the consequences of eviction. These concerns support the residents' preference for informal and relational methods of problem solving.

Residents describe these campaigns to rid the block of problem neighbors as frustrating, drawn-out, exhausting ordeals, but their battle stories typically have a silver lining. The big troubles are powerful unifiers, bringing neighbors together and giving them the experience of a collective win. One resident felt a tad wistful about her neighbors' combined efforts to bring down a crack house nearly a decade ago. "I used to know every single person that lived on my block. And I used to have most of their phone numbers. When we were having problems with the drug house, we were getting really organized, and it was really good for us."

Social Ties and Tailored Expectations

Because the "live and let live" code is primarily put into practice on the face block, social ties influence how residents manage difference. As several recent studies have shown, social network connections with fellow community members can both promote and constrain the effectiveness of neighborhood self-regulation.[18] Many Riverwest residents contextualize their decisions about managing issues with their knowledge of the person whose behavior has caught their attention.

What follows is a sampling of the many stories I heard in which social ties to neighbors influence decisions to ignore transgressions or restrict intervention to direct, informal methods. These comments demonstrate how feelings of empathy and personal connection overrode the desire to bring in the police or the Department of Neighborhood Services:[19]

- Bill's house is an eyesore and is clearly not up to code, but he has been really strapped for cash since losing his job.
- Keisha and Robert's screaming fight kept me up last night, but they're good parents, and getting the police involved would do more harm than good.
- Those new yuppies renovating their house don't have the permit required for new construction, but they seem like decent people who plan to stay on the block.
- Karina's oldest daughter and her buddies shattered the lawn ornaments in Jack's yard, but Karina will certainly deal with her daughter more harshly and more effectively than the police would.

When neighbors have exchanged favors or received some kind of assistance, the sense of social obligation or unwillingness to risk losing connection to important resources sometimes prevents formal intervention. For example, although Willie Cooper, a black resident, ran what appeared to be an illegal car repair business in a neighborhood alley, most of his neighbors ignored the questionable status of his enterprise. They found him to be affable and felt as though his presence in an otherwise unsupervised alley contributed to block safety. Willie was also generous with his expert advice and gave neighbors deals on car repair.

As the Sparrow block story demonstrates, residents may decide to pursue more formal social control strategies with neighbors who have developed reputations for being uncooperative and resistant to attempts at informal social control. But even in that situation, when it was clear that Vito Romano and his wife were the source of a host of troubles on the block, some of Vito's neighbors felt conflicted. Paul Kelley explains:

> Here is the crime of it: our neighbor Julian says, and I tend to agree with him, "If the guy was a jerk it would be a lot easier to dump him on his ear, but he could be a really good story teller and he was really very charming at times." Not when he was drunk and locked out of the house and beating down the door at three in the morning—but when he was just hanging out in front, and we were hanging out in front, and he wanted to chat about whatever was on his mind. . . . When people run away or push away from problems in society and they lose that personal connection, they don't want to help. Or the way they help is that they give to the United Way in hopes that someone else takes care of it.

Several Sparrow block residents had multiple and varied contacts with Vito that made it difficult to see him as just a problem. These multifaceted, on-the-block connections, even when relatively shallow, can steer residents toward adopting a personal and informal approach to handling nuisance neighbors.

Maliha Noor, a homeowner and landlord, wrestles with how to deal with her "sketchy" neighbor, Louis. She has her suspicions that Louis is (or was) a drug dealer and a petty thief, but she also sees that he is a caring parent who maintains his property and protects his neighbors: "You know, every once in a while it gets loud there. For a while there was a lot of traffic, a lot of cars stopping and leaving. And the police—I mean I think he spent some time in jail or whatever. We don't know if he is still dealing. I think most of the people around feel like Louis has stolen something out of their garage or yard or something like that at some point. So, on one hand he is this menace in our alley, and on the other hand he is a loving father and keeps the area clean. I like him, on some levels. He is the go-between sometimes between the really shitty neighbors who are not only dealing drugs but are probably carrying guns." Maliha's decision to directly handle her concerns with Louis is also influenced by her perception of the relative ineffectiveness of formal agents of social control. When the police have dealt with Louis, they have been overly aggressive. On several occasions, they have made a show of his arrest by barging into his home, putting him in handcuffs, and creating a spectacle in front of his family and neighbors. Each time, Louis returns home after a few days in jail. Maliha worries about the effect these episodes have on his children and doubts that the police have successfully curtailed Louis's criminal activity.

The Role of Police

There is a range of attitudes about the appropriate role of police in the neighborhood, even among those who follow the "live and let live" code. Some Riverwesterners, like Maliha Noor and Paul Kelley, have doubts about the effectiveness or fairness of the criminal justice system. Resident and community organizer Robin Lund laments that the Milwaukee police have been asked to take on the role of "policing the boundary between two cultures: the haves and the have-not-enoughs." Class bias and race bias are, in her view, built into police officers' basic responsibilities. During my time in Riverwest, I heard many stories about negative experiences with police. Residents recounted feeling harassed, intimidated, discriminated against, profiled, or discredited because of their unconventional appearance, race, class, or choice of neighborhood. Some of these residents believe that the police who serve the neighborhood have little regard for Riverwest. I met three white women who, after being the victims of a break-in or theft, were each told by the responding police officers that the real problem was her residential choice. If she wanted to be safe, she should move to a different neighborhood.[20]

Samantha Turner doesn't live in the neighborhood but spends much of her time there. She works as a community organizer for a nonprofit that focuses on crime reduction in Milwaukee neighborhoods. She goes door-to-door to talk about crime and safety with residents in her assigned area, which includes Riverwest. Samantha describes her assessment of local attitudes about police:

> There are some people who don't even think we should call the police because they think that if you went and talked to that drug dealer on the corner and told him that you don't want him to sell drugs that they would stop. There are some people with that attitude. They don't think the police do anything, and they think the police just make the problem worse, or . . . even if they call the police they aren't going to show up, or they aren't going to do what you think that they should. And I think it only takes one bad experience with the police to turn people all the way negative. Like one bad call where you get an officer who maybe isn't as professional as he should be with you, or doesn't write the ticket you want him to write, and there are all these things you think you saw. . . . But then there are other people who absolutely 100 percent believe in the police.

There is also what appears to be a small minority of residents who see police as a repressive and illegitimate force. Hazel Carver, a young white woman who grew up in Riverwest and is loosely affiliated with the DIY punk scene, is deeply suspicious of the police. When she and her friend Ike were mugged at gunpoint, they gave the "kids" a couple of dollars. The muggers, displeased with the modest sum, were reluctant to let them go. Hazel and her friend appealed to what they assumed was a shared dislike of the police. "Man, we are broke as hell. You are mugging the wrong people. Why are you doing this? We aren't going to say anything. We don't like the cops. We aren't going to call the cops on you. We don't want to deal with them either." The muggers eventually let them go.

Several residents speculate that a handful of anarchists connected to the now-defunct Cream City Collectives were responsible for spray-painting "Kill Cops" in at least two Riverwest alleyways and posting antipolice stickers around the neighborhood. The stickers, linked to an anarchist collective website, read: "COMMUNITY WATCH AREA. Trust, respect and communication are essential to healthy community. Protect your friends and neighbors from uniformed gang members and other suspicious characters. POLICE NOT WELCOME." Some residents view these actions as deeply offensive and poisonous for police–community relations, while others defend the right to question police authority. Most of the people I talked to about the stickers, including four police officers in the district, dismissed them as the work of an isolated few.

A number of residents welcome the presence of law enforcement agents in the neighborhood, reporting marked improvement in police response to local needs over the last two decades. This is due, in part, to the police district's adoption of community policing strategies, including bike and foot patrols, community liaison officer assignments, and police officer attendance at block-watch meetings. In her door-knocking campaigns, Samantha Turner has found a largely positive response to the presence of beat cops, even from some of the more police-wary residents. "People want to see police; they want to see them on the street. They want to be able to say 'Hi.' They want to know what squads—what people are, you know, patrolling their area. They know the beat cops that are in their area, and they never did before, so I can definitely see a change." Some residents have cultivated relationships with individual officers who they can now call on when situations cannot be handled with informal measures alone.

When longtime resident and social worker Rashawn Wright's sons were teenagers, he was quite worried about the "heavy hammer" that police were dropping on young black men. His attitude shifted after developing a strong connection with a community liaison officer who proved to be genuinely invested in helping the neighborhood. The officer's approach to managing local conflicts meshed with the "live and let live" code:

RASHAWN: We kind of all adopted his whole concept—we that were involved in the block clubs and organizing all that stuff over here. We kind of got that attitude. And it was good for us. That kind of helped us keep our Riverwest flavor about us. [*laughs*]

EVIE: So essentially his approach was—let's attempt to solve this in some other ways first instead of cuffs first.

RASHAWN: Right. And if all else fails, that's no problem. One phone call, I'll have enough cops here and enough wagons to haul everybody off. That's no problem. But if we can get this settled before it gets out of hand or while we've got this opportunity to change some behaviors at the same time, let's go for it.

The community liaison officers who have since served the neighborhood have largely adopted a similar strategy, but according to Rashawn, none have forged such strong relationships with residents.

Most of those who endorse "live and let live" reserve police involvement in block-level disputes for violent incidents, for drug dealing, or as a last resort. Some differences do not, in their eyes, merit criminalization or formal response. The police who work in the neighborhood are well aware of the neighborhood's normative flexibility. Don Sitko, a white police officer in the district who calls Riverwest "Milwaukee's Greenwich Village," struggled to pin down residents' attitudes about crime: "They don't want drugs [*long pause*]. They don't want crack. I don't know about the marijuana issue because that's not a drug [*sarcastic*]. They don't want crime. Maybe some, but they don't want major crime, you know what I'm saying? . . . They tolerate certain crime, and it has to be very minor stuff, but they don't want burglaries. They don't want robberies, but they're willing to turn away with some stuff. I think they tolerate things like graffiti, but they won't tolerate someone breaking into their homes. I think they will tolerate some traffic violations, stuff like that, but you are not going to rob us." The officer acknowledged that because police respond to calls for service, their involvement in any neighborhood is shaped, in part, by local standards. They recognize that what is considered unacceptable behavior or a sign of disorder in many neighborhoods may be tolerated (marijuana) or in some cases embraced (graffiti-style murals) in Riverwest. Another officer explained that when police receive a call for service, they will not discriminate; if they see a violation of the law, they will address it. In some cases, he asserted, it is not in an individual's best interest to get the police involved—especially in a "bohemian" place like Riverwest. He added that many block-level issues are not really police matters. The police therefore encourage people to handle some disputes without police intervention.

Some people in the neighborhood are concerned that those who adopt the "live and let live" code are too tolerant of crime. Rashawn Wright is a Riverwest booster. He loves the neighborhood that he has called home for over twenty years and cites the "mixture of people" as its most valuable feature. Though he largely follows the "live and let live" code, he occasionally feels the need to rein in his neighbors:

There's a remarkable tolerance in this community. And it's almost too far sometimes. That's why we have to get a little tougher with our crime stuff because people kinda let things happen to them that they shouldn't let happen to them. But they're very tolerant of all kinds of lifestyles. . . . Well, sometimes crimes go unreported. "Oh, what the heck? The guy probably needed it. He needed those things." But I think sometimes we have to report so we get the proper service that we need. Because we tend to get a little underserved because we handle things ourselves or we let things go by. . . . I'm one of those people who'll say, "Hey, you know what? Guys, we gotta do something about this." . . . And then we start making calls so we get a little bit more service. Let's face it. Where the need is comes from the reports that you make. That's when they start to give us the support that we need.

Rashawn has found his neighbors amenable to his recommendations to work with police on certain issues. However, some accuse the "live and let live" residents of being pro-crime, and these accusations are not entirely unfounded. I met a few residents who, fearful that certain kinds of neighborhood development might threaten the culture and diversity of the neighborhood, believe that "just a little crime" helps to keep potential gentrifiers at bay. For some, the threat of crime reinforces a cultural boundary, one that places limits on the kinds of diversity welcome in the neighborhood. This boundary was clearly articulated with spray paint on a sign signaling the construction of two "green" houses in the neighborhood: "Die Yuppie Scum! Get out of our neighborhood!" After construction was nearly completed, every street-level window in the structures was broken. This should not be interpreted as an indication that the "live and let live" approach to neighborhood regulation is situated in a discrete, crime-tolerant subculture.[21] Many of those who value the neighborhood's social mix were critical of the acts of vandalism. Unlike neighborhoods organized by a dichotomous set of conflicting "street" and "decent" orientations,[22] Riverwest's negotiated social order encompasses an assortment of sometimes overlapping, sometimes conflicting neighborhood orientations.

Despite varying opinions on law-and-order officials, the vast majority of residents who follow the "live and let live" code incorporate the police in their strategies to maintain a relatively safe and livable neighborhood. They may not call on the police to solve every problem, but if a situation gets bad enough, most will ask for their assistance. The everyday work of policing in Riverwest might look different from that in other District Five communities, but the police officers serving the neighborhood are a significant component of local social control.

Neighborhood Socialization: Transmission of Cultural Codes

Some residents who chose to live in Riverwest because of its diversity may be predisposed to normative flexibility. Yet as previous studies of socially mixed communities demonstrate, those who value racial or economic diversity often enforce white, middle-class standards of conduct.[23] In Riverwest, there is widespread adoption of the "live and let live" approach to difference negotiation, which extends beyond those residents who view social diversity as a key neighborhood asset. Some residents are amenable to "live and let live" because of their previous experiences in racially homogeneous but class-diverse communities where contextualized and informal negotiations of difference are one response to a lack of faith in police. Others find it a practical strategy for managing relationships with neighbors. Many residents, regardless of origin or diversity disposition, are influenced by local socialization processes.

Mary Krakowski was born and raised in the Polish Catholic community in Riverwest. A retired factory worker now in her sixties, she has witnessed many changes during her tenure in the neighborhood. She sees today's Riverwest as a friendly mixture of people "that all get along well enough." She is "not crazy about the condominiums" because she thinks they are responsible for increases in her property taxes (which are difficult to manage on her fixed income). She worries about the crime that seems to spike every few years and then fade. Mary's concerns do not include protecting neighborhood diversity or fulfilling the neighborhood's development potential. Yet she clearly adopts a "live and let live" approach to her block-level interactions. Mary generally approaches the differences between near neighbors and herself as objects of curiosity rather than concern. She addresses issues on the block directly because it is simply how things are done. I found that other residents who, like Mary, view neighborhood diversity as a descriptive statistic rather than an asset still follow the "live and let live" code.

Many relatively new arrivals to Riverwest also demonstrate an understanding of neighborhood navigation rubrics. Their reflections are particularly valuable for understanding neighborhood socialization because they can often identify recent experiences that were integral to their learning process. When they describe moments of tension—when their expectations were not met or they learned that their reactions were quite different from those of their neighbors—they highlight what many residents now take for granted.

For example, many newcomers who have previously lived in neighborhoods with less crime experience a sympathy transformation with respect to crime victimization. When they first learn of someone getting their house broken into or having a grill stolen out of their backyard, they immediately express sympathy for the victim. However, they notice their neighbors are much less willing to dole out compassion. Instead, they respond with questions: "Were the doors and windows locked?" "Was the grill chained to something?" They are communicating the expectation that in Riverwest, you are responsible for making stealing difficult for potential thieves. After a few years in the neighborhood, the not-so-new comers begin sounding like longtime renter Robin Lund: "There's what I call 'redistribution of wealth crimes,' where you've got it, they need it, they're gonna take it. So don't leave that $1,000 bike chained up to your porch, dummy. If you want to keep it, put it in your basement. Don't complain. If you leave your CD collection in the front seat of your car, they're going to break your window. I mean, c'mon. . . . Manage your life so you're not a victim." These residents have absorbed a set of understandings about their environment, what it means to be aware and responsible, and who is deserving of sympathy or scorn. They are also learning about the connections residents make between personal choices and practices and notions of neighborhood quality of life. Rashawn Wright spells out these connections: "Opportunity is always knocking, and opportunity works against you sometimes, too, if you're not careful. Always make sure that you—anyplace that you live—that you harden yourself a little bit. But now I think it's a perfect place to come and move into if you're sensible; if you're not really flashing your bling bling and everything all over the place there, it's a good place to live." If residents are willing to put some effort into awareness and prevention, they will reap the benefits of living in a good neighborhood. Leon Wade concurs: "Riverwest is a great neighborhood with lots of people who really care about it. You've gotta be careful at some points in time. You should walk through it like you've got some sense, like you've been in a city before. Carry yourself the right way, there's never a problem. But it's a great place to live."

Shared cultural constructions of the neighborhood influence how residents interpret and evaluate their social surround. To cohere and endure, culture must be shared and continuously reproduced. Although there are multiple paths of cultural transmission (how residents learn how to define and deal with nonnormative conduct), informal sanctioning by community members is particularly powerful in the neighborhood context. In casual interactions, neighbors communicate how to "live and let live." Lucy Pallotta had been in the neighborhood for a short time when she learned that Harry's Tap, a corner tavern near her home, had applied for liquor license renewal.[24] She and her husband enjoyed occasional visits to Harry's Tap for beers, and she knew it was a popular spot with neighbors. Lucy had observed that the bar owners did a poor job maintaining the sidewalk in front of their property. They rarely shoveled in the winter and were slow to clean up broken glass and trash left outside by bar patrons. She talked to neighbors about using the license renewal hearing as an opportunity to put pressure on the bar owners to be better neighbors. She was surprised by their response. Even when Lucy insisted that she did not want the bar to lose its license, her neighbors urged her not to go to the hearing. One neighbor admonished her, "Don't pick on Harry's!" Talking to the bar owners was fine; talking to city officials first was not.

Gossip among neighbors also constructs and transmits neighborhood cultural codes. Symbolic interactionist researchers have demonstrated that people clarify social norms through sharing evaluations of absent others.[25] I developed an understanding of my most immediate normative milieu by listening to neighbors gossip about other neighbors. When they complained bitterly about "that snob" Lila for calling the police in one situation and praised her for doing so in another, made distinctions between a "harmless drunk" and "crackhead thief," or fumed about Marco "ratting" on a financially strapped homeowner to the Department of Neighborhood Services, they fleshed out the proximate social order. When they teased Walter for being "soft" with his irresponsible tenants or publicly shamed Donna for screaming at her daughter, they reinforced local standards for conduct. I am not suggesting that gossiping about a particular neighbor was an effective way to change that individual's behavior. Some popular gossip targets, like Donna, seemed immune to this variety of social pressure to conform. Others were simply unaware that they were the topic of disapproving chitchat. I am arguing that gossip was an important channel for the communication of local norms. Though I encountered conflicting interpretations of events and varying degrees of normative flexibility, gossip provided general guidelines for what each of the more vocal and visible neighbors deemed appropriate problem categorization and response.

Residents may receive harsher lessons in the unwritten rules of the neighborhood. A small number of residents I met had encountered retaliation for taking action against a problematic neighbor. When Alex Dimas, a white renter, had lived in the neighborhood only a few months, he had an altercation with a group of young Latino men on his block that refused to heed his request to stop lighting fireworks on the Fourth of July. They responded by mocking him and physically pushing him down. Alex called the police, who later visited but did not arrest the men. The next day, he discovered his car had been "keyed" (defaced by using keys to scrape off paint). He decided to change tactics: "From my own knowledge of my block, I had a sense of who was the matriarch of this family and I spoke with her, sort of obliquely, about the incident, but I did tell her about what happened. Because I had good relations with her, I had a feeling that just by telling her about what happened, there wouldn't be any further trouble, and there wasn't. So there was sort of this softer way of dealing with the problem. . . . I learned it's important to have good relations with your neighbors in as much as getting to know them can cover you from some of the things that happen in the neighborhood." Alex's experience changed his approach to dealing with problematic behavior on the block. Though rare, or perhaps because they are rare, retaliation stories and their lessons tend to travel far and wide. Retaliation, gossip, and informal sanctioning teach residents about neighborhood culture and neighborhood navigation skills.

A Loose Consensus

The embrace of neighborhood diversity and the dominant cultural code of "live and let live" shape the community's internal social control strategies as well as the responses of formal agents of social control. Though the code reflects (and produces) some consensus about what constitutes a problem and the appropriate response to each problem, it is a loose consensus at best. Residents contextualize block-level incidents with information about neighbors and standards of behavior that are only partially shared. And they must, at times, navigate the tricky terrain of conflicting beliefs about the appropriate response to a particular incident. As a result, they may not be confident that their neighbors will support their chosen course of action. Residents suggest that such support is crucial.

Leon Wade is not one to shy away from confrontation with problem neighbors. Still, he knows that his efforts are more effective when he has support from his neighbors. One day Leon heard someone repeatedly beeping a car horn. As he was walking toward the car to suggest that the driver knock on the door instead of disrupting the whole block, he met one of his neighbors: "And the thing is, my neighbor came out of his house and said the same thing to them at the same time. So he came out. I came out. We're like, 'Why don't you go knock?' Always nice when someone is with you, too, because it shows a united front. Yeah. It's a big difference. It's a huge difference. When they know that more than one person is saying the same thing, it stops. Yeah, this is the standard. This is how it's supposed to be." Residents' stories often highlight the importance of critical mass consensus for enforcing block norms, yet not all those stories are happy tales. Several locals describe frustrating and isolating experiences of trying to take on block challenges without any tangible support from neighbors.

At the block level, the compromises that undergird local social control can result from direct negotiation, in which neighbors settle differences by mutual concession (e.g., no band practice past 9:00 P.M. on weeknights, but Saturday night jam sessions can extend until midnight), or, more indirectly, from tacit agreement (e.g., lack of interference). But "live and let live" also takes a more generalized form. Residents who perceive the local community code as a widely followed guideline for interaction are likely to employ the affiliated strategies (normative flexibility, compromise, direct and informal interventions first) in encounters beyond the face block.[26] Thus, the dominant rubric for neighborhood negotiation affects how Riverwest residents (and, by extension, police) deal with difference.

The Neighborhood Has Potential: Hold to a Higher Standard

While many active residents are invested in maintaining the character and diversity of Riverwest, others are committed to seeing the neighborhood improve. These residents hope that efforts to clean up the neighborhood and support responsible development will attract the kinds of homeowners who will further stabilize Riverwest. These different (although not always contradictory) visions for Riverwest's future are attached to particular strategies for difference negotiation and social control.

Riverwest residents who are invested in the neighborhood's development potential are aware of and reject the "live and let live" code. For them, tolerance of disruptive behavior is a dangerous, slippery slope. Normative flexibility ultimately condones behavior that negatively affects their quality of life. Joanne Jansen believes that Riverwest has much to recommend it, but she is frustrated by the pervasive permissive attitude that compromises neighborhood livability: "For me to live comfortably, it means that 3 o'clock in the morning someone is not outside screaming their lungs out. I'm not being allowed to live the way I want to live. 'Live and let live' is let me live however I want and let me have no consequences for my behavior. Let me not worry about being a good neighbor to other people. That's a part of that mantra of 'live and let live.' It's really not, honestly, I'm not going to interfere in your life. [It's] I'm not going to interfere in your life as long as you ignore me doing whatever the hell it is I feel like doing." Joanne feels that many residents use "live and let live" as a justification for selfish and disrespectful behavior.

Instead of engaging in loose, ongoing negotiations about what constitutes appropriate behavior, these residents hold themselves and their neighbors to a defined set of middle-class standards. These standards align with mainstream, and therefore largely taken-for-granted, understandings of the "good community"—understandings that are also reflected in municipal codes and definitions of legal conduct.[27] This social and legal support normalizes their take on desired neighborhood order: behaviors that negatively affect their quality of life are subject to official sanction. Rather than imposing conformity based on their particular tastes, they argue that they are working to make the neighborhood better.

Because these residents believe increased homeownership is essential to neighborhood stability, they are particularly concerned about what the visible manifestations of Riverwest's loose standards communicate to current, like-minded homeowners and potential homeowners. If the neighborhood looks transitional, dangerous, or neglected, these residents fear it will negatively affect local investment. Keith Bennett, a white resident, purchased his house in Riverwest in the late 1980s and spent much of his first decade in the neighborhood battling drug houses. He claims that the differences between now and then are "like day and night." Over the years, he has increasingly embraced the "neighborhood has potential" perspective. Although he sees clear, hard-won progress, he feels that Riverwest has a long way to go. He finds local resistance to upscaling baffling. Lax attitudes about property maintenance and problem behavior chafe his nerves. He can't believe that his near neighbors tolerate Willie Cooper operating his off-the-books car repair shop in the alley.

Why do you put up with that in your neighborhood? It makes you look like the ghetto, like you don't give a damn anymore! That's why I get so upset with [Willie]. You're running a business out here. Why don't you get your damn business where you can actually run your business? This guy is such a dickwad. He owes like $10,000 to the city. He's also dragging our neighborhood down with all of his crap in the yard and all these cars all torn apart. It would be one thing if the guy next door to you kept his house nice and he bought an old '57 Chevy and he's trying to restore it. When he's not working on it, he puts a nice car cover over it so I don't have to stare at the junk. There's a guy who is trying to do something positive. He's caring about what I'm doing.

For Keith, acting in accordance with middle-class standards is the equivalent of being a good neighbor. He rejects his near neighbors' arguments that Willie's presence helps keep the alley safe or that he does good work for a fair price. In his opinion, they are foolishly working against their own best interest.

Residents who hold their neighbors to a higher standard use a stable normative framework to interpret their social surround. For example, canning in the alley should be prohibited, because those who are taking material out of recycling and trash bins are engaging in illegal activity. Further, criminal activity marks suspect character. Several of these residents suggested that canners are most likely casing houses: looking for things to steal or monitoring residents' routines to identify a good window of time for a break-in. Don Sitko, a police officer who works in the neighborhood, is considered an ally by many of these residents, and he tends to share their views on local issues. He is perplexed by the level of tolerance in Riverwest: "People that can, or go through your garbage to pick cans, I don't like that. I don't trust them, and they could be, in my mind, looking into your yard—maybe they're going to steal your grill or your bike or something like that, but when you bring that up in Riverwest: 'But they're recycling. They're trying to make a living.' At whose expense? When your rain gutters are taken off your garage and sold at the junkyard, are they making a living at your expense? Is that a crime? Well, yeah, it's theft. It's very hard because what I wouldn't tolerate, they tolerate." Officer Sitko thinks that some people's judgment is clouded by sympathetic (and naive) interpretations of problematic behavior. In his view, their flexible standards and lax enforcement make the neighborhood more vulnerable to crime.

Those invested in unlocking the neighborhood's development potential see themselves as a struggling minority up against a dysfunctional culture. They believe that the "live and let live" code allows residents to ignore—and thus tacitly support—all manner of incivilities and transgressions. In contrast, these residents are quick to pursue indirect interventions, like calling the police, filing complaints with the Department of Neighborhood Services, and testifying against nuisance businesses at licensing hearings. At times, they might directly confront problematic neighbors or join block-watch groups, but they also cultivate relationships with powerful local actors (e.g., police captains and city officials), who they can call on or pressure to improve prevention services or respond to behavior or business practices that do not meet their standards.

In April 2007, a fight broke out at a birthday party held in a public park pavilion in the neighborhood. Gunshots were fired, and the crowd dispersed.

As nineteen-year-old Marques Fabian ran for safety, he was killed in a hit and run. Police later learned that the driver of the car was another teenager leaving the chaotic scene. The Chapmans, a young interracial couple who live in a condo near the park, immediately sprang into action. Megan called the sheriff, demanding information and accountability. She and her husband, James, helped coordinate a town hall meeting with the sheriff, a county supervisor, and a parks department representative. There was a strong turnout at the meeting, and they were ultimately successful in getting increased supervision at the park. However, the Chapmans are discouraged by what they see as a pervasive crime-tolerant, antidevelopment attitude among neighborhood leadership that blocks progress. A resident who shares the Chapmans' concerns is frustrated because he believes "the rhetoric of the neighborhood says nothing to support a belief system that is anticrime and pro–forward movement."

Though their critics accuse them of being intolerant, these residents assert that their rational responses to deviance and disorder will stabilize Riverwest and benefit the neighborhood as a whole. Joanne Jansen, a white professional in her thirties, carves out a distinction between prejudice and justice: "We start calling the police or making consequences for people's behavior that are against the law. I mean, they're illegal. We're not saying we don't like you or the color of the paint on your house. You know, you're doing things that are *illegal*. It is *illegal* to sit out on the street and honk your horn. It is *illegal* to play a band at 4 A.M. in your living room with amps and your windows open. It's not OK." Joanne is baffled by the fact that many Riverwesterners see her responses to crime as unreasonable. Like those residents who want to preserve neighborhood diversity, she shares an appreciation for local amenities and wants to live in a safe environment, yet their ways of interpreting and responding to neighborhood issues often clash. For Joanne, these conflicts boil down to contrasting definitions about how residents ought to behave and strategies of enforcement—essentially working with or against the formal agents of social control: "It's really hard. You can be looking for the same goal, but when your methods are so diametrically opposed, it can be very difficult to actually accomplish things. Like, working with*in* the system, working *with* the alderman versus shouting down or versus fighting and petitioning."

Sociologist Patrick Carr terms Joanne's methods the "new parochialism": the "set of practices that creates solutions at the parochial level but owes its existence and its efficacy to the intervention of institutions and groups from outside the neighborhood."[28] Carr found that this hybrid approach to self-regulation emerged in a predominantly white, working-class Chicago neighborhood to replace the more traditional forms of localized informal supervision and intervention. He argues that this shift is a response to changes in local policing and increased female labor force participation, juvenile crime, and neighborhood heterogeneity. Diversity hampers the development of social ties that are necessary for adequate informal social control. The new parochialism works in a heterogeneous context because it requires neither broad participation nor strong neighborhood social ties. Joanne's husband, Mark, speaks plainly about the efficacy of working with public officials. "We're on the inside, and we're firm believers that to get anything done, you really have to be on the inside. It sounds great to be in the opposition and against the man, but it turns out, the man runs everything. If you ain't on board, you're getting steamrolled badly."

Mark has developed skills for navigating the system. He has repeatedly reported neighbors to the authorities "for personal behavior and house stuff." As a business owner, Mark can create a flexible schedule. This enables him to testify at city hearings, even when it means sitting through long court sessions. He has found judges very accommodating to witnesses who are willing to testify. Although Mark often feels like a lone actor working against problems on the block, his connections and knowledge of official regulation processes have proven to be quite powerful. "It turns out, if you have your head on straight and your act together, you can mount a successful defense against the stupid louts in the neighborhood."

Holding the neighborhood and neighbors to a higher standard is, for African American professional James Chapman, an essential component of community building. To James, enforcing a particular set of values will attract the right kinds of people, facilitate positive changes in the behavior of some residents, and encourage those unwilling to adapt to leave:

> That's how you build a community of values that you want. You have to bring the people in who share those values. There's that constant change—so people have to make a decision. Do I want to sell my home and make some money and move to a better neighborhood or leave the city? If they want to leave the city because they don't want to adopt those cultural traits, then that's fine. Go. I don't want to live around you if you think pulling out a gun is a solution to every problem. I don't want to live around you if you don't think it's important to mow your lawn. I don't want to live around your kids if you don't think that education is a good thing or is important or [if you think] that you don't have to show up and be involved in your kids' education. I don't want to live around you. I guess I'm a little more selfish in that regard in that I

think that our priorities are the ones that are in order. I feel like we're the people who make positive changes in our community and our city, and if somebody's values are going to be adopted, I want ours to be the ones that are adopted rather than the ones that I currently see infiltrating in all the other areas. People want to say that's just right-wing bullshit. It's also the truth.

He is confident that his standards align with those that society rewards. Ensuring that community members share his values, then, is central to individual mobility and success as well as neighborhood uplift.

In Riverwest, there is the uneasy coexistence of old and new. Localized, relationship-based, block-level social control strategies persist alongside new parochial measures.[29] They are responses to a shared but differently interpreted context. In Riverwest, the adoption and validation of the strategies of new parochialism are grounded in a particular framing of the neighborhood, one that equates progress and stability with conformity to mainstream, middle-class standards and laws. These strategies are attractive to those who see formal social control institutions as legitimate and who have confidence in their capacity to make claims on representatives of the public sphere—a confidence that maps onto privileges of social class, property ownership, and, in some cases, race. Finally, because they do not necessitate strong proximate ties, these strategies may be perceived as more efficacious to residents who do not see their near neighbors as allies.

Social Organization in Riverwest

Social diversity does present challenges for local social control in Riverwest. Residents share the desire to live in a good and safe neighborhood, but they sometimes disagree about the definitions of "good" and "safe." There is also considerable variation in residents' everyday local practices. Neighbors have different ideas about leisure and work activities, parenting and communication styles, and property upkeep. At times, these differences produce tensions and conflicts that require management. Some residents attempt to enforce adherence to a set of ideal standards, but most employ malleable guidelines in their efforts to hammer out a social order. Residents' efforts are shaped by neighborhood rubrics that offer distinct organizing principles for defining and responding to problematic behavior. Sets of shared interpretations of the neighborhood are linked to differences in tolerance of a range of issues, including property maintenance, noise, alcohol and marijuana use, canning, prohibited uses of public space, and domestic disturbances. They are also linked to differences in the use of informal and formal responses to unacceptable behaviors. What some residents view as practical maintenance of a livable environment, others see as irrational compromises that make the neighborhood vulnerable to further decline.

Although residents adopt a variety of strategies for neighborhood negotiation, the local context fashions their individual efforts into a rough coherence. Together, the cultural and material conditions of Riverwest mediate the impact of heterogeneity on local social organization. The cultural packages of neighborhood and problem frames, interactional codes, and social control strategies are filtered through and re-created in block-level interactions. As neighbors accept, accommodate, ignore, and condemn others' behaviors, they (re)produce a local social order. The face block, then, grounds and organizes local culture in ways that give shape and meaning to residents' actions. Features of the built environment—including housing density, the limited supply of off-street parking, the prevalence of front porches, and the layout of sidewalks and alleys—also contribute to the primacy of the face block as a site of socialization and difference negotiation. Residents gather, chat, clash, and observe one another on the block. Block-level negotiation is an endless stream of small confrontations, resolutions, compromises, and collaborations. Through these interactions, they learn the local rules and rhythms, erect and sometimes erode social boundaries, and develop both shared and personalized expectations for behavior.

Riverwest is not a peaceful and harmonious cultural collage. Some researchers would interpret the numerous conflicts and ongoing issues with crime in Riverwest as evidence of a weak communal capacity to achieve common ends; however, my analysis of the neighborhood's social organization complicates and challenges that assessment. My investigation of the content of residents' shared goals reveals that there are competing visions of a good community (i.e., what Riverwest is or should be). The evaluation of the neighborhood's ability to reach collective goals is therefore dependent on which version of a good community one employs. Some residents hope for an improved neighborhood with increased homeownership, expanded commercial and retail development, and reduced crime. They want to see consistent enforcement of conventional standards of property upkeep and resident conduct. Viewed in this light, neighborhood diversity hinders residents' ability to maintain effective social controls. Other residents want to improve neighborhood safety while nurturing and protecting Riverwest's diversity, culture, and independence. If we assess local social organization in terms of these goals, we see that residents are able to maintain moderate stability without imposing a singular normative order on a socially mixed population. Neighborhood social regulation is relatively successful at managing the tensions between these goals by containing (although not significantly reducing) crime without insisting on assimilation to mainstream standards.

Both studies of social organization and studies of neighborhood integration have been criticized for their failure to adequately deal with issues of power.[30] In response, Sarah Mayorga-Gallo centers her analysis of social practices in a multiethnic neighborhood in relations of power and privilege.[31] She finds that white homeowners' symbolic embrace of diversity does not translate into practices that promote inclusion or equity. Their "universal" definitions of appropriate neighbor behavior, civic participation, and community development, in fact, reflect a white, middle-class understanding of neighborhood quality of life. As a result, their seemingly nonracial community engagement efforts reinforce white dominance by marginalizing people and practices that don't conform to sanctioned standards.

Living in Riverwest does not erase the habits of white people and middle-class people who help reproduce the status quo. Many residents who belong to privileged groups, including some of those who value diversity as a neighborhood strength, engage in neighboring practices or promote "common good" initiatives that fail to address or even acknowledge existing power differences. In so doing, they mask the fact that they are advancing particular interests, excluding a range of perspectives, and fortifying boundaries of belonging.

However, many people in the neighborhood, including residents with social advantages, adopt a flexible and contextualized approach to everyday interactions, which can challenge demands to assimilate to raced and classed standards. The local culture includes sets of meanings and practices that reorder the dominant cultural map, clouding or altering the lines between "good" and denigrated kinds of people and manners.[32] In other words, the widespread adoption of "live and let live" as a guide for dealing with difference produces alternatives to conventional appraisals of merit and quality of life. This collective guidebook to difference negotiation is remarkable in light of a handful of recent studies of diverse communities that, like Mayorga-Gallo's, find local dynamics that largely work against integrationist goals.[33] For example, in her study of a socially mixed Chicago neighborhood, Ellen Berrey observes that while "diversity advocates symbolically cast a wide net with their designations of who belonged and who did not, ... they failed to provide a productive conceptual framework for understanding or talking about complicated, undesirable and problematic social differences."[34] In contrast, neighborhood navigation rubrics in Riverwest do provide frameworks, though rough and contested, for interpreting, interacting with, and sometimes reframing perplexing differences.

CHAPTER FIVE

Drawing Boundaries

Disorder or Difference

Riverwest is not what it seems; it is not defined by how it is often perceived.
—Anna-Marie Opgenorth, executive director of Historic Milwaukee Inc.,
"What Is Riverwest"

"Burn it down. Riverwest is a dumpster!" This was the first suggestion offered in response to a *Milwaukee Journal Sentinel* blog post calling for input
on dealing with crime in Riverwest.[1] Another online reader of the newspaper responded to the report of a homicide outside a Riverwest tavern with
a sarcastic "nice neighborhood."[2] According to many outsiders (and some residents), Riverwest is a problem-filled community. A shooting during an
altercation between two people, from this perspective, is about more than two
individuals: it's symptomatic of a poisoned place. Neighborhood residents
feel the need to constantly defend Riverwest and combat its shady reputation. John Bauer explains that residents see their neighborhood differently
than do many outsiders: "Riverwest gets in your blood, and it's such a unique
community. And it's something that you see and something you have pride
in. Riverwest is so comforting and so nurturing. It's almost something that
people can't pick up on. A lot of other people don't see it. They see, 'Oh, it's
kind of ghetto,' and move on. They don't see the community." How do we
explain these different perceptions? First, what gives people the impression
that this neighborhood is a trouble spot? What feeds the perception that Riverwest is, according to an assortment of Milwaukeeans, "sketchy," "dangerous,"
"creepy," "crappy," and "crumbling?"

Reading the Social Surround: "Seeing" Disorder

To make sense of complex urban areas, we create and use mental maps. Our
maps break down the city into simplified, manageable chunks that facilitate
navigation and guide decision making. The boundaries we draw help us determine where to go, where not to go, which route to take, where to live, and
how to stay safe. Urban ethnographer Gerald Suttles finds that these maps
"help us make a welter of day-to-day decisions in which what we do depends

heavily on where we think we are."[3] As social cartographers, we map the material world, practices, *and* people. This kind of mapmaking requires cultural classifications—of status, safety, behavior, and beings—that help us determine who belongs where and what we should do. Mental maps, then, do much more than represent the location of places in relationship to one another; they indicate how people perceive and interact with their environment.

What signals that a particular neighborhood is a place to consider or a place to avoid? Suttles argues that safety figures prominently in city dwellers' assessments: "Above all, these cognitive maps show our preoccupation with personal safety and the need to get a quick fix on the relative trustworthiness of fellow pedestrians, residents and 'trespassers.'"[4] Picture yourself driving through a city in search of a new neighborhood to call home. How do you get that "quick fix" on your surroundings? How do you differentiate between what seems comfortable and what seems risky? What communicates community quality? If you were passing through Riverwest, you would likely find many of the visual cues of disorder that researchers have found to be salient to urban residents in their assessments of neighborhood safety and quality.[5] During my three years of fieldwork, I saw or heard residents report seeing the following: garbage and litter on the street or sidewalk; graffiti; vacant houses; badly deteriorated residential units; overgrown lawns; burned-out, boarded-up, or abandoned properties; alcohol and tobacco advertising; bars and liquor stores; public drinking and drug use; public intoxication; groups of people loitering or hanging out on the street; adults fighting or arguing in a hostile manner; drug dealing; panhandling; and street-based sex work.

Urban researchers investigate the significance of these visual cues of disorder for neighborhood evaluation and negotiation. The most widely recognized and influential articulation of this approach—the broken-windows theory—links disorder and crime.[6] The theory posits that if visual signs of physical and social disorder (broken windows, litter, public drinking) are not addressed, it indicates that residents are indifferent to the condition of their neighborhood. This, in turn, invites criminal behavior and weakens community-level controls, triggering a process of neighborhood decline. Visual cues of disorder, then, affect the behavior of residents and potential criminals in ways that increase neighborhood vulnerability to crime.

The perception of a place as disordered (and, by extension, its residents as disorderly or apathetic) generates expectations and attributions that can also influence the investment of a range of neighborhood resources. It might produce feelings of anger, demoralization, or fear among residents, which can hamper civic engagement or push residents to consider moving out of the neighborhood.[7] It might deter prospective homeowners and renters; undermine social control efforts; discourage commercial investment; or influence the neighborhood-directed actions of politicians, real estate agents, and lenders.

Disorder, it seems, figures prominently in urban dwellers' mental maps. It is a feature of place and, like place, is co-constructed by geographic location, material form (litter, an unsupervised group of teenagers on the corner), and assigned meaning (danger, residents don't care about their neighborhood). Yet much of the research on disorder assumes that signs of it are objective, clearly demarcated, and fixed in meaning.[8] Recent challenges to the supposed stability of definitions of order and disorder point out that these categories are socially constructed and therefore shaped by much more than the presence of particular objects or behaviors.[9] Their meaning varies over time, from place to place, and even within neighborhoods.[10] The fact that many public behavior norms fall outside legal criminal classification leaves various conduct standards open for debate.[11]

Legal definition does not necessarily settle these disorder demarcation contests. Laws designating which kinds of behaviors merit criminal punishment along with related strategies of law enforcement impose different frameworks for defining disorder. In some neighborhoods, "official" designations of problematic behavior may not map onto residents' definition of issues requiring intervention. For example, depending on the context, graffiti might be perceived as vandalism or art. In an assessment of the definition and measurement of disorder in research and policy, sociologist Charis Kubrin argues that "variability and subjectivity, not uniformity and objectivity, characterize perceptions of disorder."[12] If disorder is a perceptual project—something that is both seen and interpreted—it is important to investigate what disorder means and to whom.

Neighborhood effects researcher Robert Sampson argues that although the interpretation of disorder seems to be a matter of individual cognition, it is actually a socially mediated process: "Collective (or intersubjectively shared) perceptions form a context that constrains individual perceptions and social behavior."[13] In other words, those who share a social context—that is, a place *and* cultural understandings of that place—often read and respond to environmental cues in similar ways. Residents' collective perceptions create and reinforce definitions of the types of disorder that are serious threats to community life. If disorder has social, emplaced meaning, then interpretations of visual cues likely vary from one neighborhood to the next. A critical next step is to unpack this process at the neighborhood level. How does neighborhood context influence how residents "see" their social surround? In this and the following chapter, I examine how place grounds and is constituted by shared perceptions of things that typically signal disorder: graffiti, groups of young black men hanging out, public drinking, and bars.

Diversity and Disorder

There are several reasons why we might expect neighborhood heterogeneity to contribute to negative evaluations of Riverwest. First, sociologists have found that race and class factor significantly into residents' and outsiders' assessments of neighborhood quality and order. The concentrations of Latinos, of African Americans, and of poverty in a neighborhood are better predictors of perceptions of disorder than an independent measure of carefully observed disorder.[14] In other words, the racial and socioeconomic makeup of a community more powerfully influences assessments of its quality and safety than the *actual presence* of visible disorder. Notably, whites, blacks, and first- and third-generation immigrants all share these biased perceptions of disorder.[15] The proportion of African Americans in a neighborhood similarly predicts exaggerated estimations of neighborhood crime levels and disadvantage.[16] Perceptions of a neighborhood's capacity to address local problems are also tied to its racial composition. Residents of communities with larger numbers of Asian, Hispanic, and African American people are less likely to view their neighbors as capable of addressing local problems.[17]

In one study, Maria Krysan and her colleagues showed participants short videos of neighborhoods and then asked them to rate each neighborhood's quality.[18] The neighborhoods varied by social class; this was reflected in a number of visual cues, including lot size, house size, and property upkeep. The videos were shot from the perspective of someone driving slowly down a residential street, with a view of houses, their front yards, and the sidewalk. The viewer sees a few people (all of whom are actors) in each video engaged in various activities (walking down the street, chatting with neighbors, working on a car in the driveway). For each neighborhood, the researchers shot three nearly identical videos along the same stretch of street, showing the same houses and the same resident activities. The only thing that varied was the race of the residents (all white, all black, or mixed). The researchers found that study participants used observable class signals *and* the neighborhood's apparent racial makeup to evaluate its quality. The presence of black residents negatively affected white study participants' assessments of neighborhood desirability. Neighborhoods with *identical physical characteristics* were ranked lower in quality if the residents were black. It is clearly not just what we see but our shared cultural interpretations of what and who we see that matters.

These raced and classed notions of disorder are likely influenced by multiple layers of stigma. First, broadly held negative racial, ethnic, and class stereotypes (the black male criminal; the violent, gang-affiliated Hispanic immigrant; the immoral poor) may fuel negative evaluations of certain communities. Second, neighborhood-level biases play a role. For example, the association of black neighborhoods with crime, poor schools, and low property values also shapes perceptions of local order.[19] Third, neighborhood reputations are sticky and often attach to residents. This is what scholars term *ecological contamination*: the processes through which place stigma envelops and contaminates residents' identities. "Bad" neighborhoods are full of "bad" people. Loïc Wacquant asserts that territorial stigmatization and ecological contamination in "hyperghettos" skew outsiders' judgments and residents' self-perceptions. Devalued and discredited by association with the "inner city," residents experience collective demoralization and are subject to discrimination and disproportionate regulation. Race and class hierarchies (and their ranking of social and moral inferiority and superiority) are inscribed in space.[20]

Raced and classed perceptions of disorder are powerfully reinforced when they guide the strategies of formal social control agents. Studies of order-maintenance policing practices find that officers disproportionately target African Americans, Hispanics, and people living in high-poverty black neighborhoods.[21] Neighborhood stereotyping significantly colors disorder policing strategies. For example, in a study of stop-and-frisk activity across New York City, Jeffrey Fagan and Garth Davies found that police focused their efforts in the city's poorest neighborhoods with the highest concentrations of nonwhite residents, even after controlling for visible disorder and crime.[22] In a follow-up study, researchers found that disproportionate order-maintenance policing of these neighborhoods endures despite neighborhood improvements, low crime rates, or a decline in the neighborhoods' African American populations.[23]

Heterogeneous neighborhoods may also be perceived as disorderly simply because encounters with "otherness" make everyday life less predictable. One is confronted with situations that require careful negotiation—in which the rules may not be entirely clear or one's current interpersonal skill set may seem inadequate. These encounters can produce discomfort, tension, and even conflict. Richard Sennett argues that the fear-based desire to avoid difference drives people to seek out homogeneous social environments that minimize the possibility of interacting with the unknown.[24] What is lost, then, in living in communities of "unthreatening sameness" is opportunities to encounter difference. When people lack experience in negotiating difference, they rely on broad stereotypes to guide their encounters with "others." As a result, certain differences are routinely interpreted as disorder. By this logic, the link between diversity and disorder should erode with accumulated neutral or positive experiences with difference. Sennett envisions heterogeneous communities in which residents' regular interactions with "otherness" diffuse hostility.

Diversity, it seems, is disorderly. One would therefore expect Riverwest's heterogeneous makeup to contribute to negative evaluations of the neighborhood. Do residents share outsiders' perceptions of the neighborhood as an unruly and disorganized "dumpster"? How do they collectively make sense of their stigmatized environment? The numerous types of diversity in Riverwest make encounters with the unfamiliar highly likely. How does living with difference influence interpretations of disorder?

In Riverwest, interpretations of these traditional markers of disorder are contested. Broad cultural understandings of danger, blight, decline, and other troubles are filtered through collective place frames and residents' everyday experiences. How residents "see" is shaped by shared notions of how one should interpret features of the local environment and repeated interactions with stigmatized people and practices. Distinct approaches to social boundary drawing coexist in this community. Through conflicts over definitions of disorder, broad social categorization schemes and racialized notions of criminality—though sometimes reified—are often challenged.

Graffiti: Crime or Art

Riverwest Graffiti Vandals Arrested[25]

Ten young men, ages seventeen to twenty-six, were arrested and charged with thirty-five counts of vandalism. Some of this group, known as the WR Crew, lived in Riverwest. The WR—We Rock/Wall Riters/Weed Rollers/Writers Revolution—Crew left their mark (their tag) on residences, businesses, and garbage cans in Riverwest and several south side neighborhoods. Urban scholars typically treat graffiti, a highly visible public crime, as a significant sign of the breakdown of local order, but the meaning of this feature of the visual landscape is often contested. In an interview about the WR Crew, Milwaukee Police Department spokeswoman Anne Schwartz pleaded for a criminal interpretation: "Please don't call them artists. They're vandals. It makes people feel unsafe in their neighborhood."[26] Schwartz recognized that graffiti production could be viewed as either an act of artistic creation or callous destruction. The Wisconsin circuit court judge who dealt with the WR Crew favored the latter interpretation. All ten members were eventually convicted and sentenced to combinations of jail time, probation, community service, and restitution (totaling over $30,000).

I spoke with several residents and local business owners whose property had been tagged by the WR Crew. Most expressed frustration with the hassle and cost of cleaning up graffiti. Several complained about the poor artistic quality of the "scribbled" and "sloppy" tags. Riverwest bar owner John Dinon, whose business was repeatedly vandalized during the WR Crew's tagging spree, believed that the graffiti tainted the bar's image. He told a reporter, "It makes it look so ghetto."[27] Although John could have been using the "ghetto" descriptor to indicate a bad neighborhood, its use might also reflect the racialized discourse surrounding graffiti and, more broadly, "urban" youth and crime.[28] Popular representations of graffiti often bring it into a symbolic tangle with hip-hop, criminal gangs, violence, and youth of color. Seeing graffiti may therefore trigger a set of place evaluations: a community is indifferent, under siege, or out of control.

One evening at a neighborhood tavern, I overheard an African American man sitting down the bar from me ask the bartender about the recent sentencing of WR Crew members. I scooted down a few stools to join the conversation. I learned that my bar mate was Marshall Johnson, a longtime Riverwest resident and recent retiree. For him, the tagging is senseless. For the bartender, a white woman in her mid-twenties who had been in the neighborhood for several years, the tagging is harmless. Marshall explained that he doesn't feel threatened by the "little shits" who are "pretending" to be in gangs, but he worries about how their spray-painted scrawl makes the neighborhood look to outsiders. He said, "We're better than that." The bartender rejoined, "We *are* that." When Marshall gave her a quizzical look, she shrugged and turned to greet a new customer.

To me, this exchange hinted at the complexity of dealing with difference. How do you make sense of a marginalized subcultural practice in a neighborhood that identifies as a place for outsiders and a space of resistance to the mainstream? I found that in Riverwest, the definition of graffiti as disorder is contested. Residents make distinctions between deviance and creative expression, which complicates the interpretation of visual cues within the neighborhood and challenges the construction of graffiti as a problem. What looks like disorder in many communities, then, is sometimes viewed as "normal" or even valued as a physical sign of neighborhood character in Riverwest. The following examples highlight the ways in which Riverwesterners' varied encounters with graffiti complicate its interpretation.

At the annual Summer of Peace Rally, hundreds of youth from around the city descend upon Riverwest's Kilbourn Park to participate in a range of positive, educational activities that promote nonviolence. For the last few years, representatives from TRUE Skool have been invited to create a large, intricate graffiti painting throughout the course of the event. TRUE Skool is a local nonprofit organization that promotes graffiti as an urban art form that can strengthen and beautify communities and give young artists a positive outlet for their talents. Its mission, very much in line with the spirit of the Summer of Peace initiative, is to "use the urban arts as a tool to engage youth in social justice, leadership and workforce development."[29] The peace- and unity-themed canvases created by teenagers at the rallies disrupt typical associations of graffiti with deviant youth and violence. Context and content, together, channel the energy of transgression and resistance characteristic of graffiti into calls for cooperation and visions of alternative futures.

A Milwaukee green construction company acquired adjoining vacant lots in Riverwest for the construction of two single-family, energy-efficient town homes. As the company prepared to start construction, it put up a sign on the property featuring a rendering of the houses. As noted in chapter 4, someone painted "Die Yuppie Scum! Get out of our neighborhood!" on the sign. Some residents found this humorous; others fully supported the sentiment. Many people I talked to about the incident, however, were disappointed to learn about the vandalism of a project that was in line with either their understanding of the community's character or their hopes for neighborhood development. Some residents, like white homeowner Larry Neville, were angry. He suspected that the same local anarchists were responsible for making a similar statement of discontent about another construction project:

> The threat is that people might move in that actually have some
> money. There was a house built—two sets of condos, and we aren't
> talking big structures—they looked kind of like houses that belong
> in the neighborhood, not particularly great design, one of them is better
> than the other. And some of the anarchists over here wrote "CONDO
> ASSHOLES LEAVE!" And you are so full of shit. This is not the gentry that
> is moving over on the corner of Hadley. These are not people so

different than you are. You are assholes for thinking that. So this change thing is not just the educated older hippie type—it's also the younger people who want it to be some sort of thing it never was, or never could be. Where people can just do whatever they want all the time. There is some of that. And you know people doing whatever they want, whenever they want, *all* the time? I mean, nobody really lives like that.

For Larry, who largely endorses the "live and let live" attitude, these expressions are problematic because they push too far. They are out of sync with what Riverwest was, is, and should be.

In 2006, Jeremy Novy, a young artist attending University of Wisconsin–Milwaukee, pasted life-size posters of doors and windows over boarded-up doors and windows on several vacant properties in the city, including four houses in Riverwest. He hoped his street art would both call attention to and beautify neglected properties. His use of a medium that many consider representative of social disorder to combat a form of physical disorder (blight) relied on flexible interpretations of art and vandalism. Novy's technically illegal, public art installations were featured in the local media, including the *Riverwest Currents*. The positive buzz about his work resulted in requests to "decorate" additional boarded-up properties in the neighborhood.

One such request came from Marcella Morris—a white woman raising her family in Riverwest, who later adopted an art-based strategy to address a problem of her own. Marcella's garage faces the street at the entrance to an alley. Two of the four garage walls are highly visible, making an attractive canvas for graffiti writers. After repeated tagging, she decided to take a unique approach to prevention: using graffiti to fight graffiti. In the fall of 2007, she invited a street artist to spray-paint a mural on her garage during the neighborhood's annual Art Walk. As residents and visitors wandered through the neighborhood on a tour of local galleries, studios, and other art spaces, many stopped to admire the artist at his craft. The same combination of this style, medium, and space can make for crime or art. Marcella's permission changed the meaning of the activity from out of place to celebrated—yet the question remains, for whom? Although Marcella, her friends, and some neighbors view her brightly painted garage doors as a mural befitting the neighborhood, not to mention an effective crime deterrent (her garage has not been tagged since the mural was painted), it signals vulnerability, resident apathy, a lack of control, or racialized disorder to others. One of Marcella's nearest neighbors remarked that Marcella's garage is a "Welcome to the ghetto!" billboard. These varied perceptions loosely map onto different interpretations of the neighborhood: as a place worthy of celebration and protection, or a place in need of upgrading and an improved image.

The following summer, community activists organized a grassroots effort to celebrate the neighborhood, beautify alleys, and prevent crime. The Art in the Alleys project recruited homeowners interested in having murals painted on their garage doors and connected them with artists interested in creating work for broad public consumption. The project organizers wanted to revitalize alley space to encourage more and better use of areas vulnerable to neglect and criminal activity. The instructions for volunteer artists included the following guideline: "The murals, while they may be in an urban graffiti style, can't be graffiti or confused with tagging." I visited with one of the Art in the Alleys artists as he crafted a garage mural, spray-paint can in hand. He had outlined large, stylized, interlocking letters that were difficult to decipher—a form of graffiti writing known as wildstyle. I asked him how he navigated the graffiti-style-but-not-graffiti guideline. He said the organizers granted approval after the owner of the garage enthusiastically endorsed his design. One by one, the artists turned blank canvases (invitations for vandalism) into works of art and transformed alleys into galleries. That fall, the Art Walk map directed participants down three neighborhood alleys that featured seventeen murals, including several done in graffiti-art style.

Leon Wade, a black resident who owns several properties in the neighborhood, seemed pleasantly surprised when he learned about the success of the Art in the Alleys project. He explained that he had previously looked into having a graffiti muralist paint his garage, but had met resistance from the city. Although his neighbors were supportive of the mural idea, he was discouraged by the threat of fines from the Department of Neighborhood Services: "I want someone to throw up on my garage with something nonviolent, something very peaceful, very positive. That's dope. To me, you're adding value. Maybe not to the city. It'll probably devalue my home. But to me, you're valuing my home. You're like, 'Here's that piece.' And people will drop by, 'Oh shit, that piece is nice.' They'll stop [to] take a look at it." Leon felt that city officials and Riverwest residents would have very different interpretations of the mural's aesthetic worth and its effects. His hunch was correct.

In January 2009, two city alderpersons, including the chair of the Anti-Graffiti Policy Committee, proposed an ordinance to regulate mural production on private property. If passed by the common council, the ordinance would make it illegal to put up a mural without a city permit and would require annual $75 inspections. The ordinance also placed restrictions on the location of murals. They could not be within three hundred feet of an existing mural or facing an alley. Alderman Zielinksi and Alderman Wikoviak claimed that this was an effort to protect property values, reduce blight and "visual clutter," and promote traffic safety (some murals, they argued, distract drivers). The initial draft of the ordinance noted an additional justification for the legislation: "graffiti-like symbols" encourage vandalism.

Riverwest artists and other residents quickly mobilized to join the fight against the proposed ordinance. Many of those who wrote letters to the city council members or were quoted in the local media couched their opposition in the success of the Art in the Alleys project as a beautification and safety initiative. Residents repeatedly drew boundaries between illegal tagging and graffiti-art production, arguing that legitimate graffiti art *deters* vandalism. Some focused primarily on the infringement of their rights as individual property owners, but most highlighted communal concerns. They claimed that the ordinance not only threatened the expression of the neighborhood's identity as a diverse, creative, and open place, but also interfered with the community's right to self-determination—a key element of the "diversity is our strength" framing of Riverwest. The alderpersons' attempt to expand their power to control the aesthetics of public space met fierce opposition from a community invested in preserving its distinctiveness. Before the Zoning, Neighborhoods and Development Committee met in February 2009, the mural ordinance was removed from the agenda.[30]

The proposed regulation of artistic production provoked debates about meaning and power. Who has the authority to define threats to quality of life (and quality of life for that matter)? Who are the official arbiters of taste? Who gets to control the cultural spaces of the city? A year later, controversy surrounding a specific graffiti-style mural brought these issues into sharp relief.

The Struggle over Raw Love

On July 17, 2010, TRUE Skool hosted its fifth annual block party in Walker's Point, a neighborhood on the city's south side. As part of the organization's Adopt a Community Kick-Off, volunteers spent the morning picking up trash and removing illegal graffiti in the neighborhood. The block party, attended by over five hundred people, showcased multiple facets of hip-hop culture: live music, DJs, b-boy and b-girl breakdance battles, and visual art. For the live graffiti-art exhibition, a group of TRUE Skool students painted a graffiti-style mural on the side of a building. The sanctioned project was supervised by J. Bird, a Riverwest artist responsible for the creation of several murals on display in his neighborhood. Throughout the afternoon, partygoers watched artists create the words "Raw Love" in sharp, wildstyle lettering that twisted around a stylized biohazard symbol. The mural also featured a bug-eyed person in a gas mask and hazmat suit cradling a bomb. There were snippets of the Milwaukee skyline and a passing train in the background. According to TRUE Skool, the piece represented local community struggles between good and evil ("raw love" spelled backwards is "evol war"). The temporary installation was, as agreed, painted over several days later.

On the Monday following the block party, Alderman Bob Donovan held a press conference at the mural site to express his outrage at TRUE Skool's glorification of graffiti and endorsement of vandalism. In what escalated into a heated argument with TRUE Skool cofounder Sarah Patterson, Donovan referred to the mural as "garbage" and "crap" and blamed the organization for an increase in illegal graffiti tagging. Patterson described her organization's efforts to remove illegal graffiti, partner with local residents, and redirect taggers' talents into positive, community-building endeavors. Donovan, clearly exasperated, complained that he has "been through so much hell with graffiti." As he walked away from the camera, he raised his arm, shook a pointed finger, and said, "Stay out of my district!"[31]

The event struck a nerve. Reactions to Donovan's stand against graffiti buzzed in local newspapers, online magazines, blogs, and the Riverwest Neighborhood Association listserv. My analysis of the over four hundred comments generated in these discussions situates the symbolic boundary-drawing contests in Riverwest in the broader cultural context of the city. That the participants in these online discussions tend to offer either vigorous support or cutting criticism of the alderman's position (and behavior) is hardly surprising. Even when civil, dialogue in the digital public square about hot issues tends to represent the poles. Although these exchanges rarely include the voices of the deliberating middle, they still provide valuable information about the contours of local discourse and contribute to the symbolic construction of the city.[32]

Alongside largely irresolvable debates about what constitutes "real" art and the effectiveness of sanctioned street art for deterring illegal graffiti, I found arguments about the definition of unacceptable "out of place" practices (and, by extension, unacceptable "out of place" people).[33] The mural site is on Milwaukee's south side, home to the city's largest concentration of Hispanic residents (most of whom are Mexican or Mexican American). One articulation of the social problem of graffiti identifies Mexico as the source of disorder. Although a few people emphasized the role of the city's Hispanic gangs, I found general references to problematic places more common. "Aquitas" warns readers: "Give it a while, once Milwaukee has welcomed enough ILLE-GAL ALIEN PARASITES, their graffiti will have the city looking like Southern California/Tijuana."[34] Concerned that graffiti art, like the murals, will make the city look "CHEAP AND TRASHY," "Anewday" attempts to steer the next generation toward the right path: "KIDS WAKE UP, YOU KNOW WHAT'S RIGHT AND WRONG, DON'T BE MISLEAD BY ANYONE. WE ARE NOT MEXICO AND DON'T BELIEVE IN GRAFFITEE PAINTED ALL OVER IN PUBLIC." Mexicans and Mexican Americans, according to these narratives, have destabilized the aesthetic and normative order of the city. The identity of the city and its residents (the Milwaukee "we") does not include—and is indeed threatened by—what is perceived to be a foreign and deviant culture.

Other comment posters indicate that one need not travel quite so far to find the roots of graffiti and the cluster of problems it represents. They employ beliefs about another raced place—the ghetto—to erect symbolic boundaries. "Urban" culture, portrayed as a way of life cultivated in poor minority neighborhoods, is seen as incongruous with the legitimate mainstream. "Jimtherepublican," is frustrated by the burden of removing graffiti tags from his property. He has serious doubts about TRUE Skool's pedagogical embrace of urban culture. "This is just another example of failure in Milwaukee. Using hip hop as a tool? Yea right. I work with the Scouts. They teach real life skills and values. Hip hop? What does it teach? How to be a punk? A thug? A baby daddy? A drug dealer?" He draws on a set of stigmatized stereotypical black male identities to mark the line between good and bad masculinity training.

"US Citizen" also links graffiti to a dysfunctional and wholly other "urban" culture. "Cultural Projects? Why not teach them useful skills that will help make them a productive contibuting member of society not a detriment to society. Another feel good waste of working people's money. Urban art, urban culture, urban lifestyle? Why should the hard working people that pay for this culture to sit on their butts all day and then go vandalize and terrorize the comunity have to accept this behavior?" In her study of New York City's war on graffiti, Maggie Dickinson finds similar symbolic bundling of graffiti, problematic people, and place. "The construction of graffiti as a problem has significant parallels to urban poor people being constructed as a problem more generally. These contested representations effectively shut these cultural productions out of public space and defined them as invalid."[35] Several of those posting comments in support of the artists call attention to what they see as a race-tinted interpretation of the mural by, for example, suggesting what would likely be an acceptable alternative. "2fs" says, "I can't help but imagine that if the wall of this building had been painted by a bunch of fresh-faced white farm kids, and depicted a Norman Rockwell scene of apple-cheeked youth joyfully painting white picket fences, Donovan and others wouldn't have even noticed."

In Maria Kefalas's study of Beltway, a working- and middle-class, predominantly white community in Chicago, residents rally to ensure that a teenage vandal is sufficiently punished for tagging the widows of a local school. To them, graffiti threatens the community's hard-won (and precarious) order and image of respectability. "It is an assault on decent, hardworking people's way of life."[36] Fears about the encroachment of the neighboring ghetto are embedded in Beltway residents' understandings of themselves as the moral middle class—a people who value the traditional neighborhood, family, personal responsibility, and hard work. Many of the comment posters who indicated that they live on Milwaukee's south side expressed similar sentiments about graffiti as an attack on decency. "Respecteveryone" feels compassion for youth who live in violent environments, and questions why others don't extend their sympathies to families, like his, who have to defend their neighborhood. "The south side is filled with decent hardworking families who are also facing these challenges and mine is one of them. Why does True Skool advocate trashing our neighborhood? Many of these people have nowhere else to go. As for me and my family, I've worked very hard for what I have, and I won't be pushed out without a fight."[37]

Critical criminologist Jeff Ferrell unearths similar themes in his research on graffiti writers and their battles with agents of formal social control over cultural spaces in the city: "Those in power attempt to remake the meaning of cultural space, to substitute the symbols of safe homogeneity for those of diversity and threat. In each case, the politics of reaction—the illusory return to 'traditional values' and 'simpler times' when kids and other outsiders knew their place—are enforced through an aesthetics of authority, an aesthetics that seeks to remove from public view the untidy cultures of undesirable populations."[38] The threat of graffiti to social order is linked to the disruptive nature of diversity made visible. The restoration of order, Ferrell argues, often comes in the form of evicting or at least concealing out-of-place people and practices.

Graffiti threatens the middle-class way of life from below but also from above. Several comments framed mural supporters as out-of-touch elites who romanticize graffiti art but have no firsthand experience with its negative impact. The local *Art City* blog posted the following email written by Alderman Witkowiak's aide, Mike McGuire, in response to a concerned citizen:

We get calls daily from people living in inner city areas who are in real despair over gang crime and the fact that their homes and alleys are defaced by graffiti, often weekly or more. These people are severely and directly affected by this and are badly hurt. . . . Now we have others who live in much better neighborhoods and are not directly affected by this plague. Some consider themselve's [*sic*] art lovers and seem to get satisfaction by pontificating from their nearest Starbucks about how the rest of us should really appreciate "urban art." Our concern is with those living in the affected neighborhoods . . . not the arts lovers who do not so reside. And yes . . . we both consider graffiti in any form to be garbage and worse.[39]

By characterizing graffiti art appreciators as disconnected snobs, McGuire defends the concerned citizens of the district he serves against charges of provincial small-mindedness.[40] Their anxieties and anger are rational responses to the experience of being under siege. In the comments thread underneath the blog post, a Riverwest resident offers the success of the Art in the Alleys project in decreasing tagging as evidence that graffiti murals can benefit communities. "2fs" then weighs in, using the example of Riverwest to challenge McGuire's portrayal of urban art supporters. "I'm not sure why McGuire assumes the people who complain live in better neighborhoods or are better off—Riverwest is one of the city's prominent arts districts, and in terms of income and crime stats is pretty comparable to the area where TRUE Skool painted the mural." So what, then, is different about Riverwest?

The Local Lens

Residents share many of the concerns articulated by mural opponents. They are upset when their property is tagged. They worry about what the presence of certain kinds of graffiti signals to visitors, potential customers, prospective neighbors, and criminals in search of a target. However, living in Riverwest changes how many residents "see." Place shapes their cultural cartography—their understandings of who and what belong where—and their strategies for managing their environment. Again, we see that residents must simultaneously address fears about the threat of increased crime and decline, and fears about homogenizing forces of gentrification and top-down strategies for neighborhood improvement. They carve out a workable middle ground by (1) maintaining boundaries between threatening turf claims or senseless, artless tags and sanctioned street-style art, and (2) resisting attempts to sterilize and flatten the visual culture of what many consider to be an artist's neighborhood. In claiming some graffiti as a legitimate feature of their shared landscape, Riverwesterners reinforce local notions of aesthetic belonging, decency, resistance, and quality of life. The intentional inclusion of street-style art shifts interpretations of graffiti from race-coded threats and indicators of neighborhood neglect to symbols of resident investment and expressions of local character and autonomy.

By bringing together multiple, often clashing aesthetic perspectives and facilitating regular interactions across differences, socially mixed places may also create opportunities for remaking the meaning of visual cultural practices. When conflicts over the appearance of a community garden emerged in a diverse New York neighborhood, sociologist Sofya Aptekar observed that the aesthetic preferences of more privileged gardeners were supported by local organizations and government agencies. Yet the cross-class and cross-race ties formed in the garden proved useful in defending and preserving some of the less privileged gardeners' spaces, which had been deemed disorderly. According to Aptekar, this resistance was "facilitated by the characteristics of the community garden itself, including the sense of threat to its survival, the shared investment in its continuation, the parochial nature of much of the interactions, and a sense of common purpose and activity."[41] That the Riverwest community shares all these characteristics suggests that, under certain conditions, diverse neighborhoods can be sites that destabilize dominant notions of community ideals.

In Riverwest, valuing a style of artistic production signals a symbolic inclusiveness but does not directly address the issues of marginalization and criminalization of black and brown youth that are at the center of the overarching condemnation of graffiti. When controversy brings such issues to light, however, Riverwest residents' draw on a shared social context to articulate an alternative vision of social diversity as livable and nonthreatening. Otherwise out-of-place practices and people have a place in their neighborhood.[42]

Hanging Out: Black and Brown Criminality

At a block-watch meeting, Maria Pérez shared her concerns about a group of young black men who had recently started hanging out in front of a convenience store on her block. One of her neighbors pressed her to identify the specific problematic behaviors these men had engaged in: "But what are they *doing*, Maria?" When she could not identify any disorderly conduct, the group dismissed her concerns with shrugs and silence. A police officer who had been invited to attend the meeting added, "Congregating is not a crime, ma'am. We gotta be careful about the assumptions we make. If they are doing something illegal, we will take action."

Most surveys designed to assess neighborhood disorder ask residents about the presence of youth hanging out on the street. Young people lingering in public spaces with no apparent purpose can trigger perceptions of those spaces as unsecure or threatening. Popular portrayals of black and brown male criminality that perpetuate negative racial stereotypes make the congregation of certain bodies seem more menacing than others. In response to an opinion piece about a community's efforts to keep its streets clean and safe, a *Milwaukee Journal Sentinel* reader shares his observations of a Milwaukee neighborhood: "Tuesday morning at about 11:00 A.M., I drove a few blocks through an African American neighborhood. It was depressing to see that the people found it necessary to put bars on their windows and doors. I should not, I guess, have been surprised to see, in the course of 6 blocks, three separate groups of young African American males just hanging out on the sidewalk."[43] Young black and brown men hanging around is, for many, a potent visible marker of neighborhood disorder, despite the fact that this vague referent is detached from specific, problematic conduct. In Milwaukee, this reading of the social environment is sustained by a local ordinance that regulates street life.

Loitering—lingering aimlessly or remaining in an area for no obvious reason—is against the law in Milwaukee if it occurs "in a place, at a time, or in a manner not usual for law-abiding individuals under circumstances that warrant alarm for the safety of persons or property in the vicinity." In 2007, the antigang loitering ordinance was signed into law. The ordinance expanded the authority of police to disperse groups of people that include gang members. Gang members may be identified by certain criteria, such as using gang signs, exhibiting gang dress and gang mannerisms, formerly admitting to being a gang member, and claiming to no longer be affiliated with a gang but continuing to associate with known gang members. The public presence of certain individuals, independent of disorderly behavior, is a criminal offense. Those in support of the antigang ordinance claimed it was providing police with an important crime-fighting tool. The politicians and citizens' groups opposed to the ordinance raised civil liberties concerns, arguing that it justifies racial profiling and unfairly targets black and Hispanic youth. In an investigation of a similar ordinance in Chicago, legal scholar Dorothy Roberts asserts that racial disparities in loitering arrests reflect race-based understandings of criminal propensity: "The identity of 'visibly lawless' people at the heart of vague loitering laws incorporates racist notions of criminality and legitimates police harassment of Black citizens."[44] Loitering laws and their enforcement reinforce broader cultural stereotypes of groups of black and brown troublemakers.

Do Riverwesterners also perceive congregated youth of color as a significant social marker of danger? Although I encountered some stigmatizing characterizations of Latino boys and men during my three years in the neighborhood, the overwhelming majority of criminalizing commentary was directed at young black men. The widely held assumption in the neighborhood that crime comes from west of Holton Street (the boundary between Riverwest and the predominantly black Harambee) fuels racialized constructions of disorder and criminality. It locates the primary threat to residents—those criminals who prey on the Riverwest neighborhood—outside the neighborhood in the disadvantaged "ghetto." This assumption co-constructs Riverwest and the ghetto. Crime is viewed as a ghetto export; it is produced in a foreign land and migrates east in search of opportunity. This externalization of the source of neighborhood troubles is part of what sociologist David James calls a "race-making situation": "The racial ghetto sustains and nourishes the racial identifications, fears, and attitudes of blacks and whites."[45] It undergirds and is used to justify residents' suspicions of unknown, nonwhite men.[46] As Elijah Anderson observes, "Not only does the physical ghetto persist, but it also has become a highly negative icon in American society and culture, serving increasingly as a touchstone for prejudice, a profound source of stereotypes, and a rationalization for discrimination against black people in general."[47]

In Lefty Walker's eight years in Riverwest, he has seen things get better and get worse, "like the teeth on a saw." I first met Lefty, a white man in his sixties, when we crossed paths while walking our dogs. He told me he "used to be a hoodlum," as he pulled up his sleeve to show me his collection of tattoos, but now that he's "clean and sober," he has changed his criminal ways. One hot summer night, I joined a small group of white and Latino/a neighbors hanging out on the corner and talking (technically loitering). Lefty and I had just started chatting about his dog when three black teenagers walked by. One of the boys was yelling at someone on his cell phone and was clearly upset with whomever he was talking to. "Bitch, I told you not to fucking do that. FUCK YOU, bitch!" Lefty paused and watched them walk past. He turned to me and said, "That's why there's a ghetto." He then pointed west, the direction they were headed, and said, "Yeah, keep walking." He proceeded to rant about the "black thugs" terrorizing Riverwest. In Lefty's view, the neighborhood has crime because of the adjacent ghetto—a bad place full of badly behaving people with no work ethic and no ability to plan for the future. Several of those gathered on the corner dismissed Lefty's diatribe with rolled eyes or exasperated sighs, but no one directly addressed his racist tirade. When I pressed Lefty about his views during a subsequent sidewalk gathering, another neighbor, Marta Kohl, told me I was wasting my breath. Marta had previously attempted to challenge Lefty's ideas about black pathology but to no avail. "He don't even hear you."

The Hoops Hazard

Lefty's outright condemnation of young black men was hardly unique, but I found articulations of thinly veiled racial suspicion more common. Basketball hoops, for example, often serve as stand-ins for the problematic potential of gatherings of black youth. There are a number of basketball courts in the neighborhood's public and quasi-public spaces—in parks, at school playgrounds, and in some alleys. Residents sometimes couch their anxieties about certain kinds of people in their evaluations of these spaces. When Jean Harmon framed the elimination of basketball hoops as a key component of Gordon Park's improvement, she was talking about a change in the demographics of the park's users and, by extension, its perceived safety. During discussions about the plan to redesign and revitalize Reservoir Park, near neighbors debated the proposed construction of a basketball court. Key arguments both pro and con rested on assumptions about the deviant inclinations of the basketball set. Some residents viewed the court as a valuable prevention tool that would provide teens a way to positively channel their energy. Others saw it as a trouble magnet. Jamie Park, a young Asian American Riverwest parent, felt that the case against the court boiled down to racist fears and intolerance: "Why do you live here if you don't want those people playing basketball out in the park outside your house? 'I don't want those types of people playing basketball. That's only problems.' Are you kidding me? There are courts next to my house. There's never been a problem. I'm sorry, I just don't think that's a valid argument at all. That's a bunch of bullshit excuse for being racist. I'm just not going to say right out that I don't want black people playing by my house. Why do you live in Riverwest if you don't want those people around you?" Longtime residents who oppose new courts or call for restricted use or increased monitoring of existing courts also draw on their experiences with parks and school playgrounds, citing a litany of (sometimes-violent) disturbances that they connect to the use or allure of basketball courts.

Symbolic battles over the significance of public basketball hoops are not new. According to former Riverwest resident Harvey Appleton, in the 1980s a group of white neighbors who lived near Kern Park began organizing an effort to replace the basketball courts (primarily used by black park goers) with additional tennis courts (primarily used by white park goers). This was widely understood to be an attempt to make the park less attractive to black residents. At a town hall meeting, the white organizers found city officials unsympathetic to their cause. At this point in his dramatic retelling, Harvey paused and leaned in: "In the midst of that tense meeting, in that sea of antagonism and misunderstanding, the Kern Park Country Club was born!" At Harvey's suggestion, a small group of mostly white Riverwest residents met for a potluck picnic in the park every month. They set up shop next to the basketball courts. Once in a while, a few basketball players would accept invitations to make a plate. A few country club members would occasionally make their way into a pickup game. Harvey felt that the group had ultimately achieved its goals of normalizing shared park use and reducing suspicion. Over time, the picnics changed how some residents read cues of safety and belonging in a particular public space.

Intentional interventions like the Kern Park Country Club are rare, but the underlying process—the erosion of apprehension through repeated exposure— is part of day-to-day life in this diverse neighborhood. The negative perception of young black and Hispanic men is complicated when residents routinely encounter situations that contradict their expectations. Repeated neutral or positive experiences with these men weaken the association with threat. As David James argues, "All systems of prejudice and racial attitudes are shaped by the social conditions that give them daily validity. Racial attitudes and prejudices that are poor guides to everyday behaviors tend to be modified or abandoned over time."[48] These modifications are a central part of developing what Elijah Anderson terms "street wisdom."[49] As people move from making broad-brush assumptions to more fine-grained distinctions, their environment becomes more manageable. Stereotypes do not necessarily disappear, but their utility for neighborhood negotiation diminishes.

Marisol Flores moved in with relatives in Riverwest when she decided to attend the University of Wisconsin–Milwaukee. At first, she felt uncomfortable walking through the neighborhood to catch the bus or run errands for her aunt and uncle. She was particularly wary of young men congregated on front porches or the sidewalk. Some would try to engage her in conversation as she passed. Others would offer a casual greeting or simply ignore her. After weeks without incident, she began to relax. Marisol now recognized a few faces and, over time, grew confident that those individuals would assist her if there were any trouble. She couldn't explain why she felt this way. They didn't know one another—it was "just a feeling." What had triggered uneasiness now signaled security. Although these cognitive shifts take place inside individuals' heads, they are influenced by and, in turn, support shared understandings of safety and order.

As noted earlier, local sets of meaning are also constructed through discussions in public forums. Residents who participate in block clubs, neighborhood association meetings, town hall gatherings with public officials, the neighborhood listserv, or other online discussions about Riverwest observe discursive patterns in such settings. Over time, they develop a set of expectations about how certain matters are handled and which issues trigger strong reactions and spark conflict. For example, many residents anticipate that when negative racial stereotypes emerge in public or official conversations about local affairs, they will be addressed and challenged. This section opened with Maria's neighbors' unwillingness to accept her framing of the gathering of young black men as a problem absent any negative behavior. In a town hall meeting, a proposal to prohibit barbecuing in local parks was quickly rejected by those who saw it as a proposal to discourage black people's use of public spaces. These challenges sometimes make their way to informal settings like the block. As neighbors gathered on the corner before walking to Gordon Park to see the Fourth of July fireworks, a few grumbled about having to deal with disruptive "ghetto families." A neighbor retorted that if they wanted to find loud families with unruly children, they need look no further than their own backyards.

Not all who noted the expectation that, as one resident explained, "around here, people will be called out on their racist stuff" are in favor of this policing of local discourse. James Chapman, an African American professional who lives in Riverwest, is frustrated by diversity rhetoric that prevents residents from facing the realities of crime and neighborhood change:

> Things are changing. People are moving in that have money. You have an infiltration of ghetto culture. Students are getting shot. People are having shoot-outs over here. All of the diversity crap is great to talk about, but it doesn't really function if people don't feel safe. When people start getting invested in their own safety and see their property values going down and their property taxes going up and you can't send your kids to good schools or get your garbage picked up but at the same time, they're just telling you to write that check out. . . . All of this

stuff is coming together. People are getting irritated. The time that we can fool ourselves by not having a conversation where somebody can say "black" or that the public housing towers have a lot of thugs that are stealing our shit? The times that you can't say those things are coming to an end.

The pressures of tax burdens, deflated housing values, and security threats will, according to James, eventually override naive and often empty expressions of commitment to racial justice. For now, the confrontations continue with predictable regularity, particularly on social media.

In the regular online conversations about crime prevention, suggested strategies that incorporate some form of racial profiling are routinely challenged. A post in a neighborhood forum warning of a "suspicious looking black man" wandering in the alley sparks a cascade of back-and-forth comments ranging from thoughtful dialogue to snark. Such exchanges tend to include the expression of the following sentiments in one form or another:

- The comment poster is racist.
- The comment poster is legitimately concerned.
- This kind of profiling is harmful in an inclusive neighborhood.
- Such profiling is necessary given ongoing crime problems.
- Based on my extensive experience in Riverwest, this warning is nonsense.
- Based on my extensive experience in Riverwest, raising an alarm in this situation is appropriate.

Although such online debates rarely reach any sort of conclusion or reconciliation, they question the assumptions underlying the racialization of deviance and the normative authority of whiteness. As a participant in one of these heated exchanges cautioned, "Better not walk while black."

Given selective participation in such forums, the reach of these symbolic interruptions is unclear. Although they call out racism, they may also support the idea that racism is a problem of wrong-thinking individuals rather than systemic inequalities. Yet these discursive disruptions contribute to a local cultural context that can influence how residents go about assigning blame and maintaining order. When I informed Latina renter Gabriela Ortiz about a group of concerned residents' suggestion that a bar stop hosting hip-hop musicians after a fatal shooting outside its premises, her eyes widened: "You KNOW they are going to get flack for that!" She predicted that these residents would be accused of using racially coded language (i.e., hip-hop) to mask the fact that racialized notions of criminality are at the heart of their proposal for addressing violence.

Normal as Novel

> I like my block because my block provides me a place to be.
> And I don't have to front. (Leon Wade, Riverwest homeowner)

Do these individual shifts in perception add up to something meaningful and tangible to those who inhabit bodies marked as disorderly? Several of the black men in the neighborhood, well-schooled in reading the tension and fear their very presence inspires, see Riverwest as subtly, though significantly, different from other majority-white places. Marcus Zwic, a biracial artist, has spent much of the past fifteen years living in Riverwest—from his "wild wild twenties" to the current "slower" phase of his life as a parent. After travels through North America and Europe, Marcus developed a greater appreciation for Riverwest. His choice to return to the neighborhood was influenced by a sense that local mundane interactions were less racially charged: "I feel like I am treated normal in Riverwest, and that's why I stayed here as a home, because I feel like outside of Riverwest, I can feel the difference in the vibe. . . . I mean because there—not everybody so much has their guard up in Riverwest; people are more inclined to like hang out and talk to each other and say hello. It's a different type of friendly." Marcus chalks this up to "being exposed to it": "This is why Riverwest works in some ways. Because there is less culture shock for the people who live here. . . . Where you go to other communities and just being a little bit different is enough for them to be like, 'Eh, I don't know about you,' either really turned off or cautious—kind of like giving you the cold shoulder. I have been at places that didn't even want to serve me!" Marcus emphasized that normalcy is a valued, exceptional (and, in Riverwest, sometimes-achievable) status—something I would hear again and again during my time in Riverwest from residents who often felt "othered" in some way. In the midst of a list of the kinds of people who would appreciate Riverwest, Tamika Evans included "someone who just wants to be able to do whatever you do and not have people look at you, hold their purse when they walk past you because they're afraid."

Cultural sociologist Wayne Brekhus describes social categories that we (mis)perceive as neutral and generic as "unmarked" categories. He cites heterosexual and white as examples of unmarked categories. Because these are typically default, taken-for-granted characteristics, they are rarely included in descriptions of individuals or used as the foundation for stereotypes in the dominant discourse. Marked categories like homosexual and black receive disproportionate attention, and the diversity within these categories tends not to be recognized. These categorization schemes profoundly affect our perceptions and behavior. Brekhus observes that "characteristics of a marked member are generalized to all members of the marked category but never beyond the category, while attributes of an unmarked member are either perceived as idiosyncratic to the individual or universal to the human condition."[50] The price of markedness is to be rolled into a cultural monolith. The prize of unmarkedness is to be perceived as an individual. Some marked categories, like black, carry such cultural weight that their salience transcends multiple spheres of social life. Yet context matters. As John Hartigan, a cultural anthropologist, observes, race is a "relentlessly local matter. . . . Racial identities are produced and experienced distinctly in different locations."[51]

In a socially mixed neighborhood, some residents must manage marginalizing markedness in everyday encounters while others seemingly float free, ignorant of the privilege of an unearned normalcy. Most Riverwesterners, however, negotiate bundles of marked and unmarked memberships—some of which are immediately visible to others, some of which gradually unfurl, and some of which remain hidden. Residents who have found a level of acceptance and belonging in Riverwest talk about that experience and its significance in various ways. A subset of black residents' narratives include descriptions of a local resocialization process through which race fades from perceived prominence into a set of defining features, orientations, tastes, and quirks. Leon Wade, a teacher, describes some of the key lessons to be learned in a diverse community:

> I like that there's people from different backgrounds comingling with each other. It can help you understand people. If all you know of black people is the *Cosby Show*—we're not all lawyers and doctors that live in a three-story brownstone in New York. Or if all you know is what you see in the news—we don't all rob and kill. Some of us work hard every day and bitch about property taxes just like you. It's nice if people can see that other part of you, you know. . . . It's nice to have different people doing different things in the same area because you get to see other people every day. It's like socializing a dog. You leave the dog in the house all the time and it meets another dog, it's gonna be pissy and act the fool. But if it goes outside and plays with the other strange dogs on the block, then it's not an issue anymore.

Leon believes that mundane activities and conversations refashion how neighbors view neighbors of a different race because they bring other, potentially shared aspects of identity to the fore. Residents note discovering overlapping experiences as parents, caretakers, workers, students, consumers, artists, homeowners, renters, pet keepers, love seekers, people with disabilities, people living with illness, and people with a variety of shared interests.

Marcus Zwic recounted the story of witnessing the gradual transformation of a man who had recently moved to Riverwest. Over time, the attitudes of this "old school redneck guy who just seeped racism" seemed to shift. "You can feel it and see it growing out of him being in the neighborhood and dealing with . . . kids and all that stuff, and different cultures of people where he used to be like, 'Ah!' and saying derogatory bigotry remarks. And even his friendship with me was kind of like, 'Well . . . I don't know.' It's so weird that I would even think of him as a friend because he is so like that, but to see him change. He just totally did a 180 after living here for a year. . . . His heart just got soft." Marcus noticed that this man's everyday interactions with black and Latino/a people also changed. Though not exactly enthusiastic, he was less standoffish and more engaging.

Darius Hines also attaches weight to the prosaic. It's the "simple social norms"—like keeping the alley tidy and putting the garbage can back after trash pickup—"that let us know we on the same page." He sees diversity as a neighborhood asset, but for Darius, the real achievement of integration in Riverwest is the normalization (rather than the celebration) of difference. He embraces not colorblindness but a deflation of charged otherness, a dimming of the socially marked as what is shared is made visible. Our very first conversation, at a mutual friend's party, touched on this issue. We revisited it several times, months later, during a recorded interview:

> DARIUS: It's a lotta cooperation in the neighborhood . . . among
> different races and ethnicities. It is. It really is. And it's something
> that doesn't necessarily have to be talked about. It just kinda is what
> it is. You know? I'm here. You here. We here. [*laughs*]
> EVIE: We don't need to put up a sign . . .
> DARIUS: Right. Hey, white on black! Hey, we're here! Hey!

Of course, Riverwest residents do put up "diversity is our strength" signs. Darius isn't opposed to such expressions of pride, but he values the opportunity for normalcy. He believes that one thing that Riverwesterners share is "the desire to be able to walk down the street and not feel, you know, like somebody doesn't want you there." A neighborhood where many people have aspects of their identities that are stigmatized elsewhere can broaden access to experiences of belonging and being (relatively) unexceptional.

It is important not to overstate the impact of these challenges to the criminalization of black men. Block-level interactions and observations can expand residents' understandings of specific neighbors and aid in the development of an appreciation for the diversity within marked social categories of people. However, such perspective shifts do not necessarily or readily apply to encounters with unknown black men in off-the-block public spaces. Indeed, some residents assert that Riverwest's embrace of racial diversity ends at Holton Street, implying that these perspective shifts might be limited to well-known others deemed exceptions. Appreciation of diversity is sometimes overshadowed by the daily peddling of stereotypes in the media, the powerful image of the ghetto, and the reality that the majority of those found responsible for crime in Riverwest are black. White Riverwest resident Scott Horvath is pessimistic about the possibility of dismantling long-standing narratives about Milwaukee's disreputable black poor:

> Right now, the worst racist stereotypes and fears of white suburbanites and South Siders and some white East Siders and even Riverwesterners are too often in actual fact on the ground confirmed. It's too often confirmed. I would say there are a lot of people who don't confirm it, but there's a lot who do. Disparity is the ultimate cause, but what I'm saying is that disparity has caused incidents—just day to day, when certain white people walk by Gordon Park and the way two mamas yell at each other over their kids. . . . We can put it in context and talk about why it's there, but I'm not willing to qualify it. It's not a small group of people. The different standard of behavior is not isolated. Are there more stable African American families who are raising their families and keeping their doors shut than most people realize? Absolutely. But when you travel neighborhoods, you see the corner boys. There's less corner boys than those keeping their heads down, but when you look at the stats—the test scores, the graduation rates, the joblessness rates, I'm not sure that that's a small group. Yes, there is incredible variation, but unacceptable variation. I'm not disputing causes—I'm discussing effects. The institutions are so racist that they have allowed the on-the-ground racist attitudes to be confirmed. It's a feedback loop. Until that on-the-ground reality changes—and yes, it's

there because of institutional racism—but until that changes, I think we stay fucked.

As long as residents encounter people and behaviors that support negative stereotypes and enable them to justify their prejudices, Scott believes the neighborhood will have limited potential to reshape racial attitudes. Existing research suggests that reality lies somewhere between naive optimism and stark pessimism. Living in multiracial contexts corresponds with lower levels of racial animosity.[52] However, the impacts of diverse neighborhood residence are conditional: People respond differently to heterogeneous contexts. The key is to identify the mechanisms—like cultural frames and linked engagement and social control practices—that influence integration outcomes.

Remarkable Whiteness

Racial constructions are relational. Local understandings of whiteness are therefore a critical component of perceptions of raced disorder in Riverwest. Despite the pervasive diversity rhetoric, some residents view Riverwest as a white neighborhood. Although I encountered this perspective most often among nonwhite residents, a few white people also described the neighborhood as white. Racing place in this way is linked to ideas about who belongs and who has power. Elijah Anderson describes the "normative sensibility of the white space" with respect to African Americans as one that "excludes or marginalizes blacks, and in which blacks are unexpected, and when present require explanation."[53] These white spaces reflect the prevailing white normative perspective in the United States: "This perspective starts from the dominance of white worldviews, and sees the culture, experiences, and indeed lives, of people of color only as they relate to or interact with the white world. White normativity is not simply an attitude held by whites in which white people are the center of the universe. Rather, white normativity is a reality of the racial structure of the United States in which whites occupy an unquestioned and unexamined place of esteem, power, and privilege."[54]

In Riverwest, there are many practices that reinforce the white normative perspective. When residents use "diversity" as a stand-in for nonwhite people or praise the neighborhood for being "welcoming," they construct whites as hosts and "others" as guests.[55] A white resident I met at a block party implicated a normal (yet superior) white worldview when he concluded a description of his ongoing struggles with a neighboring black-owned business with, "They are from a different culture. They have different values." When white residents frame their decision to stay in a racially diverse neighborhood as a commitment to being a stabilizing or revitalizing force, their paternalism places a premium on whiteness.[56] Yet local racial understandings are complicated by the frequent marking of whiteness by both nonwhite and white residents.

In everyday conversations, some residents use *white* as a descriptor of particular neighborhood places and groups: "That block is mostly white." "It's a white people's thing." "Yeah, that bar used to be pretty white." When *white* is included in a description, it can destabilize or at least make visible assumptions about whiteness as the norm. If whiteness is worthy of note, then it becomes an object of scrutiny.

For some residents, white dominance signals a legitimacy problem in local organizations, establishments, or events, particularly those claiming to be representative. The predominantly white Riverwest Neighborhood Association is frequently critiqued on these grounds by skeptical onlookers and participants alike. Scott Horvath has participated in the RNA but questions its representativeness: "The Riverwest Neighborhood Association? Lately it's become increasingly irrelevant; although I'm not sure it's ever been that relevant. It's always been extremely white." For this resident, the measure of relevance is the racial makeup of the membership. Maliha Noor, who at one time was active in the RNA, reflects on the outreach strategies of local organizations:

> I can't tell you how many people I have heard say, "Well I want more
> black friends, but I don't know how to have them." And I think it's a
> typical white method of getting black people in their lives. Listen to
> my words, *"getting black people into their lives."* In a lot of the organizing
> I have done I see white people struggle to get black people involved.
> And the real answer to that in my opinion is to go and get involved
> in what black people are doing, instead of trying to get them involved in
> what white people are doing. But you have to have a consciousness of
> believing what they are doing is important and affects you, and I don't
> think that most people have that.

Maliha's concerns are representative of a theme I found running through a subset of engaged, white, diversity-valuing residents' attempts to make sense of race. They are sensitive to lopsided participation in various endeavors and worry about perceived or real power imbalances, but they struggle to find effective strategies to address their concerns without being patronizing.

I met a handful of residents who make whiteness visible by identifying and critiquing racialized notions of the "good" community and positive neighborhood change. Paul Kelley worries that if Riverwest faces significant gentrification pressures, market forces will prove stronger than local efforts to preserve the local social mix. But he does not see those market forces as neutral. Paul describes the assumptions that he believes guide the decisions of residential and commercial developers: "Generally the view of the developers is: 'We are going to make it a good neighborhood, because there won't be any black people there.' And that is not—I mean, there is a reality there which exists outside of the economic reality. . . . Everyone wants to live in a good neighborhood. But a good neighborhood is not necessarily determined by high housing values and, I guess for a lack of a better way to express it, by a neighborhood populated by mostly white people." In Paul's view, real estate developers rely on dominant understandings of desirable communities that place a premium on whiteness and high, appreciating property values.[57] He doubts that the alternative definition of the "good neighborhood" that he and some of his neighbors endorse would have enough support to withstand gentrification pressures.

Naming whiteness is not restricted to the group of residents grappling with the social meanings and responsibilities attached to being white. For most nonwhite residents, navigating predominantly white spaces is nothing new. For many white residents, however, Riverwest is the first place they have lived that is not exclusively white. White isolation that is produced and maintained by residential segregation reaffirms dominant understandings of racial difference and generic and preferred whiteness.[58] These understandings are potentially disrupted by local encounters with whiteness as visible, variable, and even suspect. They are further complicated by this marking of whiteness in a cultural context with flexible norms and unstable interpretations of "others" (and, significantly, not just racial "others"). I am not suggesting that radical transformations in racial thinking abound. I am arguing that emplaced challenges to the normative white perspective are linked to blurred lines of social distinction and an unsettling of racialized notions of crime and disorder.

For a few residents, living in a socially mixed neighborhood has tempered notions of threatening or hostile whiteness. For example, Jada Moore, a young African American mother I met as we were both leaving the Center Street Daze festival, told me she was surprised to find "decent" white people on her block when she moved into the neighborhood. Although I had seen Amos Sims around the neighborhood, I didn't officially meet him until we ended up sitting next to each other at a bar that is primarily populated by older locals. After telling him about my study and describing some of my burning questions, Amos treated me to an hour-long stream of stories and observations. I learned that he grew up believing that all white people are inherently bad. His now long-standing neighborly relationships with white people on his block would be a shock to his younger self (and continue to arouse his mother's suspicions). That I encountered only a handful of indicators of these shifts during my time in Riverwest might signal that they are relatively rare. It also might point to my limitations as a white researcher or my failure to develop the kind of rapport necessary for nonwhite residents to feel comfortable sharing their negative assessments of white people. Still, I think it is worth noting that the processes that soften social boundaries and disrupt negative stereotypes can work up, down, and even within groups in the racial hierarchy.

Doing Difference, Seeing Differently

As residents construct mental maps of their neighborhood, they draw boundaries between safe and dangerous, productive and destructive, asset and nuisance, different and disorderly. The lines they draw can have very real consequences for the reproduction of inequality, including reifying or reframing existing social categories.[59] Previous research demonstrates that the construction of diverse neighborhoods as problematic places is connected to interpretive biases that link racial composition with inflated assessments of disorder, crime, and disadvantage. In Riverwest, we see that residents' mental maps are also shaped by neighborhood context. Place grounds and organizes experiences and interpretations of encounters, collective understandings of the social surround, and shared strategies of neighborhood negotiation. At times, these local interactions and meaning-making processes create a legitimate space in public culture for marginalized styles of artistic expression or encourage the diversification and decriminalization of marked categories of residents. When linked to dismantling the construction of certain types of behavior or people as transgressive or threatening, these practices can challenge racialized perceptions of disorder and associated practices of exclusion.

CHAPTER SIX

Drinking
Beers, Bars, and Bad Behavior

CHEERS TO RIVERWEST! Last summer, the U.S. Government flew over
Riverwest in a helicopter, with a giant breathalyzer instrument. The results of
the test were shocking. Riverwest was five times more drunk than the average
neighborhood and the entire neighborhood was declared intoxicated. Yes,
Riverwest likes to raise a glass and give a toast to drunkenness. There are many,
many great bars of all kinds.
—Tea Krulos, "Riverwest Six-Pack Tour"

Wisconsin is famous for beer, both its production and its consumption, and
drinking figures prominently in the state's leisure culture.[1] You would be
hard-pressed to find a bar or restaurant without daily happy-hour specials.
Beer-soaked tailgating is a prerequisite for attendance at major sporting
events, such as Milwaukee Brewers' baseball games. It is not unusual to treat
the bar as an extension of the office for business meetings scheduled outside the regular workday. Holidays and celebrations of almost any kind
merit festive imbibing. Wisconsin's drinking culture is steeped, in part, in its
German heritage and related beer-brewing tradition. The city of Milwaukee
was long known as the "beer capital of the world," once home to prominent
beer barons and the Miller, Schlitz, Pabst, and Blatz breweries.[2] More recently,
Milwaukee has been given the (perhaps related) honor of being one of the
"drunkest cities" in the nation. Twelve of the cities listed in the top twenty
are in Wisconsin.[3] There is some substance behind the state's beer-swilling
reputation. Since the Centers for Disease Control and Prevention began measuring binge drinking in 1993, Wisconsin has consistently topped the state
rankings. In 2010, for example, Wisconsin had the highest prevalence of
binge drinking, with a quarter of surveyed residents reporting excessive
drinking (defined as four or more drinks for women and five or more drinks
for men on an occasion during the past thirty days). The general alcohol
consumption rate in Wisconsin is 28 percent higher than the national average.[4] The drinking culture is also supported by a substantial supply of bars,
three times more per capita than in the rest of the country.[5]

Although a source of pride for many Wisconsinites, alcohol's central place
in recreational culture is also viewed as a serious social problem. In March 2013,

Health First Wisconsin released a report that assessed the economic costs of "excessive" alcohol use. The estimated $6.8 billion spent each year on health care, lost productivity, vehicle crashes, and criminal justice garnered national media attention.[6] A 2008 community health assessment in Milwaukee found that alcohol use was a key health concern for city residents, second only to violence.[7] These tensions are not unique to Wisconsin. In the United States, alcohol use is both highly valued and deeply stigmatized. It is associated with both celebration and a host of medical, moral, and social problems. Alcohol use, then, can be the basis for social inclusion or exclusion.[8] Cultural ambivalence about alcohol consumption plays out in multiple social arenas—in policy debates about the merits of alcohol regulation; in the practices of institutions responsible for social welfare or medical treatment; and in everyday, on-the-ground assessments of people and places.

At the neighborhood level, urban scholars find that public drinking, the presence of bars, and the presence of liquor stores are significant markers of disorder.[9] Current concerns about the disruptive impact of drinking on social order are rooted in the temperance movement, which popularized the link between alcohol consumption and crime and violence. The movement framed drinkers as morally compromised deviants, and the drinking class (synonymous with the working class) as dangerous.[10] Despite the ever-shifting and contested definition of the "alcohol problem," the relationship between drinking, low socioeconomic status, immorality, and danger has retained considerable symbolic power.[11]

As I demonstrated in chapter 5, appraisals of features of the urban environment are influenced by (and produced through) the filtering of broad cultural understandings of disorder through local meanings and interactions. Making sense of practices like drinking and their interpretation requires situating those practices in specific social contexts. As Joseph Gusfield argues, "The problems of public control of alcohol are seldom those of drinking per se but rather the contexts and groups within which drinking and drinking behavior occur. It is these contexts that give meanings to and create troubles for specific parts of social structures within particular historical circumstances."[12] Do the thirty-six neighborhood bars and prevalence of public drinking create troubles for Riverwest residents?

Illicit Leisure

"Are people in the neighborhood bothersome?" A recent study used this yes/no survey question to measure perceptions of social disorder.[13] In this chapter,

I extend the examination of disorder in Riverwest to the realm of leisure. Understanding how people interpret bothersome public behavior reveals processes central to the organization and regulation of difference. Who gets to determine what or whom is bothersome? Sociolegal scholar Mariana Valverde argues that the urban legal mechanisms that shape the everyday policing of disorder reflect and valorize particular cultural preferences—namely those of middle-class, middle-aged property owners. "Enforcement work is full of culturally laden assumptions about who has the right to what 'level of tranquility' and about who is a credible complainant."[14] The application of municipal laws, Valverde concludes, regulates taste in ways that tend to denigrate and exclude the leisure activities and aesthetic preferences of marginalized groups.

Urban governance likely influences local interpretations of disorder in a socially mixed neighborhood, but most of the day-to-day management of potentially troublesome recreational practices in Riverwest happens without involving agents of the law. I find that these informal processes of drawing boundaries and regulating neighborhood space rarely add up to a clear endorsement of a particular residential ideal. Competing perceptions of leisure habits and habitats—of drinking in public and in bars—are the stuff of group marking and placemaking in Riverwest.

Public Drinking

According to societal norms and legal rules of conduct, consumption of alcohol must take place only in designated, clearly bounded social spaces: in bars, in restaurants, or at home (preferably with others). The importance of concealment reflects the contentious moral status of drinking. The containment of consumption provides at least the illusion of control. This is part of what makes public drinking—in parks, on the sidewalk, or on the front stoop—so problematic: what should be secluded is now in plain view and beyond the reach of regulated drinking spaces. In a survey of residents across forty neighborhoods in six U.S. cities, this out-of-place activity—public drinking—was the most highly ranked form of disorder.[15] Because alcohol reduces inhibition, drunkenness is associated with erratic behavior and exaggerated emotion. When intoxicated, people can become loud, aggressive, belligerent, and even violent. What is unsettling about encountering people who are inebriated—especially strangers—is that they are unpredictable.

In the warmer months, many Riverwest residents spend time on their front porches, and drinking is a popular porch activity. This semipublic consumption of alcohol takes various forms. The college students across the street sit on the front steps with friends on a Thursday afternoon, chatting and drinking cocktails. That evening, more friends join, and the party spills onto the front lawn and the sidewalk in front of their house. After a long day of work, Jordan fires up the grill and flips burgers with one hand while he holds a bottle of beer in the other. Jerry wanders down the street at noon, can of malt liquor in hand, stopping to chat with neighbors as they come and go. Amelia stands on her porch, crushed beer cans at her feet, screaming at her kids who are playing on the sidewalk. Her speech is slurred. Her sons eventually head toward home, heads hanging.

The boundary between public and private consumption in the aforementioned situations is easily blurred. The activities of porch dwellers are often visible and audible from a few doors down or across the street. Their theoretical containment is rather thin. When people take the few steps from the porch to the sidewalk or street, they cross the legal boundary between private property and public property. The legal demarcation of public and private is less significant, however, than the social demarcation between those activities that are acceptable in public and those that belong in private. Porches exist in the space in between—in the transition from domestic to public. The neighborhood's porch culture pulls what might otherwise take place inside or in the backyard into public view. Neighborhood porches host all manner of gatherings and activities—knitting circles, card games, bull sessions, barbecuing, hair braiding, guitar picking, people watching, marijuana smoking, and enjoying a morning coffee and cigarette with a friend.

Many of these porch uses would be deemed inappropriate in other neighborhoods. In certain contexts, otherwise identical everyday behaviors become "incivilities" when they move from the living room or the back patio to the porch. These lines of propriety are steeped in classed understandings of the privatization of leisure. For example, in her study of a gentrifying Chicago neighborhood, Mary Pattillo finds that some of the more affluent residents feel that barbecuing on front porches or the boulevard is distasteful and tarnishes the image of a respectable middle-class community.[16] In a newly developed mixed-income housing community in Boston, middle-class place-use norms are built into the neighborhood's official regulations. Laura Tach observes that rules against loitering and related pressure from management to socialize in backyards instead of on front stoops effectively limit the visibility of lower-class residents.[17] In these analyses, formal and informal practices of social exclusion are justified as necessary to produce a good and decent (read middle-class) community. As Joseph Gusfield argues, these practices communicate the "public worth" of one set of norms over others: "The designation of a way of behavior as violating public norms confers status and honor on those groups whose cultures are followed as the standard of conventionality, and derogates those whose cultures are considered deviant."[18] The problem of public drinking can be understood in a similar framework. Cultural geographer John Dixon and his colleagues find that residents view street drinking as a transgression of tacit place norms that pollutes or "defiles" the character of a place.[19] Such tensions and transgressions are made visible in heterogeneous neighborhoods and public spaces.

In Riverwest, porch, sidewalk, and street socializing and imbibing are valued or at least accepted aspects of neighborhood character, provided they don't disturb the peace. Revelers cross the line when they become threatening or violent or take up space in a way that makes others feel unsafe. In the course of one casual conversation, a couple laughed about putting blankets over the punk kids passed out on their lawn and lamented having to call the police after an inebriated neighbor pounded on his door for an hour, screaming at his wife to let him back in. That public drinking "troubles" are typically determined by bad behavior rather than assumed by the mere presence of a category of people suggests that neighborhood insiders and outsiders "see" differently.

Drinking Alone and Addiction

In Milwaukee, drinking is celebrated as a social activity, so encounters with the solitary public drinker are often particularly troubling.[20] Sidling up to the bar solo at the local tavern, however, does not necessarily constitute drinking alone. Since bars are social spaces, drinking in a bar is still considered a social act. When one encounters a stranger drinking by him- or herself in a public space like a park, this apparent indifference to the social norms of imbibing can be disturbing. Solitary consumption might signal a deviant relationship with alcohol, a desire to not be held accountable by others, or a propensity to drink too much.

It is not uncommon for Riverwest residents to be familiar with someone in the neighborhood whom they believe to be an alcoholic.[21] This might be a neighbor or someone they regularly run across in their neighborhood rounds. Although many have a household member dealing with substance abuse issues, I am focusing here on public encounters with individuals who appear to have a drinking problem. Despite the considerable shift in public understanding of alcohol dependence as a disease rather than a moral failing, alcoholism continues to carry the stain of stigma. In talk about local "drunks," residents alternately characterize alcoholics as sick and deserving of sympathy or weak, irresponsible, lacking self-control, and shameful. This gossip serves a purpose, helping residents determine how to factor these individuals into their assessments of environmental disorder and risk.

Consider Jerry Baum: Tamryn Keyes lives in a house across the street from Jerry. I got to know both of them, as I spent a lot of time on their block. Jerry, a white renter who has moved in, out of, and around Riverwest over the years, almost always has a beer in his hand. He has a physical disability that inhibits his ability to work. Jerry spends the majority of his time on the block. He drinks every day as he drifts up and down the sidewalk. He's loud, opinionated, and occasionally argumentative but never violent or threatening. When Tamryn first met him, he made her nervous. She was particularly concerned about the effects of his behavior on Carly, Jerry's ten-year-old daughter. Since that first meeting, Tamryn notices that Jerry, a single father, watches closely over Carly. He walks her to and from elementary school every day. Carly appears to be generally well cared for, although she sometimes looks a bit disheveled. Jerry and Carly are both strong willed and frequently have loud disputes. Some of the neighbors are friendly with Jerry. He is widely regarded as a pain, but not a serious problem. When Tamryn first expressed concerns about him, her neighbors assured her that he was shifty but mostly harmless. They gossip about his drinking habits and joke about his inebriated performances. They speculate on the likelihood of Jerry being responsible for the disappearance of items from neighbors' porches and garages. They sometimes find odd jobs for him to do for money. They begrudgingly give him cigarettes when his supply has dwindled. Some are friendly with Carly and check in with her about her issues at school. One afternoon, a couple of recent college graduates living on the block styled Carly's hair and painted her nails.

After a while, Tamryn's view of Jerry began to shift. She became more comfortable with her interactions with Jerry and even began to understand his caustic humor. She also concluded that his routine wandering up and down the block makes him a one-man block watch. Eventually, his presence became less disconcerting and, at times, oddly comforting. Her daughter and Carly have become friends. Although she won't let her daughter go inside Jerry's house, she now trusts Jerry to watch over the children's outdoor play sessions. In turn, she looks out for Carly and shares her knowledge of local family resources that Jerry might find useful.

There are many Riverwesterners, like Jerry, whose addictions are public. They experience varying levels of integration into life on the block based on near neighbors' collective assessments of their behavior and character. Although most would agree that their very presence is in some respects disorderly, their other roles (e.g., as parents, protectors, charismatic connectors, or skilled workers) or their positive contributions to (or lack of severely negative impact on) the quality of block life can soften such judgments.

One summer afternoon, Joyce Becker waved me onto her porch. Joyce, a small but tough-as-nails white woman, has been renting in Riverwest for over three decades and now has children, grandchildren, and great-grandchildren living in what she claims to be *her* neighborhood. As I approached, her little dog strained against his leash to greet me. Joyce motioned with her cigarette for me to take a seat. She had just begun to fill me in on the highlights of her recent fishing trip when neighbor Russ Hoffman bounded up the porch steps to join us. A few minutes later, Joyce's fishing tales were again interrupted— this time by a man walking down the street toward us yelling, "Russ! Can you believe they want $750 a month for that dump above the bar?" Joyce and Russ gave each other a knowing look. Russ stood up to greet our visitor. "Hey, Manny." This is just the opening Manny Castillo is looking for. He stands in the front yard, shirtless, with a two-by-four balanced on his muscular frame, and delivers a fifteen-minute, meandering monologue about apartment hunting, work, love, prison, health care, his nine children, the cost of groceries, constructing a food cart, and drugs. He "can't handle crack no more," so he's growing marijuana in his backyard. His speech comes to an abrupt end when he spots a couple he knows walking down the street and chases after them.

Joyce and Russ spend the next ten minutes piecing together a picture of Manny, a Latino resident who has been in and out of the neighborhood for years. I learn that he is a talented and reasonably priced electrician who has worked under the table for many neighbors and is currently working on a project for Russ. He is also a crack addict, who, according to Joyce, "smokes everything he makes." Neither Joyce nor Russ believes Manny's claim to have given up the pipe. When I ask if he's a bad guy, Joyce is quick to defend him. "Oh, no," she says, "he don't bother nobody."

With repeated exposure and the opportunity to gather information about a neighbor, his or her disorderly behavior may become normalized or sanitized through disassociation from threat. The unfolding of this process is dependent on a willingness to contextualize a neighbor's behavior instead of rejecting it outright as problematic. The neighborhood mantra, "live and let live," and the opportunity for ongoing block-level observation support this kind of difference negotiation.

Yet this is precisely what frustrates other residents. They believe that in tolerating Jerry's drinking and Manny's drug use, their neighbors are enabling addiction, failing to help the negatively impacted families in a direct manner, and contributing to the deterioration of local social order. Part of what can make substance abuse in Riverwest particularly unsettling is its visibility—the public nature of personal troubles. Context matters. What might be concealed in upper-class communities is in plain sight in this neighborhood. I found both subtle and overt links to social class in residents' framing of the local alcohol problem. Some formulate place-based norms that are rooted in long-standing constructions of urban, working-class drinking—rather than the "moral" middle- and upper-class drinking—as impulsive, indulgent, deviant, and disorderly.[22]

Mark Jansen, a white homeowner, is tired of seeing his neighbors spending their days at the corner taps while neglecting their deteriorating properties. He believes that local tolerance of rampant alcohol and drug use is a major barrier to neighborhood improvement: "Walk down a warm night and count how many people are sitting on their porch with a forty ounce in their hands. They are wearing it on their sleeve. They're not hiding their addictions. . . . What bugs me about the alcohol and drug thing is that it's so powerfully laid over everything, but no one wants to talk about that. But it's at the core of why a lot of people here have marginal, unsuccessful lives in Riverwest. You can go out to the suburbs and what is it filled with? Successful people. It isn't also filled with people sitting in corner bars." What might seem to be an individual-level problem is, in Mark's view, a place problem that requires dispassionate intervention.

These different strategies for negotiating difference, linked to conflicting notions of what it means to be a good neighbor, play out in the daily life of the neighborhood. The clashes are not always visible. Calls to Child Protective Services or pulling a neighbor into the backyard for a one-on-one conversation happen outside public purview.

Neighborhood Context, Social Distance, and Stigma

Despite large-scale efforts to increase public understanding of mental health issues, negative social stigmas continue to be attached to mental illness.[23] Drug and alcohol dependence have been medicalized (i.e., redefined as mental health issues), yet the particularly severe social stigmatization of addiction endures.[24] Stigma contributes to the marginalization and social isolation of people living with mental illness, constrains their quality of life, reduces the effectiveness of treatment, and undergirds individual and institutional acts of discrimination against those with mental health problems.[25]

The stigma of mental illness is not erased in Riverwest. Residents use labels like "drunk," "crackhead," and "crazy" to set themselves apart from (and as superior to) their neighbors. In on-the-block chitchat, neighbors with addictions and other mental health issues are often the objects of ridicule and scorn. Yet emplaced norms, understandings, and practices work against the outright rejection and expulsion of those living with mental illness, provided they do not seriously threaten the local order. In only rare cases did I encounter the sentiment that this broad category of people simply doesn't belong in the neighborhood. Instead, behavior that is harmful to others typically determines who loses the right to be in Riverwest.

In some cases, people with mental health problems are woven into community life. When residents on one block had the opportunity to develop more nuanced understandings of their alcohol-dependent neighbor, Marilyn Noble, "addict" became one of multiple facets of her identity. She was then able to socially engage with her neighbors as mother, artist, or political commentator—multiplying opportunities for connection, belonging, and the gift and receipt of a range of supports. Although Marilyn is aware that acceptance by her neighbors is conditional, she considers herself a proud member of the block.

One morning, I ran into Robin Lund at Fuel Café. She reported, laughing, that she had been on her way to the Riverwest Co-Op that morning when she saw Jermaine Wilson. She assumes I know whom she is talking about, and I do. Those who frequent Fuel Café or the Co-Op are familiar with Jermaine. These are two of his primary hangout spots in the neighborhood. Robin goes on to explain that she found him standing on the sidewalk, legs spread apart, rocking back and forth. She was pretty sure he was "swinging his junk between his legs." Robin noted how that wouldn't fly in most communities and would likely prompt a call to the police. "But in Riverwest, there isn't anybody we want to throw away. We know Jermaine, and he knows us." She explains that the Co-Op staff find ways for Jermaine to help out from time to time. And Jermaine knows not to hit her up for money because she doesn't have any. Robin thoroughly enjoys listening to his multiple biographies, which regularly change and sometimes include his revolutionary days with the Black Panther Party. By that time, Lucy Pallotta had wandered over and joined our conversation. She asked Robin if Jermaine is schizophrenic. Robin paused and then questioned the usefulness of diagnoses. On any given day, she said, she can be in a different place along a spectrum of mental health, and so can anyone else.

Without the context provided by regular interactions, Jermaine's behavior might seem disconcerting or even threatening. As Jermaine has been folded into the acquaintance networks of neighbors, café regulars, and local organization members, he has become a known entity—his unpredictability is predictable and bounded, and his behavior is innocuous.

When Travis Hunt, a gregarious public character on my block, fell into a downward spiral of crack addiction and legal trouble, it clearly affected his near neighbors. Some felt they had been manipulated into supporting his habit or hiding the truth from his wife and kids before they fully understood the gravity of the situation. After Travis eventually wound up in jail, neighbors stepped up to offer his wife rides or child care. When Travis returned after a stint in a drug rehabilitation center, neighbors cautiously and slowly allowed him to reintegrate into block life.

After a particularly troubling interaction with Travis when he seemed strung out and desperate, I wrote about my complex relationship with him in my field notes:

> Here's this crackhead—who isn't just a crackhead. He's a jovial neighbor who lends a little humor to the block. He's the first person to show up to help push my car out of the snow. He's the guy who would probably beat up anybody who tried to hurt Daniel or me. He's a father to kids I care about. He's the husband of someone I consider a friend. He's someone I drank beers with in the backyard. He's a carpenter who will help you out for cheap. In the abstract, of course, no one wants a crackhead on their block . . . but . . . it's [Travis].

Those neighbors who also had multidimensional and conflicted relationships with Travis struggled to find ways to be supportive without being enabling and to engage Travis without leaving themselves or the block vulnerable to trouble.

Mental health professionals that serve the community must also navigate Riverwest's complex cultural terrain. After spending several years working for a neighborhood social service organization, Jackie Wold has developed a middle-ground stance on substance abuse. She sees that there are limited resources to support the many people living with addiction and other mental health issues. She appreciates that struggling families are sometimes able to find social support in Riverwest, but worries that the "cultural community support" for some illicit drug use is linked to substance abuse problems, particularly among neighborhood youth.

Social scientists have paid increasing attention to the multiple ways in which social networks impact health. An individual's web of relationships may affect one's access to emotional and instrumental support, strategies for managing illness (including seeking help), exposure to social influences on health behaviors, levels of social engagement, and experiences of stigma.[26] Social networks also influence how people categorize and respond to illness and in some circumstances may reduce the stigma attached to certain illnesses. This exploration of responses to addiction in Riverwest demonstrates the importance of emplacing networks by situating them in specific contexts. The demographic makeup and physical structure of the community impact the formation of social ties. A heterogeneous neighborhood divided into face blocks presents opportunities to develop multifaceted connections that cross social boundaries, including those associated with stigmatized mental illnesses. And the local cultural context influences relationship management strategies and pathways to belonging, which, in turn, affect understandings of addiction, the inclusion or exclusion of those living with mental illness, and related access to support.

Bars

Many struggling, high-crime urban communities in the United States have above-average concentrations of bars and liquor outlets.[27] Although the nature of the relationship between alcohol availability and neighborhood crime is a source of ongoing debate,[28] perceptions of safety may be influenced by the density of bars and liquor stores. The appearance of being unable to support or attract businesses besides those that sell alcohol contributes to perceptions of neighborhood disadvantage.

In Riverwest, there is an abundance of locations offering the opportunity to imbibe. There are thirty-six bars in the neighborhood, and six places to buy alcohol for off-premises consumption: one liquor store, one large grocery store, several small convenience stores, and a bar (see Map 3).[29] Riverwest Stein, a microbrew named after the neighborhood, is a source of local pride. Brothers Jim and Russ Klisch started brewing beer in the basement of their Riverwest home in the 1980s. They rolled barrels of their crafted concoctions to corner bars willing to give these local boys a shot. It turns out that they were talented brewers. Lakefront Brewery has enjoyed considerable success and continues to pay homage to the neighborhood that helped give the Klisch brothers their start. The vast majority of bars in the neighborhood have Lakefront's award-winning Riverwest Stein available, including those corner taps that typically don't carry microbrews.

Bars provide some of the most utilized social spaces in Riverwest (apart from the face block). Some of the bars are clustered on the neighborhood's more commercial streets. The rest are scattered throughout the neighborhood. Many small corner taps are integrated into residential blocks. Riverwest's assortment of bars includes a tiki bar; a gay bar/art gallery; a brewery pub; a potentially anarchist bar ("We like to let people draw their own conclusions"); a romantic hideaway lounge (for both straight and gay couples);

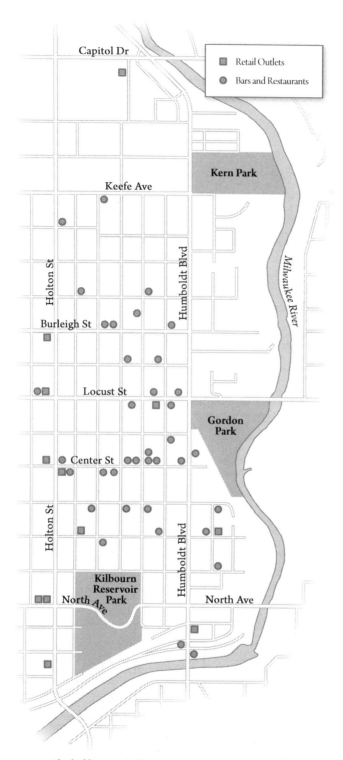

MAP 3 Alcohol licenses in Riverwest, 2010. Source: City of Milwaukee, Information Technology Management, GIS.

music and dance clubs; sports bars; third-shift bars; an African club; a Puerto Rican bar with domino tables; a Polish bar with a bowling alley and meeting hall; a cooperative bar; quite a few cozy, hole-in-the-wall taverns; and the Uptowner, Milwaukee's oldest continuously operating bar (opened in 1884). That Riverwest can support such a variety of watering holes is, for some, a reflection of its diversity. There seems to be a bar for everyone.

Many residents view the bars as neighborhood assets. They provide places for residents to gather informally and get to know one another. John Bauer has lived in Riverwest since the early 1970s. He has worn many hats during his time in the neighborhood, including walking the Riverwest beat as a police officer. Over the years, he has watched many of the neighborhood taverns close. He laments the loss of so many of these gathering spots and deeply appreciates those that have survived. He sees them as fulfilling an important role in building and maintaining communal bonds: "They are the social network. They are the fabric. They are where people meet. They are the community living room. It's not just drinking establishments; it's where you discuss what's going on, like the old general store. It's where boy meets girl. . . . It's like a warm spot on a cold winter day. It's where you find someone maybe to fix your car, or do some repair work. You get the community network through these spots." For John, bars enrich local social connections. They are what Ray Oldenburg terms "third places": essential complements to home and work that provide settings for informal public life. Third places offer accessible neutral ground for the gathering of diverse people; the enjoyment of good company; and the nourishment of the intellectual, political, and social lives of patrons and their neighborhoods.[30] Bars in Riverwest fulfill these fellowship functions to varying degrees.

Bars as Connectors

To understand the social role of bars in Riverwest, it is useful to consider them in relationship to other gathering places in the neighborhood. In the warmer months, residents tend to socialize on sidewalks, some of the most neutral spaces in the neighborhood. Bars, like sidewalks, can offer relatively open, democratic space for congregation with neighbors, but they pull from broader geographic areas (i.e., beyond the face block). Some corner taps are primarily frequented by residents in a few-block radius, but most Riverwest bars attract patrons from throughout and sometimes outside the neighborhood. Bar gatherings are thus more clearly separated from home than are sidewalk conferences. This physical and symbolic distance eliminates the potential for

hosting burden and allows patrons to largely leave behind on-the-block reputations and entanglements.

The third place function of bars takes on particular significance in the winter months, when the cold effectively shuts down on-the-block socializing.
Neighbors exchange only the briefest of greetings while shoveling, rushing
from car to home, or walking as fast as possible while bundled in layers of
clothing. To fight the winter blues, some residents will trudge through snow-
drifts toward the warm, inviting glow of steamy tavern windows. When they
push open the door, blasting cozy customers with a shot of cold air, all heads
turn to greet the brave joiner. In that moment, isolation is shattered and bonds
renewed.

Every bar in the neighborhood has a core set of regulars (a defining feature
of third places).[31] Some patrons pledge their allegiance to one establishment
and rarely, if ever, visit other watering holes. Most resident bar goers, however,
rotate through a handful of places where they feel at home and can expect to
find people they know. Marcus Zwic, a biracial artist, speaks fondly of regular
visits to his "little communities": "And it's kinda like small families. You know,
like whether you are hanging out at the Pub, or I go to the Art Bar regularly—
I became a family member over there. Uptowner? It's like another family over
there. Riverhorse? That's a whole other family over there. So if you start shoe-
stringing together, every time you just go hang out and go get a beer, there is
more of that commiserating, hanging out, family thing. It's more for the
social—and I think this neighborhood has more of that than most." I found
this to be a common narrative, one that was supported by barroom observations. Regulars are greeted by name by bartenders and fellow patrons. They
are easily folded into ongoing conversations. They tease one another and request updates about specific events or associates. Regulars seem to know what
to expect from one another. Anticipatory groans, gentle warnings, and knowing
nods communicate a casual intimacy and sometimes contribute to the collective regulation of an individual's behavior and, by extension, the bar's culture.

The level of familiarity among regulars can be intimidating to newcomers. Even the most seemingly impenetrable bar crews, however, will usually
make room for those who show up regularly and demonstrate that they are
of solid-enough character. John Bauer calls this "passing the test." This process
allows the regulars to separate the dedicated from the fickle or voyeuristic.
The design of interior space also matters. On one end of the spectrum, there
are bars with sets of clearly separated tables that cater to small groups of
friends who primarily seek the enjoyment of one another's company. On
the other end of the spectrum, there are taverns dominated by U-shaped bars

with stools that are inviting to the solo patron and encourage unplanned reunions and the spontaneous formation of new connections.

Bars have the potential to foster the development of neighborhood ties that bridge social and geographic distances. During several bar visits, just when I thought I had figured out the character of a tavern's clientele, the bartender would turn to greet a regular who fell completely outside my delineation. Bartenders can play an important role in helping patrons forge new connections. Adam Wojtkowski, a Riverwesterner since birth, fondly recalls one of his favorite barkeeps, Leo: "He wore a shirt with the collar up and a big gold medallion, and big hair—you know he was a real character. Oh, really neat! He was the best bartender that you could ever want. He would talk to you, and he would get everyone else talking to each other, too. And you would go in there and you wouldn't know somebody and he would get people talking to each other. [There] would be some of the older people who were Leo's age and my age, and then there were younger people also, so that was pretty neat, too." Some bar owners and their employees work to make their establishments inclusive. As one bartender explained, such an attitude is "good for business, and it's Riverwest. It's how we do."

Billy Croft, a self-described "rough and tumbling punk dude" and "white-trash person," is a resident and neighborhood bartender. He describes how the employees and regulars enforce conduct standards at a bar that's known as a place for the irreverent:

> You get all sorts in there. You get old school construction worker dudes that get off work and then they just drink until 8 P.M. . . . and they get shitfaced. Like really fast. And then you get crackhead dudes that come in during the day. And there are the young kids that are like "Whoa dude!" because it's totally David Lynchesque, which is the best way I have heard it described. And on top of it—it's the kind of bar that is totally un-PC and everyone will drop racist stuff or say whatever—"homo" and stuff like that. But as soon as anyone says anything malicious, everyone steps up and says "Uh-uh. Not here. You are gonna get kicked out." And there was awhile when, I don't know, like when people say the words—when they drop the N-bomb in a sentence or when it's directed at an individual, that's crossing the line.

It turns out that even at one of the most lawless dives in the neighborhood, there are, in fact, rules. When patrons' commentary turns venomous or harmful, they lose their seat at the bar.

Certain venues, particularly those featuring an assortment of live music and DJs, have a reputation of attracting diverse clientele. Although Justice Sewell, a black renter, has only lived in the neighborhood for a short time, he has already found a few local spots that he particularly enjoys. He believes that their broad appeal and openness to diverse crowds is a rarity in Milwaukee: "If you look at the night life, you'll see all kinds of people at Stonefly. At Timbuktu, you'll see all types of people. So, at the clubs, at the hip-hop shows you have at the bars or something like that, you'll have all types of people. And it's, like, cool. And speaking a certain thing and being a certain type of person, which wouldn't be cool in another part of the city, in Riverwest, that's cool. The spirit, the energy, the overall idea of diversity, is very well embraced." Although Justice used vague descriptors in this statement, he went on to describe night-life diversity in terms of race, ethnicity, age, and "style."

My own bar observations, which admittedly had more breadth than depth, revealed that most neighborhood watering holes that cultivate interaction across social divides tend to be relatively homogeneous in terms of one characteristic. For example, one restaurant and bar that attracts customers who are young and old, black and (mostly) white, and mostly middle class. Another pub fosters cross-generational ties but primarily among Puerto Rican residents. A third spot attracts punks, hipsters, hippies, queer folks, art-school students, and hip-hop heads, almost all of whom are white and under thirty years old.

Bridging Constraints

Several factors limit the integrative potential of Riverwest bars. First, for many Riverwesterners, barhopping is cost-prohibitive. It is always cheaper to purchase alcohol for private consumption than to go out. Longtime residents who view a pub's proper primary function as social (rather than commercial) find the cost of items at the more upscale bars an affront. Joyce Becker was "outraged" when she learned that a newly opened bar had committed two offenses: it offered no domestic brews, and the cost of the cheapest beer on tap was "just stupid." Cost and taste standards influence Joyce's assessment of a bar's quality and authenticity.

Perceived (or real) social criteria for membership also limit the inclusivity of bars.[32] Some Riverwesterners remember when particular spots developed practices to maintain their racial exclusivity. The policies and even the ownership of these bars may have shifted over time, but their reputations endure and continue to act as clientele filters. Residents are sometimes put off or intimidated by bars that they see as cliquish, pretentious, exclusionary, or in some way distinctly "other." I heard bars described as white, Puerto Rican, black, honky, white trash, thug, hipster, punk, snobby, gay, dive, cop, blue collar, old man, old hippie, racist, stoner, coke den (where cocaine use is thinly concealed), dirty, and shady. Related concerns about trespassing or feeling uncomfortable prevent residents from stopping in at certain places. After talking about the many reasons why she values living in a diverse neighborhood, white homeowner Karen Kelley paused for a moment and then reflected on some of the limits to her comfort with difference:

> I am feeling a little self-congratulatory. You know, like, "I love my neighborhood, we are diverse, and I love diversity." Well a lot of that is true. But I feel a little maybe disingenuous, and it's making me think. . . . I was walking with someone and we walked past Club 99, and they were like, "Have you ever gone to Club 99?" and I was like "No" and didn't say anything else, but one of the big reasons I think is because it's a Puerto Rican bar. And then it's like, wow, did I just say that? Did I just think that? Of all the places I do go in Riverwest, there are a lot of places that I have never stepped into. For what that is worth, that there is still that segregation I guess, at least in my life.

Explanations for avoiding particular spots usually touch on concerns about acceptance or the potential for a good time (e.g., "they just aren't my people"). Some residents report that a single bad experience—being given the cold shoulder by apparent regulars, receiving poor treatment or lousy service from the staff, or just feeling out of place—resulted in crossing a place off their list. A few people with class or race privilege frame their choices to stay away from certain establishments as failures to be as "adventurous" as their friends, who had accumulated exotic experiences in bars not meant for them. This indicates an approach to border crossing—the consumption of otherness—with limited bridging potential.

Although a small number of places had relatively stable and widely agreed-upon reputations, I was surprised by the amount of variation in perceptions of the character and level of exclusivity at particular establishments. What one young white woman dismissed as a "white hipster bar" a young black man described as a "place for all kinds, you name it." Neighborhood bar patrons who recognized that they were in some way a minority in a place they frequented tended to link their comfort in these places to accumulated positive experiences and a belief that the unwritten tavern rules support inclusion.

Most nights the majority of local bars will have considerably more white patrons than nonwhite patrons. Majority-white spaces, for many nonwhite residents, can't serve as third places because they are neither neutral nor

diverse. Daniel Mercado, a young Puerto Rican man who grew up in the neighborhood, was waiting for a friend outside a convenience store and, as it turns
out, listening to my conversation with Milo Rossi, a white twentysomething
hipster who worked at one of the local bars. Having recently met Milo, I asked
him where he liked to hang out when he wasn't at work. He had listed off a
couple of names when Daniel started providing unsolicited commentary of
Milo's choices. "That spot is NICE." "Nope." "Too much work." When I asked
him what he meant by "too much work," he said, "Too many white people.
Too much work." Unfortunately, I didn't ask him to elaborate, but he might
have been suggesting that he wanted to avoid the effort required for a Latino/a
resident to navigate majority-white spaces.[33]

Neighborhood elder Rashawn Wright takes it upon himself to encourage
young people to give a chance to those places they avoid: "You have some
people that might feel like they would not be accepted at some places. Like Art
Bar. I didn't have any problems when I walked in. I go into Art Bar. I go into
other places. But some, especially African Americans, may feel that they
wouldn't be accepted. Well why not? They can never give me a straight answer. I say, 'Is it because it's white people there? Is that what it is?' 'No, I go
other places . . .' 'Well yes it is. And it's OK, but think about it. Think about
why you don't go there, because you're probably missing good times. You're
missing a lot of good times.'" Rashawn recognizes that some nonwhite residents see some local bars as unwelcoming white spaces. In his experience,
those perceptions don't consistently reflect reality. Still, the assumed or real
exclusiveness of majority-white organizations and establishments limits their
potential to serve as common and integrative spaces. When white residents
see white places as "normal" and black and Puerto Rican places as distinctly
raced, they reinforce racialized notions of "other."

Good Bars and Bad Bars

Riverwest bars, particularly those located on residential blocks, are expected
to be good neighbors and community members. John Bauer links the amount
of local support taverns receive to their perceived investment in the community. A handful of bars sponsor local events or regularly offer their space at
reduced or no cost for community events, from town hall meetings with city
officials to chili cook-offs to raise money for the Riverwest Co-Op Grocery
and Café. Others sponsor local events like the Riverwest 24-Hour Bike Race
or the Locust Street Festival. Several bar owners and bartenders are held in
high esteem for their community work as connectors and caretakers. Jess
Blanc, a white woman who came to Riverwest in her early twenties and is

now raising her child in the neighborhood, has frequented the bar down the block from her home for many years. The owner, Jamal Green, is known for his big personality, his skills with a pool cue, and his guardianship: "He has had a big part in also the solidarity of the block that is up the street because he has always watched out for everyone. He is super, super protective of his customers. He knows everyone who goes into the bar, and if you walk in there and you are a stranger . . . and if he gets any weird vibes, he kicks them out. And he has female bartenders the whole time, many of them lesbians. He likes protective women. . . . He is an old man who wants to protect you like a dad. And so, it's good."

Bar owners like Jamal foster local cohesion and contribute to customers' and near neighbors' sense of security by closely monitoring the activity in and around their establishments. Their patrons describe their bars as "welcoming," "chill," and "under control." They create the space for social connection and information exchange. In those taverns that have proximate neighbors as their primary customer base, bar chats often turn to things local: block gossip, the latest break-in, the newest tenants, or the city's lousy plowing response to Monday's snowstorm. George Morris, a black homeowner, has been making the rounds to a few bars within walking distance of his house for decades. For years, his Sunday routine was "go to mass, and go to the bar after that." George has invested considerable time and energy in a variety of block- and community-level crime prevention efforts, and his bar networks include trusted sources of neighborhood knowledge.

> [The Local] is right around the corner from my house. Easy walking distance. And it's just a little neighborhood spot with a lot of neighbors in the general vicinity congregating. So I'm in there some days, whenever, have a beer, shoot a little pool, "Hey, what's going on?" It's where I get all my information about the neighborhood. People tell me things. "What happened over here with this?" "Well, you should look out for this." "You can always come to me, anything that I know I will pass along." I have been here for so long I know all these people. I go in and have a drink or two, but the thing is I know all these individuals and that's my network. And people tell me things. "I have something new, man! You always get off with this stuff!"

When bar boosters talk about their favorite haunts, their descriptions tend to feature social aspects. The activity of consuming alcohol takes a back seat. George may enjoy a few adult beverages, but making the rounds is really about seeing friends. Although the privileging of things social conveys what they find meaningful about their bar experiences, it might also reflect the ambiguous status of drinking in the broader culture.

"Good" bars are good neighbors. They are engaged, responsible, and predictable. "Bad" bars are bad neighbors. Their patrons are loud and disruptive. The staff does not regulate the behavior of their customers in the area outside the bar. Their establishments are perceived as magnets for crime. They play their music too loud and until too late. They fail to maintain their property, leaving broken glass and trash on the sidewalks. Their owners don't reach out to the neighborhood or respond to residents' concerns.

When Mark and Joanne Jansen first moved into the neighborhood, they noticed that every night at bar time, the patrons leaving the corner bar on their block poured onto the street and raised a ruckus. Many left with full "to-go" bottles of beer in their hands. The Jansens approached the bar owners about the problem and requested that they work to minimize their closing-time impact on near neighbors. The bar owners dismissed their concerns as the complaints of uninitiated residents. "We don't do things like that around here." The "live and let live" code, then, is not always tied to a valuing of neighborhood diversity. Some rely on the code as a shield for illicit activities or to justify a lack of accountability to neighbors.

Although it can be difficult to shed a bad reputation, these designations are fluid. A group of residents who live near one corner tavern claim that they can always tell when the owner is sick. As soon as the noise level and activity outside the bar increase, they know that the owner's less-responsible brother has temporarily taken over management. Ownership, clientele, and neighbor relations can all change—and the accompanying shifts in perception can be consequential.

Bars and liquor stores have good reason to pay attention to the concerns of near neighbors. All businesses that sell alcoholic beverages must regularly renew their liquor license before the city council's licensing committee. Although there is some variation in the process from one aldermanic district to the next, most alderpersons send out letters to near neighbors of the business looking to renew its license with an invitation to return a postcard with their opinions on the renewal. In numerous public meetings, I heard the alderpersons who serve the Riverwest neighborhood educate residents about the licensing process. They appreciate receiving written comments from neighbors but emphasize that it is far more impactful to show up at the licensing hearings to lodge complaints against or show support for a particular business. The committee may decide, based on resident input, to suspend or even revoke a license.

Although license revocation is quite rare, residents of Riverwest and neighboring Harambee effectively shut down Montal's Lounge, a notorious "bad" bar on Holton Street. During my time in Riverwest, I heard numerous stories about the infamous Montal's Lounge. One resident recalled driving home on Holton Street, a major thoroughfare, to find the area in front of Montal's Lounge blocked by double- and triple-parked cars. The most common complaints were about the behavior of rowdy patrons outside the bar, particularly at closing time: yelling, blasting loud music from cars, urinating on neighbors' property, and fighting. In September 2007, a twenty-four-year-old man was fatally shot while exiting the bar. Residents, with support from their alderperson and a nonprofit organization focused on crime reduction, successfully argued for a license suspension and eventual revocation.

Race, class, and gender distinctions sometimes factor into assessments of a bar's impact on the neighborhood. Montal's Lounge was known as a black bar, and racialized constructions of criminal behavior buttressed the bar's reputation as a trouble spot. Social distinctions also work their way into the world of hypothetical projections. In September 2008, the owners of three new establishments seeking liquor licenses were asked by an alderman to attend a Riverwest Neighborhood Association (RNA) meeting. In the discussion at the meeting and in related conversations (both online and offline), residents wrestled with how, if granted licenses, these establishments would affect Riverwest.

One young entrepreneur, Ali Lockhart, included a proposed menu, wine list, martini list, and floor plan in her pitch to the RNA about the Mercury Lounge. When she started to seriously consider opening a lounge at the proposed location in Riverwest, she had knocked on doors to talk with residents about what they would like to see. At first, it seemed that neighbors wanted sandwiches and standard pub fare. She then met with a small group of residents who expressed concerns about her plans to open what they saw as "just another bar." They encouraged Ali to put a greater emphasis on upscale dining. Her new menu included items like blackened tilapia and shaved ham and brie. Several of the residents present praised her for the changes. One RNA board member said that the restaurant looked like a "decent" restaurant that would "attract the kinds of people we want to attract." Another resident asked Ali if she thought most of the customers would be coming from the neighborhood. Ali said that she hoped the restaurant would draw people from the east side and downtown (predominantly white, more affluent areas). One of the RNA cochairs then read some of the emails that had been submitted by those who could not attend the meeting. In one email,

Jennifer Marshall explained her support of liquor licenses for any establishments that were primarily restaurants: "I would love to have a nice cafe/restaurant move into my neighborhood. My hope for Riverwest is that we attract more of this type of development—more restaurants, more stores—more services in general. . . . I have a child too—and I want her to grow up in a nice neighborhood and I would like that to be Riverwest if possible. If there was a proposal to add another ghetto liquor store selling forties in our neighborhood I would fight it. If we were voting to close down some of the current liquor stores, I would vote for that too. I don't think that nice restaurants selling micro beers or martinis and wine is going to attract a criminal element." Jennifer is invested in the neighborhood's development potential and sees an upscale establishment that caters to more upper-class tastes as a desirable addition to Riverwest. She would actively resist an establishment that attracted "criminal" clientele.

Jennifer was one of several people who, in the course of discussions about new liquor licenses, referenced "forties." Malt liquor—a cheap, high-alcohol-content beer—is often sold in forty-ounce glass bottles, or forties. When people express concerns about the sale of malt liquor, forties become a stand-in for their stereotypical consumers. The image of someone sipping a forty out of a paper bag triggers a set of disparaged cultural associations: poverty, alcohol dependency, homelessness, and public consumption.[34] This marker of disorder is also racialized. Beer companies have aggressively marketed malt liquor in African American communities since the 1960s. More recently, they have targeted black and Hispanic youth by using images of popular rap artists and advertising slogans that associate malt liquor with danger, violence, and masculinity.[35] This marketing strategy has helped reinforce the stereotype of the forty-drinking, dangerous, urban black or brown male. When Jennifer and others oppose bars and stores that sell forties, they are identifying categories of unwelcome clientele: poor people, alcoholics, and black and Hispanic men.

For white homeowner Mark Jensen, the problematic bars in the neighborhood "cater to the dregs. They cater to the unsuccessful people." He watches his neighbors spend their time and money, day after day, at the corner tap as their property falls into disrepair. These bars, for Mark, represent the deterioration of the neighborhood's working-class culture into "alcoholic white trash": a result of the disappearance of factory work. "When they get older, they die in that bar uneducated, fearful, marginal future, trapped. But they come with a whole belief system that doesn't involve pride in ownership, doesn't involve taking responsibility." Though I rarely encountered such overt articulations of classism, Mark's concerns about the blue-collar bars were not unique. For many of those invested in neighborhood development, these bars are unsightly scars left by decades of economic decline in Riverwest.

Riverwest's blue-collar roots are alternatively viewed as an asset. Some college-age people in the neighborhood enjoy rubbing elbows with longtime Riverwesterners at the corner bars. These gritty hangouts for retired factory workers are markers of neighborhood authenticity. The romanticization of working-class culture by this group of largely middle-class young people is part of a national trend that has elevated drinking cans of Pabst Blue Ribbon to a symbol of hipster cool. As sociologist Matthew Desmond observes, "Of the many consequences of deindustrialization, one of the most ironic has taken place in the realm of culture. It can be described as the emergence of a kind of nationwide longing for the industrial society that was destroyed."[36] It would be unfair, however, to lump all the young people who frequent these bars together. While the attraction of Riverwest's corner taps is, for some, linked to romanticized authenticity, others seek out these gathering spots for comfort and social support. For example, a young man who decided to cast off upper-class career expectations to pursue work in the skilled trades told me he has found acceptance (even if only qualified acceptance) among happy-hour regulars.

Boundaries and Belonging

To an outsider passing through the neighborhood, Riverwest's numerous bars, pronounced public drinking, and seeming tolerance of public intoxication may be seen as cause for concern. Residents' perceptions of local drinking establishments and activities, however, are more varied. Bars can be serious trouble spots or valued amenities. Those with visible addictions can be nuisances or accepted neighbors. Porch drinking can degrade the neighborhood's reputation or signal a vibrant public life. These perceptions are products of residents' social experiences in the neighborhood and are embedded in shared visions of Riverwest's past, present, and future.

In his ethnographic study of a diverse, disadvantaged neighborhood, Gerald Suttles finds that in pursuing a local social order, residents employ a set of social distinctions unique to their community. These "localisms," or place-specific forms of social differentiation, can complement or deviate from broader societal standards.[37] In this and the previous chapter I have tried to demonstrate how localisms in Riverwest can support but also challenge widely held cultural assumptions about the nature of disorder.

Definitions of uncivil or out-of-place practices are embedded in constructions of cultural membership and social distance. Riverwest residents' sense of who and what belong in their neighborhood is shaped by their accumulated experiences. For example, residents might develop multidimensional understandings of particular neighbors through repeated encounters. These nuanced portraits allow residents to develop personalized expectations and situate disorderly behaviors in context. Routine encounters with a person need not produce depth of information to influence notions of belonging or menace. At times, these encounters add up to a working definition of a person with a stigmatizing attribute as nonthreatening. Interactions with particular places matter as well. Visits to a local tavern, repeated run-ins with the clientele of a neighboring bar, or daily strolls past a crowded corner may color attributions of trouble and perceptions of order. Local discursive practices also carry ideas about cultural boundaries. In everyday conversations about Riverwest's identity, transgressions of community norms, and conflicts over the proposed regulation of practices, residents construct, challenge, and defend what fits in their neighborhood. Evaluations of the visible landscape are therefore situated in residents' framing of the neighborhood and its trajectory.[38]

These collective perceptions and customs have multilayered consequences for Riverwest. The inclusion (or conditional acceptance) of people, places, and practices that are commonly stigmatized or viewed as markers of disorder contributes to the maintenance of multiple types of diversity in the neighborhood. Since most outsiders (and some insiders) do not share the dominant neighborhood frames and social experiences that sift broader understandings of order, the apparent acceptance of public drinking, graffiti, loitering, and myriad bars negatively affects their assessments of the neighborhood. Some residents applaud the fact that this filters out those who aren't a good fit for the neighborhood. Others worry about how Riverwest's visible disorder discourages communal efforts to address problems, hinders investment and development, and undermines neighborhood stability.

CHAPTER SEVEN

Moving Up, Moving Down, Moving Out

Wherever you live, you have to learn how to adapt to that area, and so there
are just things that you have to adapt to when you come to live in Riverwest. . . .
You learn when to play your role and when to step back.

—Heriberto "Eddie" Cardenales

Neighborhoods filter, construct, and transmit cultural meanings and practices
in ways that influence how residents define and negotiate their local environment. Individual characteristics also factor into residents' perceptions of
place. This is not to say that knowing people's age, level of educational attainment, socioeconomic status, tenure in the neighborhood, and race or ethnicity
allows us to predict how they will interpret and navigate their local context.
These characteristics are bound up with individuals' accumulated experiences and the skills and preferences they develop along the way—all of which
interact with the neighborhood context to jointly affect their everyday perceptions and practices. This bundle of relationships is made visible when people
experience contextual shifts (moving from one place to another or experienc-
ing changes within a particular place). An individual's residential mobility trajectory not only tells us a great deal about that individual but also about place.
Where someone has lived, the changes that person has witnessed, and where
he or she hopes to be all affect how that person thinks about his or her neighborhood. Here I share five residents' mobility narratives, highlighting the interplay between individual place pathways and understandings of Riverwest.

Darius Hines

Although Darius Hines's family made frequent moves during his childhood,
he spent most of his elementary- and middle-school years in houses in the
Riverwest neighborhood. His assessment of the neighborhood—then and
now—is heavily influenced by comparisons to the north side neighborhoods
he has lived in. Darius has fond memories of the time he spent in Riverwest
as a child. He remembers being struck, even at a young age, by the racial mix
and the feeling of things being peaceful and low key:

> So, diversity was the main thing that stood out more so than anything.
> And it was the Hispanic or Latino culture that's down there. Then, you

know, also whites and blacks and whatnot, so it was a lot of diversity
that I didn't see at my grandmother's neighborhood. I feel like . . .
it may or may not have been more places to play and do things. Well,
diversity is the key one because no matter what you did over there,
it was always with different people. . . . But I think that, more so than
anything, if you can imagine just having some sorta sense of thinking
that what's around you is sorta calm and cool, and, you know, things are
OK. So I guess I'd say that heightened sense of danger that one might feel
in certain neighborhoods—yeah, I didn't [*pause*] I don't feel that much
at Riverwest.

When it was time for Darius to enter high school, his mother reluctantly
moved the family to the more distressed north side. During his tenure on the
north side, Darius lived in majority-black neighborhoods that had higher concentrations of poverty and more crime than Riverwest.

When Darius was in his late twenties, he moved back to Riverwest, where
he's stayed for nearly ten years. This decision was influenced by the absorp-
tion of his mother's place values. Her neighborhood preferences "kinda
trickled down into some of my own values and what I thought would be
appropriate or a nice place to live if I would decide or choose to live in the
city." His family now owns a duplex, and his son attends one of the local
elementary schools. Based on his experiences in a number of different Milwaukee neighborhoods, Darius considers Riverwest to be a good residential
choice for someone who wants to live in the heart of the city. "Some people
see it differently, but I think it's a pretty decent place, over and above a lot of
the other neighborhoods in the city. Matter of fact, it might be the best." He
appreciates the parks, neighborhood festivals, coffee shops, restaurants,
quirky commercial spots, entertainment establishments, and proximity to
relatives. When Darius talks about the neighborhood, however, the "unstress-
ful" environment and community values take center stage.

Although he acknowledges that the neighborhood has its share of crime,
he has far fewer worries about personal safety than do friends and family who
live in other neighborhoods. For Darius, two significant markers of safety are
people jogging and walking their dogs. He rarely sees these activities in other
central-city neighborhoods: "It's those little things, you know, that let you
know—those are indicators that it is a safe neighborhood." The environment
is comfortable because it is predictable—a luxury he hasn't always enjoyed,
a luxury he knows is by no means a given. When Darius draws on comparisons to other Milwaukee neighborhoods in order to identify what he values

about Riverwest, he takes great pains to frame these issues as structural or environmental rather than individual. Darius focuses on problematic places, not problematic people:

> Just the whole idea of being able to—to just pull up on your block and not worry about anything, or, you know, that sort of stuff. For me, when you sharing how you really feel, when you sharing realities, and you wanna be conscious of what you're saying or conscious of who gets the messages, it's challenging because most of the stuff get heard in small sound bites. So if I share with you that on my brother's block, he doesn't know what things are gonna be like when he pulls up at home, it would lead a person to think several things that would require further conversation to talk about. But just in a real general sense, if I compare when he pulls up and when I pull up, I think everybody would like where I pull up at versus where he pulls up in front of his house, you know? Now again, not anything against anybody. We're just talking purely environment and what it takes to live in that environment, and who lives there, and how they support themselves. You know how challenging things are right now for folks.

Part of what keeps the neighborhood calm and cool, according to Darius, is Riverwest values: residents' prioritizing working together over competition. Darius finds that residents' conduct and the "feel" of the neighborhood more powerfully convey Riverwest's character than any rhetoric about diversity:

> It's not a money-hungry community where the dollar is the main thing, you know, the end all to be all. It is really about community, and it's really about lifestyle. . . . Those sort of values around the community, you know, that stuff kinda matriculate through. People kinda get the feel of it without a lot of conversation. You just get a feel for what's around you and how people operate when you start to notice that kinda stuff. So I think that's important, too. I think you got some of these old Milwaukee socialist values down there. That's important to me though, 'cause you need to work together to—in order to be able to maintain the good things that we desire versus competing. When we start competing, well, you know, that's just based on a whole other set of priorities.

Even local businesses reflect this community orientation, seeming to care more about providing a positive service than producing sizable profits. Darius's sense of Riverwest's values mediates his interpretation of the neighborhood environment. He compares Riverwest's grassroots initiatives to broader community development initiatives on the north side:

> I really feel like it is more about community than it is about capitalism or whatever, you know, in a real way! . . . By and large, most of the small storefronts you see in the area or informal things that's going on in groups in the neighborhood, you know, it's obvious that it's a different set of values there versus what you might see in another area where you got all these different apartments going up, and vacant storefronts. And, well, over here you got a raggedy storefront, but somebody's in it doing good things. Where up North Avenue and Sherman you got a brand new building, but it's empty, and waiting ten years for a turnaround. So the values are totally different. What's important and the priorities are just—they almost like diametrically opposed in comparison to some other communities. And that's pretty darn interesting. That's pretty darn interesting when you think about it.

What an objective observer might take as a symbol of neighborhood disadvantage and decline, Darius sees as a representation of community strength. The shoddy facade belies the positive, neighborhood-building activities he assumes are taking place inside. He sees Riverwesterners as intensely invested in their community and prepared to stand up to those who threaten the neighborhood's well-being. Although he tends not to take an active role in neighborhood affairs, he has faith that his fellow residents can and will appropriately respond to serious problems.

Shortly before I met Darius, there was a homicide outside Quarters, a Riverwest bar. Although Quarters has been in the neighborhood for decades, recent activities around the bar had near neighbors concerned. Darius was confident that the matter would be handled before it could escalate: "I guarantee you, that if it persists to any degree, that there will be some changes made. It won't necessarily be changes coming out of city hall. It just won't happen that way. We live in a neighborhood where people voluntarily decide, 'This place isn't working for the neighborhood anymore. Let's shut it down and try it again in two years.' . . . You gotta do what you have to do, especially if that kind of behavior persists. And it ends up being good for everybody, even the people who potentially get in trouble in those environments." Darius believes engaged residents have real power and that they tend to use it for the common good.

In Darius's residential mobility trajectory, Riverwest is a step up—a step toward stability, collective responsibility, and calm. He is careful not to denigrate the residents of the north side neighborhoods he has lived in. River-west is not a better neighborhood because its residents are somehow better; its advantage is cultural diversity. Other neighborhoods in the city are shackled by disadvantages that are a result of socioeconomic and racial segregation, including cultural homogeneity: "You get that land of everybody, of all the different cultures and ethnicities, down there. And so, with culture come values and social norms, and when you segregate it, you can't do nothing but have your own set of social norms, your own set of values. In these different places or different neighborhoods, that's what you find. But in Riverwest, those values—compared to some of the ones that are kinda segregated out—it's totally different." In Darius's view, segregation constrains some communities' potential by limiting exposure to alternative ideas about things like community power and the role of police. In contrast, Riverwest's community values and engagement grow out of having to incorporate the multiple perspectives that a diverse population contains. He argues that perceptions of neighborhood character influence the evaluation of neighborhood quality and property value assessments, even absent objective differences in appearance and physical condition:

It's a testament to how community involvement—whether real or the appearance of it based on how people interact—has power and influence, not only on the community but [on] the people who have to serve it. . . . There's a general attitude in the neighborhood. You don't get the feeling that somebody's looking at you like "What are you doing over here?" I guess that relates to how the property values stay high and are maintained. It's based on community. The conditions of houses a block or two blocks away from Humboldt [in Riverwest] are no different from the condition of houses on 15th and Center [in a nearby north side neighborhood]. Same condition, but of course, different appraisals. And that's just purely based on community.

Darius's Riverwest is constructed through comparisons to a handful of Milwaukee's north side neighborhoods. The things that struck him as a child—the relative diversity and feelings of security—still figure prominently in his perceptions of the neighborhood. Over time, he has developed a nuanced understanding of what Riverwest is and what makes it distinct. Darius sees a place that encourages residents to take ownership of their neighborhood, prioritize the common good over private gain, and generally benefit from living among multiple ways of operating in the world.

Frank Schmidt

Frank Schmidt grew up in a predominantly white, upper-middle-class suburb near Riverwest. In high school, Frank and his friends liked to venture out
into other parts of the city but avoided the Riverwest neighborhood. He was
first introduced to the neighborhood in his early twenties, when he dated a
woman who lived in Riverwest. Her experiences largely confirmed his suspicions that the neighborhood "was not a desirable place to be." She called
the police on a regular basis about problems on her block, and it seemed that
most of her friends had been robbed or had their cars stolen. When the couple
became more serious and started looking for a house to buy, Frank refused
to consider Riverwest. They ended up purchasing a home in Frank's home-
town suburb. After their relationship ended, Frank was pulled back to the
neighborhood by another relationship, the allure of cheap rent, and signs of
promising changes. In the short time that Frank had been away, there was an
influx of interest and investment in what now appeared to be an up-and-
coming neighborhood.

In 2003, Frank moved his business, and later also his residence, to Riverwest, but the neighborhood never really became his home. Although he
found "cool" people in Riverwest and enjoyed some initial local buzz around
his business, Frank became embittered by clashes with neighbors over what
he perceived to be fundamental lifestyle differences:

> I'm not used to a neighborhood where the parents go to work and the
> kids run the neighborhood. . . . There's kids banging on the window
> and throwing rocks, and when I go out there they call me a fat fag like a
> hundred times and throw rocks at me and call me a faggot over and over
> and over [*chuckles*]. This isn't how kids [from the suburb I grew up in]
> act. I've never met kids that act like this. Or, like, up the street the family
> that's been there, and the second generation is still living with the first,
> and they've got nasty furniture on the front porch and crazy pit bulls
> and they're just like—you don't even know what decade they live in.
> It's bizarre. And there's that tension.

The social and cultural distance between Frank and many of his neighbors
was too vast to bridge. He found many of his neighbors to be frustratingly
tolerant of all manner of bad behavior on the block.

Frank was also uncomfortable with what he observed around his home.
He saw sex workers and drug dealers plying their trades nearby. Some of the

rentals on his block housed a steady rotation of bad tenants. Feeling under siege, Frank appealed to formal social control authorities to deal with the problems on his block. He attempted to work with the police and the Department of Neighborhood Services to address local concerns but was frustrated by the seeming futility of his efforts:

> And then you start to really realize how little power the police have and how little power you have and you're just like, "Why am I wasting my fucking time?" You start to get into this Wild West mentality. There's a new drug dealer in the neighborhood and I think, "Should I just hit her in the face with a bat? I mean, that would probably take care of it. If I start shooting the drug dealers is anybody going to give a fuck?" You get to that point. It doesn't do a fucking thing. Or sitting on my roof trying to take pictures of a drug deal that happens every Friday the same time, for months. And you call every week. And you call every week. And then one day there's a different car meeting with one of the usual cars but not the other car, and that's the day three squad cars fly up, and of course they find nothing that time. What can you do? And then neighbors organize. They're like, "Oh, there's been a lot of robberies, so now we're all going to walk our dogs at this time on this day, or every night at six we're gonna walk our dogs." That lasts for like a month and things get better, and then people are like, "Oh, this is boring," and they give up and crime starts again.

Frank saw many of the community's attempts at intervention as weak and ineffective. Residential instability presented additional obstacles to effectively dealing with his concerns. He constantly had to assess the character of new neighbors and attempt to forge constructive relationships with those few people who seemed to be on the same page: "Part of it, too, is that it changes. You build that relationship and all of the sudden those people move, being here for almost four years now. People get swapped out and you build the relationship and then the next person comes in and you're like, 'Now what do I have to deal with?'"

Despite high residential turnover on his block, Frank did eventually create strong, positive connections with a group of his neighbors. They regularly communicated about block affairs and looked out for one another. Frank believes that neighborhood challenges provide a strong incentive to build relationships with near neighbors. "I think because it is so shitty [*laughs*], I think that, like, we do all the work. We are forced to know our neighbors, which I think is amazing. Because I never lived anywhere where I talked to my neighbors. Never. And the nicer the neighborhood, . . . the more the neighbors hate each other—[and] the more property they have to insulate themselves from having any real relationship from anyone around them." Frank and this tight-knit group of neighbors looked out for each other and worked together to address issues on the block, but many problems proved too big to handle. "I feel like I really love the people I am around. It's just the other people who come into this neighborhood make it so hard to be here. . . . It grates away, and you just don't have anything left."

The limited effectiveness of formal and informal efforts to maintain a livable level of order wore Frank down and left him feeling vulnerable. After a frightening encounter with a group of young men, Frank viewed his proximate environment as unpredictable, out of control, and immune to intervention:

> When you live in a neighborhood like this, you have to be on the defensive all the time. Like I have a baseball bat behind my desk. I have never pulled it out, but I am glad I have it there. Certainly I have thought about buying a gun. If I could afford one I probably would have. You just get into situations like I can't even fucking walk the dog. Everyone you meet, everyone I know has been jumped. . . . It's the feeling [of] the loss of control. Feeling like there's nothing I can do. Nobody can help me, and nobody will help me. Like walking my dog down the street and seven guys are across the street and I'm ignoring them and they're just sitting on somebody's car and in this yard, and they're like "Yo, you fat ass nigger, we're gonna kick your fuckin' ass." And you're like, "What?" And you look over and they're like, "You better keep walking, mother fucker." And you're like, "What the . . . I'm just walking my dog, you know." And you think, "I have to feel scared walking in my neighborhood. That was a block and a half, two blocks from my house, and I have to feel unsafe in my neighborhood?" And then you can't just call the police. I have a friend that worked at the YMCA. There'd be a huge fight, and the kids would be beating the shit out of each other. And if he called, they wouldn't come. Or they'd come in an hour. He'd have to be like, "One guy has a gun. I think I saw a grenade." Then they'd come. So like, in that situation, I was like—yeah—then I start to lie to the police. I was really emotional. I was fucking freaked out. Fuck, this might be it. I'm gonna die a block from my house. . . . They were probably all fucking drunk, sitting around—"Who is this guy? White rich fucker, whatever." They probably just don't give a fuck, just wanted to fuck with me.

Fed up with fighting a losing battle, he moved out of the neighborhood to the east side and eventually closed his business. He was relieved to walk his dog without constantly turning around to check for approaching danger. Frank found that the police had a much quicker response to his calls, even though his new neighborhood was in the same police district as Riverwest.

Frank's early impressions of Riverwest as a step down were largely confirmed. His time in the neighborhood chipped away at his hopes for Riverwest's potential as an up-and-coming neighborhood. He primarily experienced the neighborhood's diversity through conflicts, from visual manifestations of class clashes to what he saw as threats of violence fueled by racial and class tensions. Frank neither had nor developed the tools to navigate the dizzying jumble of lifestyles and related standards of behavior on his block. Those tools that served him well in "better" environments, namely the sense of entitlement necessary to call on public servants, proved relatively ineffective in Riverwest. The social distance Frank perceived between himself and most of his neighbors hindered the development of informal strategies to address matters of concern. The supportive relationships Frank developed with a tight-knit group of like-minded neighbors, though valuable, were ultimately unable to provide enough of a buffer against the barrage of criminal activity and incivilities. He had little faith in what he saw as feeble, halfhearted community organizational approaches to safety. In the end, the uneasy coexistence of conflicting cultures created an environment that was impossible to control and too unstable to ever become livable.

Nikki Klein

Like Frank, Nikki Klein grew up in a predominantly white, upper-middle-class Milwaukee suburb. In the early 1990s, she moved to Riverwest. At that time, she knew little about the neighborhood. Her motivations for the move were primarily practical: Riverwest was close enough to the University of Wisconsin–Milwaukee (where she was attending college) and had cheaper rents than the east side. She stayed in the neighborhood, bouncing from one rented place to the next, throughout and after college. Nikki and several of her friends eventually realized that Riverwest housing was affordable—even cheap—and that it made more financial sense to own a home in the neighborhood than to rent. The hints that neighborhood property values were on the rise proved to be accurate. She bought her first home in 1997 for $31,000 and was able to sell it for a considerable profit just a few years later. Her reflections on this investment reveal lingering ambivalence. Did Nikki and her friends participate in inevitable change or contribute to an increase in housing prices and property taxes that adversely affected some residents? Part of what makes this a difficult question to answer is uncertainty surrounding River-west's status as a gentrified or gentrifying community and the extent of related displacement.

Nikki got married and started her family in Riverwest. After a few years, she and her husband decided to move to a neighborhood just northwest of Riverwest. Drawn by the location and the historic housing stock, they settled on a beautiful Craftsman home with wooden floors and leaded glass. As a biracial family with experience living in a racially mixed environment, they felt comfortable moving to a predominantly African American neighborhood. They knew that there were some crime issues in the neighborhood, but they weren't prepared for the amount of drug dealing and gun violence they encountered. Nikki attempted to organize the community to address crime, but her efforts failed to generate much interest or investment from her neighbors. Even her neighbor who was a city alderman at the time paid little attention to her concerns. Nikki suspects that her white outsider status played a role in her inability to create connections with her near neighbors. She also believes that the social ties (often family ties) between her neighbors and those responsible for the violence presented significant challenges to dealing with local issues. Nikki learned important lessons during her brief time in the neighborhood. She decided she would never again live in a place where she "doesn't have community," where she isn't connected to her neighbors, where she doesn't fit in, where she feels alone.

It was clear the family needed to move, but Nikki and her husband had no interest in returning to the homogeneous suburbs of their youth. When a friend heard that they were considering returning to Riverwest, she told them that the house in the middle of the three properties she owned on her block was for sale. They bought the house and soon created what they jokingly refer to as the "commune" by joining the backyards of the four properties. They had a fire pit, a communal garden, an area for shared meals, a swing set, and lots of open play space for the kids. Some of the houses were duplexes with rental units. Although this meant that there was a rotating commune membership, the carefully selected renters were brought into the fold. The commune parents did their best to ensure that the adults in their children's lives were good role models. Nikki felt fortunate to live in such a supportive and connected environment.

She also felt lucky to have landed on a good block. There were many long-time homeowners, now retired, who had worked hard to create a positive and stable place for raising their children. They joined newer arrivals, many with young families, to deal with problem houses on the block. After years of living in Riverwest without being the victim of crime, Nikki was hit with car and home break-ins. Though shaken, she remained confident in her block's collective capacity to generally keep things safe. The cohesion and support of the commune also mitigated the impact of the crime that did happen. During both of my interviews with Nikki, she repeatedly returned to the importance of connection for her sense of well-being in the neighborhood.

Riverwest has been "magical" for Nikki's kids. She believes her children are fortunate to have spent a significant chunk of their childhood in a strong, proudly diverse neighborhood. In their neighborhood interactions and at their local, dual-language public school, La Escuela Fratney, they are developing the skills to communicate and collaborate with different people—skills that Nikki sees as increasingly valuable in a globalized world. In Nikki's view, Riverwest's cultural heterogeneity fosters open-mindedness and tolerance. She has watched her kids grapple with making sense of differences in both race and sexual orientation:

> Yeah, I think it's been a really great experience. They know a lot of interesting people. Issues of race? In general, until recently, I would say they were almost colorblind. Now they're not, and I think it's been really, really good. They are just really comfortable around all different people. They check back in about things. It took a long time for them to totally accept people being gay. It was so interesting. They would check back in. "So a boy can kiss a boy?" "Yeah." "Can a boy get married to a boy?" "Yeah." Now, again, they are getting more sophisticated. My older son—these two ladies will be talking to him, two friends of mine, or whatever. And he'd be like, "Oh, are you two girlfriends?" "No, we're friends." This whole thing of trying to figure it out but being very open to it. I think they are going to be very accepting people, and I think Riverwest has something to do with that.

Nikki had assumed that raising her kids in Riverwest would shield them from some of the class issues she faced growing up in an affluent suburb. Yet she has found that her children must also negotiate the markers of difference in family resources. Some of their friends have access to expensive experiences—like hockey league participation or vacations to theme parks—that their family cannot afford: "They still deal with some things that on the flip side are funny that I think suburban kids deal with. There's a number of boys in the neighborhood that play hockey. Hockey is a great example of something I thought I was going to escape by not living in the suburbs. It's $2,000 per kid per season. I don't know how people do it. And so then I'm telling my kids—and this is how I grew up, and now I'm doing the same thing to them—'Well, we really can't afford that.' That's one of the funny things. And then the number of Riverwest families I know that went to Disney World. Who are you people? I thought I was escaping this by living in Riverwest." Ultimately, Nikki believes that confronting class differences—grappling with what it means to have more than some and less than others—is a valuable learning process for her kids.

The local environment also contributes to her children's development and identity formation in important ways. Nikki believes that because there are so many local models of who to be and how to be, her kids will feel free to experiment with different expressions of who they are. Living in a place "where you can let your freak flag fly" sends her kids key messages about acceptance and, she hopes, tempers pressures to conform. In a socially mixed neighborhood, they rarely encounter requests to explain their biracial family.

Many families ultimately decide that the benefits of living in Riverwest do not outweigh the costs. Based on nearly two decades of observations, Nikki has identified four key exit triggers for families: when they have a child, when the child is school age (and they don't want their child to attend Milwaukee Public Schools), when a family member is a victim of a crime, or when a significant crime, usually a homicide, happens in the neighborhood. Nikki's family's commitment to and overwhelmingly positive experiences in Milwaukee Public Schools and the buffers provided by a cohesive social community and a protective proximate community have helped root them in place. Nikki was frustrated by those who framed her choice to live in the neighborhood as "just a phase" or a kind of intentional arrested development. "I am not continuing to live some college dream. This is who I am."

Nikki sees herself as a Riverwest ambassador, working to combat the neighborhood's sketchy image by providing alternative narratives to the local media coverage that "squelches the positive" and "inflates the negative." The critics she encounters are rarely willing to identify their race-fueled concerns as such, so her responses tend to emphasize the value of racial diversity. When speaking to Riverwest residents, however, Nikki is critical of the neighborhood's stunted economic development. After seeing countless homegrown storefront businesses fizzle, she hopes Riverwest will do a better job of incubating new businesses and attracting established Milwaukee businesses seeking growth. Although some of her friends reject this as "too corporate" for the do-it-yourself neighborhood, Nikki believes it will bring stability and encourage other local businesses to shift from base-level maintenance to investing in enhancement: "I think Riverwest is stuck. I do. It can't quite get to the next place. The thing is, I don't think anybody knows what the next place is. 'Cause I certainly don't mean that there should be chain restaurants. I don't even know how to measure success, but I want a place to eat breakfast. There's room for another Nessun Dorma [a small bar and restaurant]. There's room for more—like La Lune [a rustic furniture-making company]. We need a little bit more of this happening. . . . It just didn't quite get there. And maybe it just is what it is. That's fine, but I always wanted a little bit more. I love Riverwest, but I want just a little bit more."

After nineteen years in Riverwest, Nikki moved out of the neighborhood. She and her husband decided to divorce, and Nikki needed to find a new home. Renting a place in Riverwest that met the standards of space and quality she had grown accustomed to turned out to be cost-prohibitive. She was determined to find a house in good condition for less than $40,000. Although Nikki looked for properties in Riverwest, she expanded her search to a few additional neighborhoods, including neighboring Harambee. She eventually found her new home in Walker's Point, an industrial neighborhood on the near south side that had begun to attract new residential and business investment. Part of what made this neighborhood attractive to Nikki is its social mix. It is home to a cluster of gay bars. The addition of upscale apartments and condominiums is creating more of a social-class mixture in this traditionally working-class community. The majority of residents are Hispanic, and there are significant white, black, and Asian populations as well. After years of living with moderate levels of crime in Riverwest, Nikki was undeterred by others' warnings about crime and safety issues. Nikki's decision to move to Walker's Point was clearly influenced by her experiences in Riverwest:

I felt like it was a good fit because it felt like Riverwest in a lot of ways. It feels really comfortable. . . . I think it's like where Riverwest has been trying to go for a long time. . . . There's more restaurants, more successful small businesses, more going on, but I feel like it's a lot of the same types of people. It feels really similar to me. I didn't look at any of the crime numbers, but I feel like it's probably similar. I don't know, and I don't really care. And I know from talking to enough people over there that it's similar, it's [a] block-to-block kind of thing. I live on a good block— three churches and all these nuns, lots of cats. It's just like anywhere else. My friend lives on kind of a bad block and struggles with all these other issues. It's comfortable because it feels very similar. I call it "Riversouth" sometimes because it really does feel like it.

In Riverwest, Nikki found what neither the suburbs nor the other urban neighborhoods she lived in could provide: connection, strength of community, and meaningful social diversity. She has developed an appreciation for the neighborhood as a co-parent—a key influence on her children's values development and identity formation. She has figured out what she needs to manage moderate levels of crime and risk—namely a core of neighbors committed to keeping just enough order. She is cognizant of the creative energy she received from Riverwest's "edge" and the importance of discomfort for sparking growth. Nikki's Riverwest experiences and lessons helped fashion her definition of a "good" place and, when it was time to leave, helped point the way to Walker's Point.

Heriberto Cardenales

Heriberto "Eddie" Cardenales has deep roots in the community. Three generations of his family have lived in Riverwest. His grandparents bought a house in the neighborhood where his mother was born and raised. His father was born in Puerto Rico and eventually made his way to Riverwest. Eddie has fond memories of growing up in a tight-knit, vibrant, and proud Puerto Rican community. As a child, he would ride his bike up and down Holton Street, looking for playmates, spending his nickels at the candy shop, and stopping to greet community elders with a request for their blessing. He describes the constant movement and social energy on the street: "Old Puerto Rican women used to just walk down the street and would go from house to house to house—visiting, drinking coffee to coffee to coffee, having a chat, then coffee, chat, coffee, chat." Eddie also recalls festive displays of Puerto Rican pride. When Puerto Rican boxer Tito Trinidad beat Oscar De La Hoya in what had been billed "the Fight of the Millennium" in 1999, there were huge celebrations in the streets of Riverwest. "I remember Holton Street being lines of Toyota Celicas! You know, just Toyota cars with the little Puerto Rican flags and everybody's playing their music, and waving their, you know, their Puerto Rican flags through their sunroofs. *That* was Holton Street."

Eddie clearly feels nostalgia for his childhood in Riverwest, but that doesn't mean he glosses over the challenging aspects of life in the neighborhood. At a young age, Eddie had to figure out how to manage a potentially dangerous environment: "Being Puerto Rican kids, light-skinned Puerto Rican kids, I mean, we used to get jumped every summer and, you know, come home with bloody noses and stuff like that. You've gone through enough stuff where, you know, a mother would say, "We have to get out of this neighborhood." But my mom was always one to tough it out and say, "Be the better person. Be the bigger person." And so that's what we always did. Growing up, we always tried to be the bigger and better person. Well it wasn't, you know, take a beating to take a beating. It was—if you're gonna take a beating, defend yourself. And I learned that from my mom; I learned that from my dad. That's just how we lived." To this day, Eddie views summer as the most volatile season in the city. "I mean summer? It's a whole 'nother world." During his adolescence, he confronted a world of complex and contentious allegiances both on the block and at his school: "It was tough, though. I mean, I had to hold my own. . . . I hung out with the wrong crowds. I got to, you know, know people, know things, learn about drugs, and hang out with kids and their older brothers, and get in fights, and—the first gun I ever got pulled on me was in sixth grade, and the last one was maybe about a week ago." When Eddie was a teenager, he started running with a powerful local gang. His parents decided to intervene. They sent him to Puerto Rico, where he stayed for nearly a decade.

Eddie's time away from home was a period of intense personal growth. He got involved in the arts, religious practice, teaching, and service work, which eventually took him around the world. His formative experiences in Riverwest proved useful in his travels:

EDDIE: All the places that I've traveled to, all the places—all the other experiences outside of Milwaukee that I lived, because I have this foundation, I have never had a problem with eating different foods in different countries. I've never had a problem of, you know, adapting to a different culture. I've never had a problem in socializing or learning something new from somebody else's culture, you know, like, it was all—

EVIE: And you credit this place with that?

EDDIE: Oh yeah! Because it was, I mean—like I said, you have to learn how to live wherever you live. And because there were so many different things here in Riverwest, I got to learn a lot of things. You know, I got to learn how the grungers hang out. I got to learn how the hippies hang out, you know? I got to learn how to crochet from a ninety-five-year-old woman. You know, there was a lot of things. I got to hang out and play. I know how to play basketball with the black kids, you know what I'm saying? That's just what we did, you know? And then I have my white friends that we would all go to Kern Park or whatever! And just go down to the river and catch tadpoles. Those are my memories, you know. Those are the things that I grew up learning. . . . I used to go to the [Urban] Ecology Center right there. They used to have like camps and stuff like that during the summer, and they would take us down to the Milwaukee River, learning about, you know, different animals, and, I mean—there was just so many different things that I did in my childhood, in this neighborhood. Swimming lessons at Riverside, like all these different things. And it just made me into a more complete person.

When he first started traveling to different parts of the world, he realized that he was better able to adapt to new environments than were his peers. He was surprised when he discovered that not everyone shared his enthusiasm for diving into new cultures. Eddie believes that growing up in a socially mixed environment gave him the skills and confidence to engage across difference.

In his mid-twenties, Eddie chose to return to Riverwest. Although there are still red, white, and blue Puerto Rican flags waving on Holton Street, his neighborhood has changed. The Puerto Rican spirit in Riverwest has not disappeared but has been diluted, as the heart of the Puerto Rican community has shifted to Milwaukee's south side: "There were so many Puerto Ricans here. And now, you know, little by little, they've all moved more down to the Spanish-friendly south side. And that's just because it's a Latino area, but it's just Spanish-friendly, you know. And so the people that are coming from Puerto Rico now are finding a more comfortable place to settle." Notably, the Puerto Rican parade that once marched down Holton Street every June has relocated to the south side. There is still enough of what he loves in Riverwest, however, to keep Eddie there: "I don't really go to the south side as much as I could. But it's because of how faithful I am to this community. Because this is home. This is my Puerto Rican culture here in Milwaukee. I don't need to go anywhere else for it."

Eddie observed two additional significant changes: less crime and more white people. "In terms of violence, drugs, prostitution, it's cleaned up a lot. I mean, I remember it how I left and, you know, when I came back, it was a whole 'nother picture. . . . I mean, I used to live on the block with three prostitute houses, two crack houses, and maybe a weed house. You know, like, one every other house. That's what I saw coming out of my front door. . . . You don't see that anymore." Upon his return home, he was immediately struck by the lack of a visible gang presence:

I don't even see gangs anymore in Milwaukee. Like, I remember growing up, and the East Side Mafioso [a prominent Latino Milwaukee gang] . . . used to call meetings, you know. On a certain corner, there'd be fifty, sixty, seventy people out on one corner. . . . You knew that was a gang meeting. Nobody said anything. Nobody did anything. Nobody called the cops. . . . They were meeting in an organized fashion; they were in a public space. They were speaking, you know, amongst themselves, not causing any harm to anybody. And people knew that they were there. Now you don't see gangs anymore, like, it's weird. It's really weird to not see that as much in Riverwest or in Milwaukee period. I mean, sure you have people that, you know, throw up signs and, blah, blah, blah, but it's not like how it used to be, where it was actually an organized system, you know, where you could see what was going on in the neighborhood because it was so organized.

Although Eddie has seen considerable improvements in terms of neighborhood safety, he finds it strange to no longer have the visible markers of gang organization that once provided a meaningful orientation to local affairs. He acknowledges that it still takes work to keep things under control. In his view, it is essential to have a "big mama on the block": someone who keeps neighbors connected and important information flowing.

Eddie assures me (a white woman) that having "a *lot* more white people" in Riverwest isn't necessarily a bad thing. He suspects that having more white people might be related to improvements in neighborhood safety. Riverwest has "flourished" and feels more "homey." He describes it as "more of an enjoy-the-day kind of neighborhood" than it once was. Still, it's clear that he feels ambivalent about the differences between the place he left and the place he returned to. "I mean, it *is* different, so it isn't the same experience. But at the same time I still love Riverwest, and whenever I get the chance, I try to ride my bike through and just be here, you know, just exist in the neighborhood. . . . It still feels—yeah, it feels good. Well, I mean, I've always enjoyed it because of the different people in it. But it's just quieter." He misses the intimate, dynamic, buzzing public life that characterized the Riverwest of his childhood. He worries that some newcomers are not interested in creating deep local connections and investing in the neighborhood. The young, mostly transient students and hipsters that Eddie sees moving in are "people who just wanna chill but not fit into the actual community of Riverwest." He wants to see even more people sitting on their porches or gathered on the sidewalk, and fewer people glued to their cell phones.

Although Eddie accepts and in some ways appreciates how his neighborhood has changed since his childhood, he misses the dense web of interconnected families and Puerto Rican traditions that defined his youth.

His departure from the neighborhood for an extended period of time influences his perspective on local conditions. What many of his neighbors have experienced as gradual changes, Eddie experienced as dramatic shifts. Although he values his time away from Milwaukee, he laments missing the opportunity to develop an extensive network of local ties: "I didn't get to enjoy Riverwest the way Riverwest was before I left as an adult, you know, because I think I would've enjoyed it ten times more. You know, it would've been . . . it would've been my place. It would've been, you know, 'Where's [Eddie]?' 'Oh, he's in Riverwest somewhere.'" Like some of the key figures of his parents' and grandparents' generations, he would have been one of the local public characters that everybody knows. This lost opportunity to preserve or build community relationships intensifies Eddie's experience of neighborhood change. He vigorously maintains that Riverwest is the place he wants to be: "Riverwest is a really rich area to live in, just because of the diversity, because of the culture, because of the history. And for me, I mean, it ties into family history." Yet for this recent returnee, it seems the neighborhood is less *his* than it once was.

June Jones

June Jones describes herself as "compassionate, colorful, and bright." She grew up and lived in what she calls the "inner city" (Milwaukee's predominantly black urban core) until she was in her late twenties. In 1998, June moved to a rented duplex in Riverwest with her two children and the man who is now her husband. After renting for many years, the couple eventually bought a property from their landlord. During her time in the neighborhood, June has grown to love Riverwest for its "acceptance of diversity." June experiences this acceptance as freedom. The social mix and tolerance are, for her, the key features that distinguish Riverwest from the other neighborhoods she has lived in. As a black woman in an interracial marriage, she feels more comfortable in this neighborhood than anywhere else in the city:

> It's a safety zone. That's where you feel most free at. You walk down the street and you see anything and everything. It's been like that, but now it's more so than ever. . . . You know, crime is everywhere, but there's also a thing called comfortability. You feel that in Riverwest. If you come there, you're gonna see a lot of different types of people there all the time. More of a variety. Oh my God, variety! [*Laughs heartily*] I like variety. I don't like a lot of one this, one that. I'm very creative, too, so

it's part of my personality. Like cross-dressers: I don't believe in their lifestyle, but I accept who they are and respect them because they respect me. Here, you are respected for who you are. . . . I learn a lot from all lifestyles—that will enhance me. It's like, we learn from each other. But if you get that one type, you're not going to learn anything or grow if you're just around one type or style.

Like Nikki, June appreciates that Riverwest is both an affirming and respectful place that brings comfort and a challenging place that encourages personal growth. During the interview, June returned several times to the relationships she had developed with a few individuals with nontraditional gender presentations. She holds these friends in high esteem, even as she struggles to reconcile their "lifestyle" and her religious beliefs.

The neighborhood has proven to be a decent place for June's family. She is proud of who her children, now young adults, have become, and she worked hard to steer them along the right path. After seeing so many young people "stray," June was well aware that the neighborhood contained multiple cultural models that could influence her children's identities and choices. She consistently intervened to direct her son and daughter away from what she determined to be dangerous and opportunity-crushing pathways: "I would say it's a good place to raise kids. You've gotta constantly teach them to make the right decisions. I would say basically keeping them from doing the negativity. Because there is negativity here. It's still in the process of getting better. My children turned out OK. I can honestly say that 'cause they could be in a lot worse places than where they at now. They not in jail, and that's a good thing, you know what I'm sayin'? They not six feet under. My children are good children." Parenting in Riverwest means never resting on her laurels. In the end, the positive and supportive forces of the neighborhood outweighed the negative, but not without diligent monitoring.

Considerable block-level troubles have also required her attention and perseverance. For June's first few years in Riverwest, the area around her family's rented duplex unit was relatively peaceful and quiet. Then a number of absentee slumlords with properties on her block and surrounding blocks began renting to problematic tenants, and things quickly deteriorated. Groups of teenage boys started "taking corners," claiming stretches of the block as their territory for drug commerce. The "riffraff" were disrespectful to neighbors. They were out in the streets at all hours of the night making their presence known. June regularly heard or witnessed fights. She worried about her children's safety. "If a deal go down bad, my babies were gonna get shot. I did not want that." One group of young men who occasionally conducted business in June's yard posted an advertisement outside her house. "I woke up one morning gettin' ready to go to work, walked outside. One of them had put a sign out. He had to have been dealing drugs all that night while I was asleep. They put up a big ol' sign that said 'Drugs are sold here.'" June was shocked. She couldn't believe that the homeowners in the area were willing to let these "outsiders" come in and terrorize their neighborhood. Because the dealers met little resistance, they simply took over.

At that time, June never saw police patrolling the neighborhood. She began calling the police to report the problematic behavior and appeal for a more visible police presence in the neighborhood. These early requests for assistance were largely ignored. June felt as though the police were working against rather than with Riverwest residents. They didn't see the residents as potential allies. This antagonistic police–community relationship was typical of her experiences in other Milwaukee neighborhoods. One day, a representative of the Children's Outing Association—a local youth and family center—knocked on June's door as part of an effort to make Riverwest residents aware of the organization and its services. He listened to her concerns and introduced her to Officer Beau McGuire, her police district's community liaison officer (CLO) at that time. The CLOs are the Milwaukee Police Department's public relations workers. They organize block-watch groups, attend neighborhood meetings, work with community prosecutors to deal with nuisance properties, coordinate crime prevention and education efforts, and act as a conduit of information between residents and police. June and Beau developed a strong working relationship. "[Beau McGuire] and me kinda made like a little relationship where we just—I talked to him, he talked to me. We just like—we was working together to help clear up a lot of stuff that was going on. And it got to the point where the closer I worked with him and the closer we worked together, things started clearing up." June credits the CLO with educating her on how to effectively use a range of public resources to address neighborhood issues. "He was my backbone."

Over the next few years, June worked quietly behind the scenes to evict problem tenants, hold landlords accountable for nuisance properties, and shut down gang and drug activity. She became an expert in navigating a range of complex public systems, including the Department of Neighborhood Services, the Bureau of Milwaukee Child Welfare, and the district attorney's office. June learned to use the police as a last resort and, when requesting police involvement, to modify her expectations about the time it takes to see results. "You gotta let those officers do what they gotta do, what they are *trained* to do. If you feel like it's taking too long, it's for a reason." June sees the residents and police officers as mutually responsible for maintaining neighborhood stability and believes that residents should strive to protect those who protect them: "Our job is to be on top of things. My job is to warn—if I see something that's coming towards these officers' way, I'm on the phone. I hear a lot of conversations, see how they do things, 'cause the intruders always changing. I'm not gonna let nothing creep up on Officer [Jablonski] or none of them that I know that's gonna harm them, 'cause I need them to protect me, keep me here 'til I'm seventy. My job is to forewarn them." June maintains that she has an important and valuable role to play in creating a safe and stable neighborhood.

Not all of June's neighborhood improvement efforts, however, have been behind the scenes. June works with the block watch that eventually formed by sharing information and advising those with whom she has built trusting relationships. Over time, her once scared and withdrawn block has developed the collective capacities that promote social control. June has also reached out to some of her most down-and-out neighbors like Clarisse, a young drug addict. Although others would avoid Clarisse, June would talk to her, pray with her, and encourage her to seek counseling. With June's support, Clarisse eventually moved into a residential substance abuse treatment facility in the neighborhood. "I'm a mother hen. We need more mother hens in the neighborhood. . . . A lot of women go through so much. Sometimes you are in the neighborhood by yourself. You don't know no one. You can be their sister or [the] mother they don't have."

During her tenure in Riverwest, June feels that her block, community–police relations, and the neighborhood as a whole have dramatically improved. For the most part, order has been restored to her piece of the community. She'll make the occasional call to the city to pick up a couch left on the curb, but that's about the extent of her current disorder-maintenance activity. She jokes that because her block has been so calm and quiet for the last few years, she's been put out of work. "Beforehand, it was bad. I was like, 'Oh my god!' I would say I had a vacation when the wintertime come, when I was doing the block captain, but when summertime come, my vacation was over with. But now it's like, shoot, I'm on vacation all year round!" June doesn't worry about the "small stuff"—the lifestyle differences that get some people worked up. She feels respected and free in Riverwest and believes in giving others room to live as they choose (provided no violence or drug dealing is involved).

June's perception of her environment is shaped by her experiences of successful individual and collective intervention in a place worthy of her investment. She has witnessed and directly participated in transforming her community into a safer, calmer, and more predictable place. But it is not only the improved results that matter; her experiences also reduce the intensity of possible threats. June's confidence in her relationships with neighbors and formal agents of social control and her knowledge of tested strategies provide a framework for, if needed, restoring order to her local surround.

Pathways, Perceptions, and Pluralism

These five residents' mobility pathways interact with the neighborhood context in ways that *jointly* shape their assessments of difference, local assets, risk, and control. Darius's experiences living in more dangerous, unpredictable, and socially fragmented environments and his sense of neighborhood character (privileging collective good over personal gain) shape his evaluation of Riverwest as calm, strong, and prepared to handle challenges to the community's well-being. Frank's suburban upbringing and understanding of a good community influenced his perception and negotiation of the social distance between himself and some of his neighbors. His understanding of the neighborhood as improving intensified his frustration with the neighborhood's inability to uphold mainstream norms. The addition of his experiences as the witness to or the victim of crime and the failure of both formal and informal social control efforts contributed to his ultimately seeing Riverwest as unstable and uncontrollable. The suburbs of Nikki's youth and her brief stint in a struggling neighborhood helped her define her criteria for a place to live. Her perception of Riverwest as an engaged and strong community and the solidarity and stability of her block contributed to her sense of the neighborhood as relatively safe and under control. Nikki associates the social diversity in Riverwest (and now, Walker's Point) with a range of benefits to herself and her family that are unavailable in the stifling, conformist suburbs. Although Riverwest might have been the type of place for Nikki to step up from, it is, instead, the type of place she considers a desirable destination. Eddie's extended hiatus from his native neighborhood and locally embedded relationships bring contrasts between the "old" and "new" Riverwest into sharp relief. Though he sees value in some of the changes, he also grieves the loss of his childhood community on Holton Street. His travels revealed the tangible benefits of growing up in a heterogeneous neighborhood, but the place he returned to feels less familiar. Eddie welcomes increased safety but is disoriented by the disappearance of the palpable gang presence and strong social networks that once ordered his community. June's experiences living in places less tolerant of difference influence her perception of Riverwest as comfortable and liberating. Her experiences of improving life on her block through alliances with her neighbors and formal agents of social control contribute to her confidence in their collective capacity to keep the neighborhood peaceful and safe.

People select neighborhoods for a variety of reasons, and these neighborhoods, in turn, shape their opportunities and perceptions. Darius, Frank, Nikki, Eddie, and June came to (or returned to) Riverwest with distinct lenses that influenced their initial expectations and perceptions of the neighborhood. Their stories illustrate place effects: how cultural framings of the neighborhood, block-level observations and interactions, and the neighborhood's in-between location together organize experience and interact with individual predispositions to influence their assessments of neighborhood quality of life and how they are incorporated into the local social order.

Their stories also reiterate a key theme running through this book: the heterogeneity of neighborhood effects.[1] Neighborhoods matter in different ways for different people at different times. Clearly, the lived experience of integration varies among Riverwest residents. The challenge is to unearth patterns and processes that help us explain observed differences in responses to residential contexts. The preceding analyses suggest several promising avenues for further investigation.

First, interrogating residential pathways reveals how people bring particular orientations and skills that shape the way they read and respond to a new or changing setting. Experiences in previous neighborhoods (or previous versions of the same neighborhood) generate sets of expectations and comparisons that affect evaluations of a community's quality and livability. The habits and skills residents develop to manage previous environments may or may not be effective in a new residential context. This leads to a second factor, behavioral adaptations to the challenges and opportunities in particular environments.[2] Some residents in Riverwest learn how to collaborate with neighbors, organizations, city officials, or police to deal with local issues. In a socially mixed neighborhood, such collaborations often entail working through different ideas about means and ends. For some, this requires unacceptable trade-offs. Others develop place-specific skills and practices as they fumble their way toward working solutions. Participation in such efforts and the relationships developed through these alliances point to established sources of effect heterogeneity: community engagement, interaction with neighbors, and the strength and nature of social-network ties.[3]

Residents' satisfaction with the results of these strategic partnerships is embedded in sets of cultural understandings of the neighborhood as it is and should be. Cultural heterogeneity, then, is a third variable linked to differing responses to a particular community context.[4] In diverse neighborhoods like Riverwest, there are multiple frames available for interpreting and navigating local life. A number of factors influence which neighborhood frame a particular resident latches on to. Again, experiences in previous places—be they different neighborhoods or different versions of a changed neighborhood— influence the resonance of particular frames. Cultural adaptations for neighborhood negotiation, as the previous narratives show, are linked to behavioral adaptations—from responses to troubles to the use of public and private spaces. These shifts toward sets of local understandings and practices have consequences for individuals as well as neighborhoods. They may, for example, affect one's access to resources, experiences of belonging, capacity for navigating other environments, or direction of future residential moves. They also, in aggregate, impact community regulation, neighborhood development, and processes of inclusion and exclusion.

CHAPTER EIGHT

Living Together

How is it possible to build a chain of solidarity out of multiplicity?
—Ash Amin, "The Good City"

"Is Riverwest doomed?"[1] This question started a thread in a city-data.com forum in the fall of 2009. The website pulls together myriad data sources to create profiles of cities and neighborhoods in the United States. The site also hosts forums for discussions about places. In the post that sparked this particular thread, the author questioned the future of the neighborhood in light of the murders of two University of Wisconsin–Milwaukee students during the previous summer: "Its future was iffy anyway because it is so close to crime ridden areas. All it takes is a few violent crimes to clear out honest renters and make way for the criminal elements." Later that day, a poster responded with a very different interpretation of Riverwest's questionable future: "At first I thought this thread might be addressing a threat to the character of the neighborhood, e.g.: will it still be as diverse and interesting ten years from now. On that question I would agree that Riverwest is on iffy ground."

Riverwest has maintained its "iffy" in-between status for decades. Throughout that time, residents and onlookers have warned of impending racial and economic transition. They predict that the neighborhood will be swallowed by the "ghetto" one day, then warn of (or celebrate) gentrification the next. Yet Riverwest has neither tipped nor flipped. How do we understand the durability of the neighborhood's social diversity? Its geographic location as a buffer neighborhood certainly plays a role. Situated between the more affluent, white east side and the poorer, predominantly African American north side, Riverwest must negotiate the countervailing pressures of development and disinvestment. But that is only part of the story.

The local culture that organizes public life in the neighborhood enables Riverwest to reproduce itself as a distinctive and diverse place. Residents that adopt a "live and let live" approach to negotiating difference use flexible categories of transgressions. These residents also tend to take considerable responsibility for supervising activity on their face blocks. This affects how the Milwaukee Police Department and other agents of formal social control interact with the neighborhood. The high level of tolerance coupled with a neighborhood code that encourages working out local conflicts informally

affects residents' determinations of when and how to call on external authorities for assistance. Yet when things get bad—when a resident is killed or
when a group distributes hate literature—the neighborhood responds with
passion and force. Riverwest residents are thus able to keep the neighborhood
relatively safe without demanding conformity, a trade-off most find acceptable enough to live with. For some who have tried to make Riverwest home,
however, such a precarious balance requires too much sacrifice and provides
too few tangible benefits. Several of the residents I interviewed who were enthusiastic about the neighborhood's potential left the neighborhood in the
years following the study. They were fed up with widespread tolerance of bad
behavior, concerted efforts to block neighborhood development, and the failure of engaged community members to effectively address issues of crime
and decline. The perception of elevated investment risk (both personal and
financial) also discourages many middle- and upper-class homeowners from
moving to the neighborhood.

At the same time, confidence in Riverwest's resilience serves as a check on
the flight of more privileged residents. Those who have by virtue of financial
means or race more residential mobility opportunities choose to stay because
they believe Riverwest is strong enough to resist the threats to neighborhood
safety and stability and because they feel they are a part of this unique, defined community. Others who have their eye on the neighborhood's development potential stay in spite of what they see as its progress-hindering local
culture. They have enough confidence in their efficacious ties to local authorities and the power of the market to improve the neighborhood.

That Riverwest's character is maintained in the face of high population
turnover (as a majority-renter neighborhood) speaks to the power of local
culture. It acts as a migration filter—in terms of both who moves in and who
moves out. Riverwest is a magnet for those outside the mainstream or those
seeking a comfortable step up from neighborhoods of concentrated disadvantage, but a repellant to those seeking middle-class stability. The culture
supports efforts to oust the biggest troublemakers, affirms the right of assorted residents to stay put, and attenuates the out-migration of some of the
more mobile.

The perceived ongoing threats of racial, economic, and cultural transition
that come from both sides of Riverwest bolster residents' sense of place. Each
challenge brings an opportunity to reassert the neighborhood's identity. In
a packed town hall meeting prompted by the unsolved murders of two college students that had taken place in Riverwest less than two weeks apart, a
middle-aged woman with long dark hair in a sweatshirt and jeans rose to

speak. With a slight Spanish accent, her voice trembling with emotion, she spoke about how she knows every person on her block. She makes sure to say hello to everyone who passes her house. If they don't respond, she looks them in the eye and repeats her greeting. Her welcome is sincere, but she is also letting them know that she sees them and is watching. There have been times when she has wanted to pack up and leave the neighborhood, "but it would be impossible to find such a fine community with so many kinds of people anywhere else." This unique place takes work but is worthy of protection and celebration.

Residents' management of perceived external threats to Riverwest's heterogeneity is linked to the negotiation of social diversity on the ground in day-to-day interactions with difference. The chief site of social connection and difference management is the face block. The forced intimacy of a proximate environment with dense housing and limited options for off-street parking produces myriad opportunities for observation and social exchange. Though some choose retreat and detachment, many interact with their local social surround. On the block, they navigate the vicissitudes of disputes, compromises, antagonisms, and alliances. Along the way, residents develop nuanced understandings of their neighbors, which enable the contextualization of their conduct.

Over time, the unemployed Puerto Rican neighbor with all those loud teenagers on the porch becomes the father of three, who spends an awful lot of time tending to his magnificent garden but clearly needs new siding on his house.[2] Then he becomes Raphael, who was laid off last year and has been living off the money he had set aside to work on the house while he looks for a new job. His oldest son is seventeen, and Raphael encourages him and his friends to hang out at the house so he can keep an eye on them. Then he becomes the protective neighbor, who walks up and gives you a loud greeting as you are getting out of your car after working late because he just saw two men he doesn't recognize move from behind that tree when they saw you pull up. Then he becomes the first person you call after seeing his son and his friends in the alley loading a pair of road bikes into the back of a truck.

Once in a while, expanded knowledge of a neighbor lays the groundwork for a friendship that crosses class, race, or other social divides. More often, neighbors become acquaintances. Deep connections are not required to keep order. A resident's casual familiarity with those in her proximate surround allows her to develop a sense of what to expect from her neighbors. These relationships, though varying in depth, add up to making block life somewhat predictable and comfortable. So, back to Raphael: Apart from sidewalk chats, you don't hang out with Raphael. In fact, you've never been inside each other's homes. But you are connected. His house looks different to you now that you know his story (less blight, more in-process). It brings you some peace knowing that he is often on the block and working outside while you are at work. You are confident that he has your back. And you have his.

Such shifts in understanding may not extend beyond making individual exceptions for a few neighbors who don't meet one's standards for appropriate conduct. In a neighborhood where residents regularly deal with difference, contextualization and flexibility sometimes prove to be practical tools for navigating the environment and, over time, become habit. When a resident's new habits of engagement interact with local cultural narratives about worthiness and belonging, living in Riverwest can change how that resident perceives and responds to status-based social differences.

Constructive Conflict

Block-level interactions multiply the axes of differentiation residents use to make sense of their surroundings. These interactions increase opportunities to find common ground on which to build new relationships.[3] They also heighten the potential for conflict. This is precisely what concerns both lay and scientific observers of urban life. They argue that difference produces conflict that makes diverse neighborhoods unstable and presents obstacles to the creation and maintenance of local social order. Although discord can be destructive, classical theorist Georg Simmel argued that it can also be constructive: "Conflict itself resolves the tension between contrasts."[4] In Riverwest, I find that conflict is central to local social organization.

First, conflict can induce cooperation and coalition formation. Numerous neighbor relationships have been formed, developed, and solidified in the process of coming together to deal with a problem on the block. Shared fate produced by an immediate threat proves to be a powerful integrator. When seemingly different people find themselves on the same side of a local battle, their experience of "we," even when only temporary, can bridge social divides. However, these responsive coalitions can also exclude. Opposition to residential or commercial developments viewed as harbingers of gentrification that takes the form of "Die Yuppie Scum!" identifies a category of unwelcome people. But the diversity-affirming "live and let live" culture in Riverwest places limits on most large-scale efforts to achieve social closure. As Annick Germain and Martha Radice find in their study of multiethnic neighborhoods in Montreal, "conflicts seem to be contained by the commonly held acknowledgement that the Other has a right to be there."[5]

Conflict can sometimes crystallize and sometimes complicate group boundaries. In broader, community-level disputes about development proposals or the use of public space, core groups of engaged residents might discover that they tend to take the same position on neighborhood issues. I found that block-level conflicts produced different coalition configurations depending on the issue. Neighbors Ed Hamilton and Marcella Morris are a formidable team when they pressure Walter Pearce to evict his most recent set of troublesome tenants, yet they are completely at odds about how to respond to a string of problems at the corner pub. There has been enough trust and goodwill generated through years of neighboring and periodic collaboration for their relationship to survive occasional rifts. When alliances shift based on the nature of block clashes, it also increases social-bridging opportunities and prevents the development of a rigidly defined "us" and "them."

Second, smaller conflicts can prevent larger conflicts. Directly articulating one's grievances with a neighbor doesn't have to result in agreement to positively impact the proximate social order. Such confrontations can provide opportunities to share important context about the experiences of both the disrupted and the disrupter. When neighbor conflicts are public or travel through gossip chains, they facilitate discussions that clarify local social norms. These collective renditions of local rules can defuse interpersonal disagreements by affecting either party's confidence in support for his or her position. Finally, by signaling a willingness to work things out informally, direct confrontation can avoid the escalation or disproportionate responses that sometimes accompany bringing in the police or city officials.

Third, conflict can produce unique opportunities for the expression of dissent, for mutual criticism, and for challenges to the legitimacy of dominant understandings.[6] When a socially mixed group of renters and homeowners come together to battle a nuisance property on their block, disagreements emerge about the definition of problems and their solutions. Some are forced to reevaluate their insistence on "obvious" community standards when neighbors argue that enforcing such standards will be impractical or unfairly affect particular households. When residents fight about whether or not prohibiting live hip-hop shows at a local bar is an effective way to address recent violence at the establishment, stereotypes are openly aired and challenged. Through the processes of conflict and conflict resolution, broad social categories and associated cultural assumptions are sometimes reinforced, but they can also be disrupted and destabilized.[7] At times, disputes refashion understandings of deviance into difference, creating the space for the emergence of new norms.

Of course, neighborhood conflicts are not always constructive. They might reinforce oppressive and marginalizing practices, deny people access to resources, hinder the progress of various initiatives, or end in violence. They can also drive people and other types of resources out of Riverwest or deter investment. Most conflicts in Riverwest produce a combination of harms and benefits. That there is often an upside to local clashes is due, in part, to an interactional context that privileges bargaining over enforcing absolutes.

Many of the concerns about diversity are linked to its discordant quality: It makes it difficult to achieve consensus. It breeds uncertainty. Yet we rarely question the assumptions about community ideals that underlie these concerns. Are unity and consensus reasonable or achievable goals for all neighborhoods? Interestingly, suburban communities are typically held up as models of organization and stability. However, research suggests that the appearance of suburban order and harmony is largely maintained by conflict avoidance, not normative consensus.[8] In a socially mixed community, conflicts large and small require residents' continual collective management. Many local norms are negotiated, challenged, and renegotiated. The flexible strategies for neighborhood negotiation support the production of a tentative social order. But it is not chaos. There are patterns and rhythms that make most local encounters familiar and navigable. The price of maintaining local culture that resists a uniform normative structure, in this particular neighborhood, is living with conflict and a degree of ambiguity. Yet as I have argued, this tentative order also contributes to the durability of neighborhood heterogeneity. Thus, instability in Riverwest produces stability.[9]

Place and Power

The considerable enthusiasm for the potential of diverse neighborhoods to address injustice and inequality can lead us to mistake the very existence of such places for the realization of that potential. In a society structured by multiple interlocking systems of oppression, the residential coexistence of people who are different in terms of race, class, gender, age, ability, citizenship status, and sexual orientation does not necessarily lead to transforming the social relations of power. As a handful of in-depth studies of socially mixed communities demonstrates, white residents, homeowners, and neighborhood decision makers who claim to value diversity often act in ways that largely reinforce—rather than challenge—existing social inequities.[10] They make symbolic gestures of inclusion that make them feel worthy, open minded, and a part of the solution. Yet local struggles over resources, rights, and definitions of acceptable behavior reveal privileged residents' commitment to maintaining a status quo that preserves their comfort and advantages and marginalizes nonwhite and lower-class residents. At times, Riverwest residents (including some of those who champion diversity) act on behalf of a definition of common good that masks their privilege and interests and excludes other perspectives. Yet as I have argued, living in Riverwest shapes how residents "see" disorder and the "other" in ways that can blur boundaries and disrupt the status quo.

Boundary maintenance is one of the key interactive processes through which inequalities are reproduced.[11] In essence, the powerful draw and enforce symbolic, social, and geographic boundaries to maintain their advantages. For example, racial residential exclusion and the normalization of whiteness help preserve white privilege. Boundary drawing expresses a type of cultural power: the power to define. The struggles of socially diverse communities are, in part, struggles over the power to organize difference. Social theorist William Sewell argues that dominant actors attempt to impose coherence through the ordering of meanings:

> They are constantly engaged in efforts not only to normalize or homogenize but also to hierarchize, encapsulate, exclude, criminalize, hegemonize, or marginalize practices and populations that diverge from the sanctioned ideal. . . . When authoritative actors distinguish between high and low cultural practices or between those of the majority ethnicity and minorities or between the legal and the criminal or between the normal and the abnormal, they bring widely varying practices into semiotic relationship—that is, into definition in terms of contrasts with one another. Authoritative cultural action, launched from the centers of power, has the effect of turning what otherwise might be a babble of cultural voices into a semiotically and politically ordered field of differences. Such action creates a map of the "culture" and its variants, one that tells people where they and their practices fit in the official scheme of things.[12]

Dominance is expressed through the imposition of a framework of meaning that orders relations, drawing boundaries that normalize or marginalize categories of people and behavior. Those in power may, for example, work to maintain clear distinctions between deserving and undeserving, credible and untrustworthy, or civil and uncivil to justify their elite status, affirm a superior worldview, or regulate access to valued resources and opportunities. These comparative evaluations of types of people, then, help legitimate the concentration of resources in the hands of people who are deserving because they are "better."[13]

Riverwest does not exist in a vacuum. Local social relations are structured, in part, by existing social inequalities and the classist, racist, sexist, and homophobic frameworks of meaning and constructions of difference that help sustain them. But places can filter and modify prevailing cultural frames. Ethnographer Gary Alan Fine argues that "local settings are sites where processes of stratification are generated, reproduced, and transformed."[14] In Riverwest, place grounds a shared rubric for neighborhood interactions that facilitates boundary-blurring processes—processes that can grind down the categorical boundaries erected to distance and exclude.

We can see this blurring in multilayered alternative classification schemes and definition disputes. The neighborhood is a supportive enclave for many who are in some way marginalized or outside the mainstream. Some, for example, take comfort in the acceptance or normalization of interracial or same-gender relationships. Others feel valued in a local prestige hierarchy that places creativity, self-sufficiency, and conservation above consumption and the accumulation of wealth. Riverwest is a place where mainstream rules can be bent and even broken. This includes challenging widely held perceptions of disorderly people and practices. Riverwest is what cultural geographer Ash Amin calls a "space of cultural displacement." This everyday heterogeneous site of encounter "disrupts easy labeling of the stranger as enemy and initiates new attachments, . . . offering individuals the chance to break out of fixed relations and fixed notions."[15] It not only disrupts fixed notions of others but also disrupts fixed notions of self. Residents find that their experiences of status are inconsistent. They may find acceptance and unquestioned inclusion in some neighborhood spaces and conditional acceptance or even outright exclusion in others. This may be particularly agitating for those who have rarely had their relatively privileged statuses challenged or even identified as such. Through these processes, neighborhood residents produce their own cultural map that reorders and resists some of society's dominant system of meanings. These processes do not *erase* boundaries; they dim their power to wholly define people and decrease their utility for managing local encounters.

At the same time, Riverwest's diversity generates internal cultural contests. A relatively small but invested group of residents challenge the dominant neighborhood cultural frames and difference-negotiation codes in an effort to improve local conditions. Their response to normative flexibility is the regulation of local behavior according to broadly accepted middle-class standards. Though a minority, their community-engagement practices are crucial for the reproduction of neighborhood culture: "Dominant and oppositional groups interact constantly, each undertaking its initiatives with the other in mind. Even when they attempt to overcome or undermine each other, they are mutually shaped by their dialectical dance."[16] Riverwest's culture is constructed through these dances—through battles over the organization of difference that take place within the neighborhood and in dealing with forces outside the neighborhood.

Cultural cartographies are at the heart of difference making, but redrawing boundaries alone isn't the difference maker. The connections between borders, practices, resources, and opportunities are the stuff of stratification. When collective ideas about difference, deviance, and what it means to be a good neighbor guide everyday encounters, they can affect what is shared, who is sanctioned, and whose interests are served.

Paradox Redux

I began the book with an introduction to the apparent contradictions of integration. While there is some evidence to suggest that heterogeneous neighborhoods can improve relationships and attitudes in ways that bridge social divides, much research indicates that we are not very good at living with difference. Robert Putnam's recent research on the downsides of diversity has caused quite a stir. He finds that diversity negatively impacts trust, community engagement, socializing, and civic collaboration. "There is a tradeoff between diversity and community."[17] This sentiment is echoed in the literature on social organization that approaches racial/ethnic heterogeneity as a key factor (along with poverty and residential instability) in the troublesome trio of neighborhood conditions that is linked to constrained capacity to achieve shared goals. The prevailing view among urban researchers is that diversity affects local social organization by posing challenges to the regulation of residents' behavior according to collective ends.

Perhaps our unchecked normative assumptions about what good communities look like and what well-regulated communities want have limited our understanding of heterogeneous neighborhoods. The analysis of social control in Riverwest, a diverse and relatively well-regulated neighborhood, challenges researchers to interrogate how their notions of conventional or ideal communities and their assumptions about the goals of neighborhood social organization influence their evaluations of neighborhood regulation.

If we assess local social organization in Riverwest in terms of "mainstream" standards, we would conclude that neighborhood heterogeneity hinders residents' ability to maintain effective social controls. The "neighborhood has potential" residents would concur. Normative flexibility and disagreement about appropriate standards of neighborly behavior may prevent a significant and sustained reduction of disorder and crime, compromise the quality of life for some residents, and repel potential investors and home buyers.[18]

Those who see Riverwest's diversity as one of its primary strengths, however, are guided by a different set of collective goals—goals that, at times, conflict with one another. If we evaluate local social control efforts in light of these goals, we see that residents maintain a relatively orderly environment while preventing the imposition of a singular normative order on a diverse community. Few rules can be uniformly applied, as assimilation proves impractical or is discouraged by local culture. Legality is often less useful for assessing conduct than are shared notions of whether an action or a behavior causes harm or is just. Instead, residents rely on flexible, contextualized, and sometimes personalized assessments of behavior. Thus, they are able to keep their community relatively safe without sacrificing the widely shared goal of maintaining the neighborhood's unique culture and social mix. The persistence of a flexible and complex normative order is itself, in this evaluation, a marker of relative success. In Riverwest, diversity does require trade-offs, but when viewed through the lens of the everyday "doing" of difference, many of these trade-offs look more like mutual adjustments in the service of neighborhood livability.

After all, consensus can be costly; it can deny or essentialize difference. Communities can reach harmony at the expense of excluding or oppressing less advantaged groups.[19] For example, in Mary Pattillo's examination of the gentrification of a poor black neighborhood by middle-class black people, she finds that the middle-class residents are successful at developing local social-control strategies (e.g., quality-of-life policing) that enforce their understanding of responsible and respectable behavior. But this success comes at a cost. Pattillo concludes, "The benefits of gentrification do not flow equally, and established poorer residents feel, and indeed are, increasingly supervised and disciplined so that the new residents can fully enjoy the neighborhood as they desire."[20] Such models of social control manage difference through exclusion and censure.

One could argue that the preservation of Riverwest as a protective enclave for the marginalized is a form of subordinate adaptation that ultimately maintains inequality.[21] Orientations deemed valuable in the local culture may be negatively assessed in the dominant culture. The skills residents develop to manage neighborhood interactions may not be effective in other settings. And the acceptance that those outside the mainstream experience in Riverwest may not extend beyond neighborhood boundaries. Several residents referred to Riverwest as something other than the "real" world. They suggested that some of their neighbors would inevitably encounter a rude awakening when they realized that their community is vulnerable and their way of life unsustainable. But most residents operate in multiple social contexts, giving them myriad opportunities to develop an understanding of the reach of their Riverwest ways.[22] The neighborhood is not walled off from the world. It is affected by and therefore must engage with forces external to the neighborhood. Riverwest is, then, very much in the urban mix—responding to and shaping the social dynamics of the city.

What, then, are the characteristics of a successfully integrated community? Cultural geographer Ash Amin calls our attention to working toward balance in socially mixed places: "The key challenge is to strike a balance between cultural autonomy and social solidarity, so that the former does not lapse into separatist and essentialised identities and so that the latter does not slide into minority cultural assimilation and Western conformity."[23] Such a balance opens up possibilities for justice: for difference without exclusion. In Riverwest, the small changes that occur through boundary blurring, relationship building, and mutual accommodation reorganize difference in ways that challenge existing inequality. Has Riverwest achieved an ideal balance? No. Are the goods of neighborhood integration equally distributed? No. But the stretches and strains that local culture make viable and visible are evidence of balance work.

I am not so much resolving the paradoxes of integration, then, as embracing them. Yes, socially mixed neighborhoods have their share of tension, conflict, and challenges. This is to be expected in a highly stratified society. As Orlando Patterson has argued, tension is not a sign of the failure of integration but a necessary accompaniment to progress and meaningful change.[24] I have approached diversity as a dynamic lived set of processes rather than a static state. It is useful to similarly treat some of the downsides of diversity as process barometers rather than outcomes. Social discord may overwhelm a community's capacity to create stability and livability, yet it might create opportunities to build a working solidarity without enforcing sameness or denigrating difference.

Some traditional indicators of community are simply not a good fit for heterogeneous neighborhoods, at least not without additional context. For example, measures of trust, neighbor networks, and willingness to intervene in hypothetical situations provide important information about community regulation but may fail to capture alternative forms of neighborhood organization. Studies that also incorporate investigations of (rather than assumptions about) residents' definitions of quality of neighborhood life, local problems, and related goals of social organization will be better equipped to evaluate a neighborhood's capacity to realize shared aspirations for their community.

This is not to suggest that we should ignore the concerns of researchers who have linked neighborhood integration to alienation, social fragmentation, and community disengagement. Our task is to determine the neighborhood conditions that are more or less likely to produce these negative consequences. To this end, place-sensitive analyses have considerable promise. This approach situates neighborhoods in their broader geographic and social contexts, attends to the built environment and local material forms, and takes seriously the meanings people attach to places and their everyday negotiation of community life. A complementary approach is to evaluate place effects through residents' mobility trajectories and related processes of neighborhood selection and adjustment. Ideally, these approaches will generate productive comparisons of heterogeneous neighborhoods that (1) reveal patterns in social organization, social stratification, and the balance work of integration, and (2) identify additional mechanisms that moderate the effects of neighborhood diversity.

For example, the circumstances by which communities become socially mixed likely matter. Studies of neighborhoods that are diverse by virtue of policy implementation (i.e., mixed-income redevelopment of public housing) indicate that the organizations involved in managing these developments influence residents' approaches to dealing with conflict, social control, and difference.[25] This mediating organizational layer tasked with promoting integration enforces rules and attempts to "mainstream" poorer residents in ways that often reproduce exclusion.

Residential integration is one tool, albeit not a consistently effective tool, for promoting a more just and equitable society. Making diversity work is about creating the space for productive dissonance and creative compromise. It is about negotiating order through mutual engagement. It is about being open to being unsettled and changed. It is about creating radical and disruptive alternatives to business as usual. Making diversity work is fundamentally about recognizing and addressing inequalities. Riverwest gives us some ideas about how such work is thwarted or advanced on the ground in daily life. I found symbolic and substantive challenges to key mechanisms (e.g., boundary maintenance and othering) that maintain unjust class and race hierarchies. It is unclear, however, if—and if so, how—these shifts in the interactional dynamics of inequality are linked to broader structural changes in the distribution of resources and power. Sociologist Cecilia Ridgeway argues that to "open up" the study of inequality, researchers need to better understand how cultural mechanisms operate (as I have tried to do here) and to examine the connections between cultural and material dimensions of inequality and between interpersonal and structural processes.[26] Future studies of socially mixed communities will undoubtedly take up these tasks to advance our understanding of living with difference and the potential of residential integration.

Speculation: The Future of Riverwest

> How to describe Riverwest without using the word *diverse*, which is way overused? There are a bunch of different elements that include activists, entertainment, environmental, and cultural differences that somewhat come together and form a very interesting blend. There's a lot of—you could say—stew, and it changes all the time. . . . This is one of those places that I think people would want to come and be because of the tolerance and variety of things to do and see and maybe a feeling that it's not all done. And I don't know how long you can keep that, because there will be change, and we might arrive at a time where Riverwest is seen to be a finished product, which of course would only be a phase in time. Neighborhoods change by becoming high-end, or having that kind of stability that means that there's not that mix going on, but I don't see that happening soon. [*laughs*] Right now stuff comes together here, and there is always this edge, okay? Rich people, poor people, educated people, and drunk people and [*laughs*] anarchist people. And there are sparks! That makes for something exciting, doesn't it? You know, it's like—I have cats. Nothing like a little fight to spice up your day. (Larry Neville, Riverwest homeowner)

I expect that in the short term, Riverwest will remain a socially diverse neighborhood, albeit of a different sort. First, the tensions related to Riverwest's buffer status will likely persist. The collapse of the national housing market and the economic recession slowed the condominium construction boom of the 1990s in Milwaukee's downtown. A ripple effect of this market trend was a decrease in gentrification pressures in Riverwest and other Milwaukee neighborhoods situated near downtown. However, many of the foreclosed homes in Riverwest that went on the market were purchased, according to local gossip, by real estate speculators. Although this news delights residents seeking neighborhood improvement, others interpret this interest and climbing housing values as evidence of the persistent threat of gentrification.

The necessary ongoing balance work of living with difference makes its preservation precarious. Place features help sustain the neighborhood's social mix by facilitating regular cross-difference interaction and cultural continuity. Although these social and cultural protections are significant, there are few substantive policy protections in place. Without established equitable development agreements, affordable housing protections, increased access to housing assistance (including public housing) for low-income renters and home seekers, vigorous enforcement of fair housing laws, or other stabilizing measures, the neighborhood is vulnerable to gentrification pressures and the potential displacement of low-income residents. This vulnerability is deepened by the fact that many powerful institutional and organizational entities (developers, departments of city planning, and neighborhood services) are likely to support the neighborhood improvement visions of more advantaged residents. For now, however, gentrification pressures appear to be rather weak, and those best positioned to leverage resources for a "revitalized" Riverwest are often discouraged by a neighborhood they find to be frustratingly resistant to change.

Neighboring Harambee was hit particularly hard by the housing crisis. Many vacant homes in the neighborhood were boarded up, and residents reported concerns about squatters, vandalism, break-ins, stripping (stealing aluminum siding and copper wires), and property neglect. There are, however, signs of progress. Harambee residents and community organizers have worked to reclaim public spaces and manage the lasting negative impacts of foreclosed and vacant houses. There are also a number of public, philanthropic, and community-based organizational entities targeting the neighborhood for the strategic investment of resources, from crime reduction to economic development. Still, the intense challenges presented by marked neighborhood disinvestment will likely continue to affect Riverwest's near neighbor throughout the next decade. Riverwest will no doubt continue to encounter opportunities to reaffirm its identity through managing the perceived pressures from the east and the west.

There is some chatter among residents that the sharp geographic and symbolic borders between Riverwest and Harambee are softening. They claim that former or would-be Riverwest residents are settling in Harambee or that recent neighborhood improvement initiatives aimed at both neighborhoods are opening up collaborative possibilities. But the legacies of residential segregation endure. Place reputations persist, even in the face of substantial neighborhood change. Until the powerful notion that Holton Street marks the entrance to the "ghetto" is seriously disrupted, it will continue to shape residents' perceptions and practices. It is disheartening that the boundary-blurring processes at work in Riverwest rarely reach past Holton Street. Although perceived threats bolster neighborhood identification and attachment, they can also sustain oppressive "othering." As long as most residents maintain a simplistic and monolithic view of neighboring Harambee, they will limit the potential of integration to create positive social change.

Second, the features of local culture that contribute to the durability of heterogeneity in Riverwest are flexible and should be able to adapt to neighborhood change. "Live and let live," for example, provides a framework for a local public order that is not dependent on consistency or consensus. The culture of Riverwest can incorporate new categories of "others"—even as it reproduces the neighborhood as a distinct place. There are signs that the ingredients of the local social mix are shifting. New neighborhood leaders are emerging, many of whom benefit from intergenerational mentoring that passes along tools for innovation and change without dictating perspective or course. As Riverwesterners draw on unique local resources as they work to reshape their neighborhood, they will need to confront challenges both internal and external to the neighborhood. As they push, place pushes back. Though neighborhood change is inevitable, Riverwest will likely remain a heterogeneous community for the near future.[27]

Appendix
In the Field

I grew up in Whitefish Bay, a middle- and upper-class suburb in Milwaukee's North Shore area. This community is also known as "Whitefolks Bay" because it is overwhelmingly white and viewed by many as unwelcoming to people of color. The public school district in Whitefish Bay is among the best in the state, evidenced by consistently high standardized test scores and college-enrollment rates. The schools I attended were more diverse than the suburb's residential population because of the Chapter 220 Program. This school choice program, established in 1976 to promote racial integration of Milwaukee's metropolitan schools, still exists (albeit in a different form). In essence, it is a voluntary public school integration program. State aid follows students who transfer from school districts with more than 30 percent minority students (i.e., the Milwaukee Public School district) to those with less than 30 percent minority students (surrounding suburban districts), and vice versa. The vast majority of 220 Program participants are students who transfer from the Milwaukee Public School district into suburban districts. Busing is provided to participating students.

In practice, the 220 Program created a more diverse student body in the Whitefish Bay schools I attended. By the time I entered high school, about 20 percent of my classmates were minority students, most of whom traveled every day by bus from their neighborhoods in the city to a supposedly benevolent school district in a sometimes-hostile suburb.[1] Although school integration offered benefits to all students, the burdens were not evenly distributed. The Chapter 220 Program also conveyed significant messages about place. There was something wrong with city neighborhoods and something right about the suburbs (a reductionist view that remains largely intact today). This widely held interpretation of the daily out-migration of "lucky" students from the central city to superior suburban schools was one of my many early lessons in segregation.

I left Milwaukee after high school to attend college in Colorado. As an undergraduate student of sociology, I regularly returned to the issues of race, place, and privilege that had puzzled me as a kid. During visits home, I spent time in Riverwest, visiting friends who now lived in the neighborhood. I was intrigued by this in-between place, this weird place, this exception to Milwaukee's seemingly intractable segregation. Many years later, in the summer of 2007, I moved to Riverwest to conduct what would be a three-year ethnographic study of the neighborhood.

Ethnography

Gary Alan Fine asserts that "ethnography opens social mechanisms to examination, particularly when ethnographers focus on how participants respond to group contexts in shaping social organization."[2] I employed the tools of urban ethnography to explore particular aspects of the lived experience of integration. Specifically, I conducted fieldwork and in-depth interviews. Over time, I began to see patterns in local meaning making and interactions. In my analysis of the observational and interview data, I assessed the mechanisms through which the neighborhood's social mix shapes how residents make sense of the neighborhood, negotiate local interactions, and produce local social order.

The Case

Though one of very few, long-standing diverse neighborhoods in Milwaukee, Riverwest shares characteristics with a growing number of communities in the United States. Recent research indicates that the number and stability of racially mixed neighborhoods have increased steadily in the last few decades.[3] In addition to demographic characteristics, Riverwest has other features found to be common among diverse neighborhoods. In the 1990s, research teams studied fourteen neighborhoods in nine cities that had maintained their racial/ethnic mix for at least ten years. In their overarching assessment of the study, the lead researchers and community-based leaders conclude that, despite considerable differences, the neighborhoods in their sample shared a number of characteristics.[4] Riverwest, like the neighborhoods in this study, has attractive physical characteristics (e.g., proximity to downtown and highly regarded parks), social seams (e.g., neighborhood festivals and schools that facilitate interaction across race and ethnicity), resident awareness of the community's stable diversity, community-based organizations committed to maintaining diversity, and common challenges (e.g., crime).

Although Riverwest shares these characteristics with other diverse neighborhoods, I do not consider it to be a typical diverse community. I concur with Mario Small's assertion that a single neighborhood cannot be representative of a population of a neighborhood type.[5] Treating a neighborhood as a statistically average place, he argues, can cloud rather than clarify our understanding of neighborhood processes: "Fundamentally conceiving of neighborhoods as homogenous institutions undermines a serious effort to assess both similarities and differences."[6] Claiming statistical representativeness as a basis for generalization makes little sense when $n = 1$. Instead, Small advocates approaching the neighborhood as a specific configuration of conditions, some of which may be found in other neighborhoods. This approach facilitates analysis that is in-depth and context dependent without sacrificing the potential for fruitful comparisons with other cases. "The conditionalist tends to focus on the context at hand but . . . pays special attention to those conditions at least theoretically capable of manifesting themselves elsewhere."[7] In line with this approach, I aimed to identify mechanisms to help us better understand how a particular configuration of neighborhood conditions (including a racial and economic mix of residents) affect local social organization and difference negotiation. Ideally, my findings help us unpack why some—but certainly not all or even most—integrated communities look like Riverwest.

This approach also makes it impossible to mask the identity of Riverwest. The idea that neighborhoods matter sociologically is fundamentally rooted in an appreciation of the emplaced nature of social life. Places are socially constructed and, in turn, structure social processes. Conducting a place-sensitive analysis—that is, treating place as a social medium rather than a backdrop—necessitates attention to its material and symbolic conditions.[8] The decision to identify the neighborhood presented challenges to maintaining the confidentiality of study participants. The trade-off involved including less detailed or slightly altered information about the individuals I describe and quote. For example, in a few instances, I changed a resident's occupation, though I was careful to select a fictional occupation that was similar in terms of occupational prestige, requisite education, and training or pay. Several study participants gave me permission to include identifying information.

Participant Observation

The introduction provides a description of my entrance into the field and my approach to participant observation. Here I provide more information about managing my relationships with people living and working in Riverwest, describe how I documented observations, and discuss how my volunteer work influenced the study.

I was generally embedded in neighborhood life—but with a level of intensity and intention not typical of Riverwesterners. I was hyper-embedded. I got involved in a wide range of neighborhood activities and social networks in an attempt to get the broad view, and routinely revisited specific spots and groups of people to get the deep view. Some people in the neighborhood don't get along with, dislike, or loathe other people in the neighborhood. Although this was hardly surprising, it meant that I experienced occasional tensions in managing incorporation into multiple groups and settings. Empathy— understanding the connections between another person's circumstances, feelings, and outlook—is both an invaluable tool and an important goal of ethnography. Although the capacity to identify with another's situation does not require shared beliefs, residents may have sometimes interpreted my interest in understanding their stories and perspective as agreement with their point of view or indication that we were on the same side of an issue. When I was able to identify that this was the case (usually after multiple interactions), I attempted to make clear my familiarity with alternative and sometimes conflicting points of view. In these situations, my goal was not to eliminate tensions by presenting myself as objective. Rather, I worked to demonstrate that I was struggling to make sense of how they understood complex issues.

After (and often during) each day in the field, I returned home to write extensive field notes of my observations, conversations, and experiences. To structure my field notes, I used Bill Corsaro's recording conventions, separating documentation of field notes, personal notes, methodological notes, and theoretical notes.[9] I concentrated on the documentation of interactional detail and participants' categories, meanings, and processes of sense making.[10] I was particularly sensitive to variation in processes of interest. I also "emplaced" field notes by describing the geographic location of observations and the ways in which residents negotiate and interpret the built and natural environment of the neighborhood.

During two of the years that I was in the field, I served as a volunteer coach for the Milwaukee Mosaic Partnerships Program. Mosaic pairs community leaders across race/ethnicity in an effort to improve race relations and build a diverse coalition for community development. Each year, Ossie Kendrix— my African American coaching partner—and I were responsible for guiding a group of partnered pairs through a ten-month process of building the trust and understanding necessary to strengthen their relationships and engage in productive dialogue. This experience provided me with a rich picture of race-, ethnicity-, and class-related issues in Milwaukee—one that incorporated diverse perspectives of the city. Given the centrality of maintaining confidentiality for the relationship-building process, I never documented my observations of Mosaic gatherings. However, my understanding of intergroup relations in Milwaukee was substantially deepened as a result of my participation in the program.

In-Depth Interviews

From the moment I started exploring Riverwest as a potential case study (winter 2006), I asked residents to identify those who "know a lot about the neighborhood." In the fall of 2007, I began interviewing individuals whose names came up most frequently. I conducted interviews with a wide range of knowledgeable informants, including lifelong residents, neighborhood organization leaders, business owners, block-watch captains, journalists, social service providers, police officers, activists, school staff, prominent artists, and church clergy. After approximately forty interviews, I adjusted my approach to respondent selection. Up to that point, my neighborhood contacts had primarily identified the more visible and vocal people in organization-affiliated positions of leadership. My fieldwork, however, indicated that there were additional sources of local knowledge and leadership that I had not tapped into with my interviews. For example, many blocks had central figures—central because of their long tenure on the block or their role as news hub, social connector, or mediator. Others were public characters, people who seemed to be known to everyone by virtue of being planted in a place that facilitated contact with many residents (e.g., a convenience store clerk) or making the rounds of a wide variety of neighborhood spots.[11] I therefore began seeking out and interviewing these other kinds of knowledgeable informants. All of the people I interviewed were, in some way, active participants in the social, civic, commercial, or organizational life of the neighborhood. Those residents who have extremely limited neighborhood interactions are not represented in the interview or observational data.

In the end, I interviewed thirty women and thirty men. My research assistant, Jenny Urbanek, took the lead on conducting two of the interviews. My knowledgeable informants included thirty white people, fifteen African Americans, ten Latino/as, two Asian Americans, two biracial people, and one Arab American. The racial makeup of my interview sample roughly coincides with that of the neighborhood population. This meant that the interview data produced a more fully developed picture of the range of perspectives among white knowledgeable informants than among African American, Latino/a, and other groups of nonwhite residents. This weakness of the research design is addressed, in part, by the fact that the findings presented in this book are also based on the analysis of my observations and experiences in the field, which included building relationships with a heterogeneous set of residents, many of whom are not in the interview sample.

In-depth interviews are particularly useful for developing an understanding of social processes and meaning systems and gaining a holistic view of respondents' experiences.[12] I used these interviews to identify salient neighborhood issues, to further develop an understanding of how people make sense of and negotiate the neighborhood, and to complement and complicate my analysis of fieldwork data. In these semistructured, audio-recorded interviews, ranging from one to four hours in length, I asked informants to tell me the story of how they came to live in the area and to describe the neighborhood, its boundaries, its residents, its best and worst features, the ways it has changed, their hopes for its future, neighborhood tensions, and so on. The interviews elicited a range of neighborhood frames and categorization schemes that, while not fully capturing the heterogeneity of sociocultural orientations in the neighborhood, indicated some clear patterns that I explored in more depth in my field observations. In most cases, I interviewed one participant. I interviewed three couples and had one interview that organically bloomed into a kind of focus group with five residents. All of the interviews were transcribed by me or my research assistants.

Local Media

Because I was interested in interpretive constructions of the neighborhood, I also collected local media accounts of the neighborhood. I read and analyzed every issue of the local monthly paper (*Riverwest Currents*) printed during the study, as well as select past issues. I also collected Riverwest-relevant articles in local media, including the online versions of the major daily newspaper (*Milwaukee Journal Sentinel*) and two alternative weekly print newspapers (*Shepherd Express* and the *Onion*, Milwaukee edition), online-only magazines (OnMilwaukee.com and ThirdCoast Digest), and blogs. I subscribed to the Riverwest Neighborhood Association's listservs and the email lists for both alderpersons who represent the neighborhood, and I joined RiverwestNeighborhood.org, a community news hub and network that is now defunct.

Most of this online media content allows for virtual interaction, and I often found readers' comments (to authors and to one another) as illuminating as the content of the articles themselves. Sharon Zukin makes a case for including analysis of this Internet-based discourse in her study of the construction and consequences of authentic urban experiences: "It is important to understand how web-based media contribute to our urban imaginary. The interactive nature of the dialogue, how each post feeds on the preceding ones and elicits more, these are expressions of both difference and consensus, and they represent partial steps toward an open public sphere."[13] In the case of Riverwest, participation in any of these online forums is limited to a small minority of residents and an unknown smattering of outsiders. The makeup of anonymous consumers of these media is anybody's guess. Still, these media publicly communicate reactions to and constructions of place and are therefore worthy of real, if cautious, consideration. These sources provided a substantial amount of data, more than I could analyze for this stage of the project. To manage the data, I typically focused on analysis of specific incidents, coding all relevant media accounts from multiple sources to reveal significant patterns.

Analysis

Throughout the data collection process, I summarized and analyzed the data by writing integrative memos in which I explored emerging themes and attempted to synthesize discrete observations.[14] My approach to the linked processes of data analysis and theory building was both inductive and deductive, driven by an ongoing conversation between the data, evolving concepts, and existing theory and research.[15] I did not, as some advocate, enter the field with a blank theoretical slate. Instead, guided by the aforementioned theories and approaches, I was sensitive to, for example, how residents framed their neighborhood. However, my approach to data recording—separating observational data from theoretical reactions—also allowed for grounded theory: the emergence of theoretical concepts from the fieldwork data.[16]

After entering the data (field notes, interview transcripts, and media memos) into Atlas.ti (software for analysis of qualitative data), I coded them for general themes, analyzed them, and, after arriving at some preliminary theoretical insights, reassessed the data using these initial insights and further developed the conceptual categories. Throughout this process, I examined the relationship between the emergent theoretical framework and the extant literature. I found comparisons with existing case studies of socially mixed neighborhoods invaluable for making sense of my data. These comparisons sparked new questions, forced me to consider alternative explanations, and helped me to more clearly articulate theoretical connections between concepts. I also used comparisons and striking contrasts with existing case studies to support my claims about the role of place in shaping perceptions and practices in Riverwest.

I regularly returned to the data to search for negative cases and retain, refine, or reframe emerging theoretical insights accordingly.[17] Gary Alan Fine's characterization of the analytic process resonates with my experience: "As citizens we are never interested in the description of social scenes to the exclusion of other concerns. We are interested in how we might pragmatically utilize what we learn. Theoretical analysis is not something that occurs only before entering the field or after one has been in the field, but is a continuing recursive process. Induction leads to deduction, which leads to induction, and on and on and on."[18]

My research design included several strategies to minimize threats to validity, particularly reactivity and researcher bias. I have indicated some of these key strategies here, including the use of multiple methods, adoption of a theory-building approach that allows for the emergence of alternative explanations, identification and analysis of negative cases, audio recording and transcription of interviews, and attention to and documentation of how my insider and outsider characteristics influence data collection and how residents construct my role. In addition, the practice of separating personal, theoretical, and methodological notes from strictly observational notes provided a mechanism for documenting and monitoring assumptions that may influence data collection and interpretation. Further, I strove for breadth in data collection.[19] As themes emerged, I sought out multiple sources of data on a range of potentially relevant factors. For example, initial fieldwork and interviews suggested that crime mattered a great deal to residents and that there was considerable variation in residents' perceptions of what constitutes crime and disorder and how to best deal with it. To further explore this theme, I examined police department crime statistics, interviewed police officers, attended police-led and citizen-led crime meetings and block-watch meetings, documented observed prevention strategies and block-level responses to crime, asked residents about crime in unstructured and in-depth interviews, and archived and analyzed local media articles and online discussions about neighborhood crime.

Although several of these strategies address threats to validity *and* reliability, I employed additional measures to maximize reliability. In fieldwork and interviews, I avoided leading questions and biases that could arise from question order. I also probed for descriptions of specific incidents, which are less vulnerable to the influence of the interview setting.[20] Throughout the research process, I carefully documented (in integrative and analytic memos and field notes) the data collection strategies and the development of analytic categories and theoretical constructs.

Over the course of the study, I developed a deep fondness for Riverwest. As a result, I found it important to attend to specific countervailing threats to the validity and overall quality of my sociological accounts of neighborhood processes: erroneous romanticization and erroneous normalization.[21] To work against the tendency to idealize this place, I paid attention to power: to winners and losers, to different levels of vulnerability and risk, to processes of inclusion and exclusion. Though I challenged the bias of mainstream notions of the good community, I was careful to avoid using an equally distorting lens, one that forced a normalizing view of local categories and practices. To protect against imposing a normative framework, I consistently attended to residents' meanings, including their evaluations of their actions and their awareness of and response to outsiders' views.

Riverwests

I learned very quickly that there are many versions of Riverwest—many more than those I attempted to capture or create in these pages. I do not claim that this is *the* story of the neighborhood. As much as I tried to grasp the multiple, complex, and contradictory Riverwest tales, in the end, this is a partial and singular accounting. It is the product of filtering my observations and many peoples' stories through my brain using a particular set of sociological tools. Many of those whom I met during my time in the neighborhood offered astute analyses of Riverwest that sometimes clashed with and sometimes complemented my evaluation. Some of them were gracious enough to read and critique versions of this project. I would like to think that the many capable Riverwest sociologists, philosophers, observers, critics, boosters, and believers rubbed off on me a bit. Their potpourri of insights certainly colored my interpretations of Riverwest living. I am grateful for their generosity.

Notes

Chapter One

1. Riverwest is not a pseudonym. Many ethnographers give the neighborhoods they study fictitious names, but my decision to conduct a place-sensitive analysis made it necessary to identify the particulars of this place. I use pseudonyms for all study participants.

2. Ellen, Horn, and O'Regan, "Pathways of Integration."

3. See, for example, Charles, "Dynamics of Racial Residential Segregation"; Dreier, Mollenkopf, and Swanstrom, *Place Matters*; Massey and Denton, *American Apartheid*.

4. Schelling, "Dynamic Models of Segregation"; Wilson and Taub, *There Goes the Neighborhood*.

5. Ellen finds that nearly one-fifth of all neighborhoods were "racially mixed" (10–50 percent black) in 1990 and that over three-quarters of the neighborhoods that were mixed in 1980 remained so in 1990 (*Sharing America's Neighborhoods*). From 1980 to 2000, the number of what Ellen categorizes as "integrated" neighborhoods (over 40 percent white with one minority group accounting for a minimum of 10 percent of the population) increased from one-quarter of all neighborhoods to one-third of all neighborhoods ("How Integrated Did We Become"). During this same period, Iceland finds general declines in multigroup segregation (*Where We Live Now*). Fasenfest, Booza, and Metzger find that nine out of ten metropolitan areas saw an increase in mixed-race neighborhoods ("Living Together").

6. Iceland, Weinberg, and Steinmetz, *Racial and Ethnic Residential Segregation*; Logan, "Ethnic Diversity Grows"; Logan and Stults, *Persistence of Segregation*; Logan and Zhang, "Global Neighborhoods"; Turner and Ross, "How Racial Discrimination Affects the Search for Housing."

7. Ellen, Horn, and O'Regan, "Pathways of Integration."

8. Fischer, Stockmayer, Stiles, and Hout, "Geographic Levels and Social Dimensions of Segregation"; Fry and Taylor, *Rise of Segregation by Income*; Massey and Fischer, "Geography of Inequality."

9. In "Growth in the Residential Segregation of Families by Income," Reardon and Bischoff find that the number of families living in neighborhoods classified as either affluent (neighborhoods where the median income is greater than 150 percent of the median income in the metropolitan areas) or poor (neighborhoods where the median income is less than 67 percent of the metropolitan median income) jumped from 15 percent to 31 percent between 1970 and 2007.

10. Fry and Taylor, *Rise of Segregation by Income*.

11. Sharkey and Graham, *Mobility and the Metropolis.*

12. Dreier, Mollenkopf, and Swanstrom, *Place Matters.*

13. Bonilla-Silva and Embrick, "Every Place Has a Ghetto."

14. Ibid.

15. Sean Reardon and Kendra Bischoff, "No Neighborhood Is an Island," New York University Furman Center, November 2014, http://furmancenter.org/research/iri/reardonbischoff.

16. See, for example, Chaskin, "Integration and Exclusion"; Ludwig et al., "What Can We Learn about Neighborhood Effects"; Oakley, Fraser, and Bazuin, "Imagined Self-Sufficient Communities"; Sampson, "Moving to Inequality"; Sharkey, "Residential Mobility."

17. De Souza Briggs, "Interracial Friendships"; Laurence, "Effect of Ethnic Diversity"; Oliver, *Paradoxes of Integration*; Oliver and Wong, "Intergroup Prejudice in Multiethnic Settings"; Sigelman and Welch, "Contact Hypothesis Revisited"; Welch, Sigelman, Bledsoe, and Combs, *Race and Place.*

18. Bellair, "Social Interaction and Community Crime"; Guest, Kubrin, and Cover, "Heterogeneity and Harmony"; Hipp, Tita, and Greenbaum, "Drive-Bys and Trade-Ups"; Kubrin, "Making Order of Disorder"; Oliver, *Paradoxes of Integration*; Putnam, "*E Pluribus Unum*"; Sampson, "Collective Regulation"; Sampson and Groves, "Community Structure and Crime"; Sampson, Raudenbush, and Earls, "Neighborhoods and Violent Crime"; Warner and Pierce, "Reexamining Social Organization Theory"; Warner and Rountree, "Local Social Ties."

19. Laurence, "Effect of Ethnic Diversity"; Oliver, *Paradoxes of Integration*; Patterson, *Ordeal of Integration*; Stolle, Soroka, and Johnston, "When Does Diversity Erode Trust?"

20. Young, *Justice and Difference*, 234.

21. Bell and Hartmann, "Diversity in Everyday Discourse."

22. Mary Pattillo, "The Problem of Integration," New York University Furman Center, January 2014, http://furmancenter.org/research/iri/pattillo. Emphasis added.

23. The emphasis on outcomes—or what social mixing accomplishes—is, in part, driven by the kinds of findings that are valued in sociology (generalizable patterns that hold across contexts) or considered policy relevant (predictions and evaluations of policy impacts). See Brown-Saracino, "How Places Shape Identity," for a discussion of the merits and limitations of a sociology of generality.

24. Oliver, *Paradoxes of Integration*, 135.

25. For reviews on neighborhood effects on individual and communal outcomes, see Ellen and Turner, "Does Neighborhood Matter"; Sampson, Morenoff, and Gannon-Rowley, "Assessing Neighborhood Effects"; Small and Newman, "Urban Poverty."

26. Gieryn, "Space for Place."

27. Ibid., 472.

28. Borer, "Location of Culture"; Fine, "Sociology of the Local"; Gieryn, "Space for Place"; Gould, *Insurgent Identities*; Gregory, *Black Corona.*

29. Small, "Culture, Cohorts, and Social Organization."

30. Brown-Saracino, "Social Preservationists."

31. Kefalas, *Working-Class Heroes*.

32. Anderson, *Code of the Street*; Anderson, *Streetwise*; Brown-Saracino, "Social Preservationists"; Deener, *Venice*; Gans, *Urban Villagers*; Lofland, *World of Strangers*; Pattillo, *Black Picket Fences*; Sennett, *Uses of Disorder*; Suttles, *Social Construction of Community*; Suttles, *Social Order of the Slum*; Wilson and Taub, *There Goes the Neighborhood*.

33. In a review of the social scientific literature on boundaries, Lamont and Molnár ("Study of Boundaries") find that symbolic boundaries may reinforce or contest social boundaries.

34. Tamika is referring to National Public Radio.

35. Emerson, Fretz, and Shaw, *Writing Ethnographic Fieldnotes*.

36. Gieryn, "Space for Place."

Chapter Two

1. Neighborhoods may not be the most meaningful place category for all residents. See, for instance, Brown-Saracino, "How Places Shape Identity," for a study of how cities are meaningful for lesbian, bisexual, and queer women's identities, and Small, *Villa Victoria*, for a study of how narratives about a subsidized housing complex affect levels of community participation.

2. Gieryn, "Space for Place."

3. US2010 Dissimilarity Index Rankings, http://www.s4.brown.edu/us2010 /SegSorting/Default.aspx. The metropolitan area ranks 116th in white–Asian segregation.

4. Logan, Stults, and Farley, "Segregation of Minorities."

5. Levine, *Racial Disparities*.

6. Levine, "The Two Milwaukees."

7. Levine defines extreme poverty neighborhoods as those in which 40 percent or more of the residents are poor (*Racial Disparities*).

8. In *Racial Disparities*, Levine argues that Milwaukee's remarkably low black suburbanization rate is largely due to discriminatory lending practices and strong political resistance to integrating the area's suburbs (i.e., widespread and systemic racism).

9. Margery Austin Turner, "How Wide Are the Racial Opportunity Gaps in Your Metro?," *Urban Wire* (blog), Urban Institute, February 2, 2012, http://blog.metro trends.org/2012/02/wide-opportunity-gaps-metro/.

10. Swanstrom, Casey, Flack, and Dreier, *Pulling Apart*.

11. Kneebone, Nadeau, and Berube, *Re-emergence of Concentrated Poverty*; Zeidenburg, *Moving Outward*.

12. Richard Florida and Charlotta Mellander, "Segregated City: The Geography of Economic Segregation in America's Metros," Martin Prosperity Institute, February 23, 2015, http://martinprosperity.org/content/insight-segregated-city/.

13. Fry and Taylor, *Rise of Residential Segregation.*

14. Gurda, *Making of Milwaukee.*

15. Ibid.; Jones, *Selma of the North.*

16. Gurda, *Making of Milwaukee*, 386.

17. Ibid.; Jones, *Selma of the North.*

18. Jones, *Selma of the North*, 257.

19. Gurda, "Milwaukee's Historic South Side."

20. Levine, *Suburban Sprawl.*

21. Levine, *Economic State of Milwaukee.*

22. "Wisconsin's Median Income Plummets, Census Figures Show," *Milwaukee Journal Sentinel*, September 21, 2011, http://www.jsonline.com/news/wisconsin/13032 5653.html. Note: income adjusted for inflation.

23. Levine, "Race and Male Employment in the Wake of the Great Recession," 2, 3.

24. Although white and Hispanic male employment rates have also taken a hit in the recession, African American male workers are doing far worse. In "Race and Male Employment in the Wake of the Great Recession," Levine notes: "In 1970, the black male employment rate among 25–54 year olds in Milwaukee was 9.7 percentage points lower than the white rate; by 2009, that gap had more than tripled, to 32.4 percentage points. In 1970 the black male employment was 5.4 points lower than the Hispanic rate in Milwaukee; by 2010, it was almost 20 points lower," 6.

25. In *Wisconsin's Mass Incarceration*, Pawasarat and Quinn assert that racialized mass incarceration in Milwaukee has been fueled by mandatory sentencing laws, ballooning nonviolent drug arrests, and targeted policing in poor black neighborhoods.

26. Pawasarat and Quinn, *Wisconsin's Mass Incarceration.*

27. Gilbert, "Divided Wisconsin."

28. Public Policy Forum, *Race Relations.*

29. Gurda, *Making of Milwaukee*, 437.

30. Tolan, *Riverwest.*

31. Gurda, *Making of Milwaukee.*

32. Ibid.; Schmidt, "Practices and Process of Neighborhood."

33. ESHAC began buying, renovating, and renting properties in Riverwest and, by the mid-90s, was one of the largest landlords in the community. The organization overextended itself in the housing market, fell behind on housing payments, and eventually dissolved due to financial challenges in 1998.

34. Schmidt, "Practices and Process of Neighborhood."

35. Although researchers employ different neighborhood typologies, Riverwest meets the criteria for diversity in recent studies of residential integration. For example, in "How Integrated Did We Become," Ellen categorizes neighborhoods as "integrated" if they are over 40 percent white with one minority group accounting for a minimum of 10 percent of the population. According to Fasenfest, Booza, and Metzger's typology in "Living Together," a "mixed multiethnic neighborhood" is one that is over 40 percent white, at least 10 percent black, and at least 10 percent other.

36. Levine, *Economic State of Milwaukee.*

37. Schmidt, "Practices and Process of Neighborhood."

38. Data on household income and educational attainment from American Community Survey, 2006–2010, U.S. Census Bureau, prepared by Social Explorer. The median household income estimate is based on data from five census tracts. All other statistics based on data from five tracts and one block group.

39. Hubka and Kenny, "Workers' Cottage"; Daniel O'Grady, personal correspondence, 2015.

40. I am referring to the area of the neighborhood between Humboldt Avenue and the river. The area north of Keefe Avenue along the river is more sparsely populated, is predominantly African American, and has more multifamily dwellings and a higher poverty rate than "Riverbest." Data on population density and race from 2000 census, U.S. Census Bureau; and data on family poverty from American Community Survey, 2005–2009, U.S. Census Bureau. Prepared by Social Explorer.

41. Data on household mobility from American Community Survey, 2006–2009, U.S. Census Bureau; and data on tenure (owner-occupied vs. renter-occupied) from 2010 census, U.S. Census Bureau. Prepared by Social Explorer.

42. Harding, *Living the Drama.*

43. I do not consider Beerline B as part of Riverwest, because most residents did not include it in their definition of the neighborhood. However, the Beerline B data is included in descriptive demographic statistics because the area is part of a census block group that includes blocks that are in Riverwest.

44. The socially constructed boundaries of the ghetto vary from person to person. Some Milwaukeeans use majority-black as the singular criteria for inclusion in the ghetto. Some situate Riverwest in the ghetto. Others assert that the ghetto truly starts farther west than Harambee, on the west side of I-43. Still others refer to the entire north side or northwest side as the ghetto.

45. Gurda, *Milwaukee: City of Neighborhoods.*

46. Borowski, "Rejuvenation Resentment"; Kenny and Zimmerman, "'Genuine American City.'"

47. Nachmias and Palen, "Membership in Neighborhood Associations."

48. In "What Is Gentrification?," Brown-Saracino observes that while most descriptions of gentrification include "an influx of capital and resultant displacement, and the transformation of local 'social character,' culture, amenities, and physical infrastructure" (12–13), scholars disagree on the relative importance of gentrification's causes, outcomes, or features of the process. Riverwest residents don't agree on a singular definition of gentrification. I encountered conceptualizations of gentrification that focused on the displacement of poor people; the displacement of nonwhite people; the arrival of condominiums, white people, or yuppies; cultural whitewashing and other forms of cultural displacement; changes in the economic character of the neighborhood; and changes in local aesthetics.

49. Peterson and Krivo note the importance of paying attention to the influence of neighboring communities: "Spatial location relative to more or less powerful and

more or less disadvantaged communities is critical to the dynamics that underlie and reproduce violent crime" ("Macro-Structural Analyses," 349).

50. I documented three instances of police officers who work in Milwaukee Police District Five characterizing the crime in Riverwest as primarily coming from west of the neighborhood. This information was shared at a block-watch meeting, a town hall meeting, and a District Five crime-trend-analysis meeting.

51. "Riverwest 24," *Decider*, Milwaukee edition, July 23, 2009, 31.

52. Kane, "Deaths Put Riverwest on Alert." This excerpt is from an article that considers the Riverwest community's response to the shooting deaths of two college students in the neighborhood within ten days.

53. "Garden at Kilbourn Park," http://victorygardenmke.wordpress.com/.

54. Levine, Williams, and Madison, "State of Black-Owned Businesses."

55. Cream City Collectives, "About," accessed March 1, 2010, http://creamcity collectives. wordpress.com/about/. Cream City Collectives was evicted and effectively shut down in 2012.

56. Greenbaum and Greenbaum, "Ecology of Social Networks"; Hunter and Suttles, "Community of Limited Liability"; Jacobs, *Death and Life*; Taylor, Gottfredson; Brower, "Block Crime and Fear."

57. Taylor, "Social Order of Street Blocks," 119.

58. Fine, "Sociology of the Local," 356.

59. In "Good Neighbours in Bad Neighbourhoods"—a comparative study of neighbor relations in a diverse "problem" neighborhood and a homogeneous, affluent neighborhood—Eijk finds overwhelming similarities in neighboring practices, despite the prevalence of narratives of difference and dissociation in the diverse neighborhood. She also finds that, much like in Riverwest, shared space powerfully shapes neighbor relations, and that the balance of proximity and privacy is central to such relations.

60. Jacobs, *Death and Life*; Taylor, "Social Order of Street Blocks."

61. Suttles, *Social Construction of Communities*.

62. Gieryn, "Space for Place," 477.

Chapter Three

1. Fine, "Sociology of the Local."

2. Ibid.; Harding, "Cultural Context"; Small, *Villa Victoria*.

3. Small, *Villa Victoria*.

4. Berrey, "Divided over Diversity"; Rich, "Neighborhood Boundaries"; Tach, "More Than Bricks and Mortar."

5. For example, Berrey, *Enigma of Diversity*; Marti and Emerson, "Rise of the Diversity Expert"; Mayorga-Gallo, *Behind the White Picket Fence*.

6. Berrey, *Enigma of Diversity*.

7. Ibid., 3.

8. Smith, "Racist Fliers."

9. Kane, "Deaths Put Riverwest on Alert."

10. Tolan, *Riverwest*, 187.

11. Wauwatosa is a city directly west of Milwaukee that many consider to be more stable and desirable than central-city neighborhoods like Riverwest.

12. Schmidt, "Practices and Process of Neighborhood."

13. Ibid.

14. Bushell and Geraci, *Riverwest Strategic Plan*.

15. "About the *Riverwest Currents*," *Riverwest Currents*, accessed May 1, 2015, http://www.riverwestcurrents.org/about.

16. "Riverwest Neighborhood Association Bylaws," article 3, section 1, http://my-rna.org/by-laws/. (Mission statement amendment approved August 14, 2007.)

17. Hunter and Suttles, "Community of Limited Liability."

18. Krulos, "Riverwest Six-Pack Tour"; Tolan, *Riverwest*.

19. *Shepherd Express*, "Locust Street Festival," June 13, 2010, http://shepherdexpress.com/article-11218-locust-street-festival.html.

20. Hart, "Neighborhood Spotlight: Jeremy Prach."

21. Riverwest 24, "The Goal Is to Strengthen Our Neighborhood," accessed May 1, 2010, http://www.riverwest24.com/about.

22. A.V. Club, "Events: Riverwest 24," accessed July 20, 2011, http://www.avclub.com/milwaukee/events/riverwest-24,254378.

23. Bell and Hartmann, "Diversity in Everyday Discourse."

24. In her study of diversity discourse in the Rogers Park neighborhood of Chicago, Berrey finds that some uses of diversity downplay racial and class inequalities or cloud out issues that poor people care about. As she argues, "Diversity discourse may be a rhetorical tool that elites wield at the expense of marginalized groups. It may be trope that white, middle-class people use to justify or downplay their place in a community" ("Divided over Diversity," 166).

25. Brown-Saracino, *Neighborhood That Never Changes*.

26. *Riverwest Currents*, "Neighbors Seek Answers from Candidates," February 2008, http://riverwestcurrents.org/2008/02/neighbors-seek-answers-from-candidates.html.

Chapter Four

1. Tönnies, *Gemeinschaft und Gesellschaft*; Durkheim, *Division of Labor*; Simmel, *Conflict*; Weber, *The City*.

2. For reviews of the literature on neighborhood effects, see Ellen and Turner, "Does Neighborhood Matter"; Sampson, Morenoff, and Gannon-Rowley, "Assessing Neighborhood Effects"; Small and Newman, "Urban Poverty."

3. Shaw and McKay, *Juvenile Delinquency*.

4. For a meta-analysis, see Pratt and Cullen, "Assessing Crime."

5. Bellair, "Social Interaction and Community Crime"; Guest, Kubrin, and Cover, "Heterogeneity and Harmony"; Hipp, Tita, and Greenbaum, "Drive-Bys and Trade-Ups"; Kubrin, "Making Order of Disorder"; Oliver, *Paradoxes of Integration*; Putnam, "*E Pluribus Unum*"; Sampson, "Collective Regulation"; Sampson and Groves, "Community Structure and Crime"; Sampson, Raudenbush, and Earls, "Neighborhoods and Violent Crime"; Warner and Pierce, "Reexamining Social Organization Theory"; Warner and Rountree, "Local Social Ties."

6. Small and Newman, "Urban Poverty."

7. Sampson, Morenoff, and Gannon-Rowley, "Assessing Neighborhood Effects," 473–74. Urban ethnographers have been particularly effective at identifying and refining hypothesized social mechanisms by illustrating how neighborhood conditions affect residents' lives in specific contexts. See, for example, Anderson, *Code of the Street*; Carr, "New Parochialism"; Duneier, *Sidewalk*; Gans, *Urban Villagers*; Harding, *Living the Drama*; Pattillo, *Black Picket Fences*; Small, *Villa Victoria*; Suttles, *Social Order of the Slum*; Venkatesh, *American Project*; and Whyte, *Street Corner Society*. Although urban scholars have made progress in illuminating social processes that explain how concentrated poverty produces a range of negative effects, we still know relatively little about why or how neighborhood heterogeneity matters for social organization. This may be due, in part, to the dominant focus on economically disadvantaged or racially homogeneous communities in urban ethnographic research.

8. Kornhauser, *Social Sources of Delinquency*.

9. In "Assessing Neighborhood Effects," Sampson, Morenoff, and Gannon-Rowley underscore the importance of looking to culture to shed light on key social organization mechanisms: "Although much effort has been put into understanding the structural backdrop to neighborhood social organization, we need a deeper focus on cultural, normative, and collective-action perspectives that attach meaning to how residents frame their commitment to places" (473–74).

10. Sampson, "Collective Regulation."

11. Sampson and Bartusch, "Legal Cynicism."

12. Becker, *Outsiders*, 9.

13. Feagin, "Community Disorganization."

14. Sampson, "Organized for What?"

15. Bell and Hartmann, "Diversity in Everyday Discourse."

16. In *Streetwise*, Anderson also finds the adoption of a "live and let live" credo associated with an acceptance of diverse lifestyles in a socially mixed urban neighborhood.

17. Neighbors sometimes name their tight-knit face block. I encountered the Pierce Street Pirates, the Booth Street Buccaneers, and the Pierce Street Parallelograms.

18. Browning, Feinberg, and Dietz, "Paradox of Social Organization"; Pattillo, "Sweet Mothers and Gangbangers"; Warner and Rountree, "Local Social Ties."

19. All of these examples are from conversations that I described—but did not directly quote—in my field notes.

20. I never heard about a police officer questioning a Latino/a or a black resident about his or her "choice" to live in Riverwest. This may reflect a broader racialized construction of residential fit: the belief that brown and black people belong in less-advantaged neighborhoods whereas white people choose them.

21. Sampson, "Organized for What?"

22. Anderson, *Code of the Street*.

23. See, for example, Pattillo, *Black on the Block*; Mayorga-Gallo, *Behind the White Picket Fence*; Berrey, *Enigma of Diversity*.

24. Harry's Tap is a pseudonym. I use pseudonyms for restaurants and bars when doing so is necessary to avoid identifying respondents.

25. Fine, "Adolescent Gossip"; Eder and Sanford, "Development of Interactional Norms."

26. Fine argues that local group meanings and practices extend beyond group boundaries, as people have ties to other networks and places. He advocates for "treating the local interaction scene as a means through which wider cultural relations and behavioral commonality are built" ("Sociology of the Local," 370).

27. Valverde, *Everyday Law on the Street*.

28. Carr, "The New Parochialism," 1252.

29. In *Turf Wars*, Modan finds that residents of a multiethnic gentrifying neighborhood in Washington, D.C., employ a similar set of neighborhood regulation strategies: the social control method and the institutional authority/law-and-order method. The latter method is associated with wealthy residents and an individualistic and suburban orientation.

30. Sampson, "Organized for What?"; Mayorga-Gallo, *Behind the White Picket Fence*.

31. Mayorga-Gallo, *Behind the White Picket Fence*.

32. In "The Concept(s) of Culture," Sewell uses the notion of an "official cultural map" in his theoretical exploration of how dominant groups exercise power through organizing difference (56).

33. Berrey, *Enigma of Diversity*; Chaskin, "Integration and Exclusion"; Freeman, *There Goes the 'Hood*; Mayorga-Gallo, *Behind the White Picket Fence*; Tach, "Diversity, Inequality, and Microsegregation."

34. Berrey, *Enigma of Diversity*, 150.

Chapter Five

1. Comment responding to Sharif Durhams, *Hubbub* (blog), *Milwaukee Journal Sentinel*, July 29, 2009, http://www.jsonline.com/blogs/news/51872397.html.

2. Dave Umhoefer, "1 Dead, 1 Wounded in Separate Overnight Shootings," *Milwaukee Journal Sentinel*, March 28, 2010, http://www.jsonline.com/news/milwaukee/89358107.html.

3. Suttles, *Social Construction of Communities*, 4.

4. Ibid.

5. For example, see Ross and Mirowsky, "Neighborhood Disadvantage"; Sampson and Raudenbush, "Seeing Disorder"; Skogan, *Disorder and Decline*; Swaroop and Morenoff, "Building Community."

6. Wilson and Kelling, "Broken Windows."

7. Skogan, *Disorder and Decline*.

8. Ibid.

9. Harcourt, *Illusion of Disorder*; Sampson and Raudenbush, "Seeing Disorder."

10. Hipp, "Resident Perceptions of Crime."

11. Skogan, *Disorder and Decline*, 5.

12. Kubrin, "Making Order of Disorder."

13. Sampson, *Great American City*, 131.

14. Sampson, "Disparity and Diversity"; Sampson and Raudenbush, "Seeing Disorder."

15. Sampson, *Great American City*.

16. Krysan, Farley, and Couper, "Eye of the Beholder"; Quillian and Pager, "Black Neighbors, Higher Crime?"

17. Drakulich, "Perceptions of Local Danger."

18. Krysan, Farley, and Couper, "Eye of the Beholder."

19. Ellen, *Sharing America's Neighborhoods*; Harris, "Racial and Socioeconomic Determinants of Neighborhood Desirability"; Harris, "Why Are Whites and Blacks Averse to Black Neighbors?"

20. Wacquant, "Urban Desolation."

21. For example, Harcourt and Ludwig, "Broken Windows."

22. Fagan and Davies, "Street Stops and Broken Windows."

23. Fagan, Geller, Davies, and West, "Street Stops and Broken Windows Revisited."

24. Sennett, *Uses of Disorder*.

25. Brien, "Graffiti Vandals Arrested."

26. "11 Arrested in Vandalism Spree," *Milwaukee Journal Sentinel*, January 17, 2007.

27. Brien, "Graffiti Vandals Arrested."

28. Dickinson, "Making of Space, Race and Place."

29. True Skool, "About True Skool," accessed May 20, 2016, http://www.true skool.org/#!about/ccjb.

30. The removal of the proposed ordinance from the committee's agenda effectively signaled its failure at that time.

31. Alderman Bob Donovan, press conference, accessed September 13, 2010, http://www.todaystmj4.com/news/local/98814684.html.

32. In *Naked City*, Zukin asserts that online media discourse shapes contemporary urban experiences in multiple ways. She acknowledges that analyzing this type of data and assessing its impact present numerous methodological challenges. Still, she asserts that "the circulation of images about the city, and about who has the right to be in

specific places in the city, from neighborhoods to public spaces, is fueled to a great extent by the self-referential online conversations in local blogs" (27).

33. In "'Litterers,'" Murphy finds that residents of a suburb use physical objects of disorder (i.e., litter) to construct the "other" as a subject of social disorder. Murphy asserts that this process is linked to residents' constructions of themselves as moral community caretakers.

34. Comments posted in response to Mary Louise Schumaker, "Alderman, Cultural Group Clash over South Side Mural," *Milwaukee Journal Sentinel*, July 19, 2010, http://www.jsonline.com/news/milwaukee/98797164.html. All quotes and online aliases are exactly as posted.

35. Dickinson, "Making of Space, Race and Place," 42.

36. Kefalas, *Working-Class Heroes*, 84.

37. Comments posted in response to Mary Louise Schumacher, "Witkowiak's Aide Calls Graffiti Art 'Garbage,'" *Art City* (blog), *Milwaukee Journal Sentinel*, July 29, 2010, http://www.jsonline.com/blogs/entertainment/99573669.html.

38. Ferrell, "Youth, Crime, and Cultural Space," 32.

39. Comments posted in response to Schumacher, "Witkowiak's Aide Calls Graffiti Art 'Garbage.'"

40. Such charges were launched in several of the discussions about the mural, including the thread associated with McGuire's email. For example, Mike Brenner posts, "if you can't tolerate living in milwaukee, leave! we don't want your small town ideas and 1950's thinking here anyway. you're just bringing the rest of [us] down with you."

41. Aptekar, "Visions of Public Space," 224.

42. In "The Good City," Amin also acknowledges the difficulty in assessing the impact of the use of public art to celebrate heterogeneity: "How successful these public expressions of ethnic and racial solidarity are in combating race hate is a matter of conjecture, but they provide a powerful official signal for what the public culture of a city should be" (1020).

43. *Milwaukee Journal Sentinel*, "Comments," March 31, 2010.

44. Roberts, "Race, Vagueness, and Policing," 790.

45. James, "Ghetto as a Race-Making Situation," 427.

46. Those residents who lived in Riverwest when gang activity was a dominant force in neighborhood life (late 1980s to '90s) recall a time when a group of young black or Latino men was a potent indicator of threat. The neighborhood is not entirely free from gang-affiliated violence and trouble, but the perception that active gangs are no longer based in Riverwest has complicated local interpretations of danger. For example, the East Side Mafioso, a Latino gang with many Puerto Rican members, once controlled Holton. Although there are signs that the gang still exists, most of the Latino gang activity is now concentrated on the city's south side. Riverwesterners today see black gangs as a more significant threat because of their presumed proximal location—just across Holton.

47. Anderson, "White Space," 13.

48. James, "Ghetto as a Race-Making Situation," 427.

49. Anderson, *Streetwise*.

50. Brekhus, "Sociology of the Unmarked," 36.

51. Hartigan, *Racial Situations*, 14.

52. Oliver, *Paradoxes of Integration*; Oliver and Wong, "Intergroup Prejudice in Multiethnic Settings"; Sigelman and Welch, "Contact Hypothesis Revisited."

53. Anderson, "White Space," 19.

54. Bell and Hartmann, "Diversity in Everyday Discourse," 907.

55. In "Diversity in Everyday Discourse," Bell and Hartmann offer this useful framing of the implied "we" (i.e., hosts) in their analysis of diversity discourse in the United States.

56. I acknowledge that some of those who talk about a white neighborhood presence as a stabilizing force may be referring to the dynamics of a housing market in which the value of whiteness is reflected in housing values.

57. Paul's assessment of dominant cultural understandings of the "good" neighborhood is supported by the research I describe at the beginning of this chapter, which finds that the racial composition of a neighborhood significantly influences its desirability rating and perceptions of disorder.

58. Bonilla-Silva, Goar, and Embrick, "When Whites Flock Together."

59. Bourdieu, *Distinction*; Newman, *No Shame in My Game*; Schwalbe et al., "Generic Processes in the Reproduction of Inequality."

Chapter Six

1. Romell, "Drinking Deeply Ingrained in Wisconsin's Culture."

2. Gurda, *Making of Milwaukee*.

3. Sawyer, "Drunkest American Cities."

4. Kanny, Liu, and Brewer, *Binge Drinking*; Black and Paltzer, *Burden of Excessive Alcohol Use*.

5. Romell, "Drinking Ingrained in Wisconsin's Culture."

6. The Black and Paltzer *Burden of Excessive Alcohol Use* report was covered in several national media outlets, including National Public Radio: Audie Cornish and Eliza Barclay, "Binge Drinking Sticks Wisconsin with a Hefty Tab," *All Things Considered*, March 14, 2013.

7. City of Milwaukee Health Department, http://city.milwaukee.gov/MAPP-Community-Health-Assessment.

8. Room, "Stigma and Alcohol and Drug Use."

9. Hipp, "Resident Perceptions of Crime"; Ross and Mirowsky, "Neighborhood Disadvantage"; Sampson and Raudenbush, "Seeing Disorder"; Sampson and Raudenbush, "Systematic Social Observation."

10. Gusfield, *Contested Meanings*.

11. Ibid.

12. Ibid., 79.

13. Hipp, "Micro-structure in Micro-neighborhoods."

14. Valverde, *Everyday Law on the Street*, 67.

15. Skogan, *Disorder and Decline*.

16. Pattillo, *Black on the Block*.

17. Tach, "More Than Bricks and Mortar."

18. Gusfield, *Contested Meanings*, 173.

19. Dixon, Levine, and McAuley, "Locating Impropriety."

20. Social Issues Research Centre, *Social Aspects of Drinking*.

21. Ten percent of residents responding to a neighborhood health assessment survey identified "alcohol misuse" as an issue that negatively impacts their personal or family well-being (Riverwest Health Initiative, *Riverwest Community Health Assessment*, 2004–06).

22. Gusfield, *Contested Meanings*; Mattson, "Urban Ethnography's 'Saloon Problem.'"

23. See Pescosolido et al., "Rethinking Theoretical Approaches to Stigma," for a summary of research findings on the stigma of mental illness.

24. Schomerus et al., "Public Attitudes about Mental Illness."

25. White, "Long-Term Strategies"; Link and Phelan, "Labeling and Stigma."

26. Pescosolido et al., "Rethinking Theoretical Approaches to Stigma," and Berkman et al., "From Social Integration to Health," draw on theoretical and empirical work to develop conceptual models of the ways in which social networks influence health and health-related stigma.

27. Dilulio, "Broken Bottles."

28. See, for example, Block and Block, "Space, Place and Crime"; Gruenewald et al., "Alcohol Outlets and Violent Assaults"; Roncek and Maier, "Bars, Blocks, and Crimes"; Roncek and Pravatiner, "Taverns Enhance Crime"; White, Gainey, and Triplett, "Alcohol Outlets and Crime."

29. The number of these types of neighborhood establishments fluctuated during my multiple years of fieldwork. These are based on counts in 2010.

30. Oldenburg, *Great Good Place*.

31. Ibid.

32. In "Urban Nightlife," Grazian argues that urban scholars' recent emphasis on the social capital-building potential of third places like bars and clubs has directed their attention away from race and class barriers to participation in certain nightlife scenes.

33. In "The White Space," Anderson describes this work as an individual's performance or "dance" to demonstrate that negative stereotypes about race do not apply (13).

34. In "Characteristics of Malt Liquor Beer Drinkers," Bluthenthal and colleagues give some substance to these stereotypical associations based on their study of alcohol consumers in a low-income Los Angeles neighborhood, finding that malt liquor drinkers had higher rates of daily or near-daily drinking than did hard liquor or regular beer drinkers, and were more likely to be homeless and unemployed.

35. Alaniz and Wilkes, "Pro-Drinking Messages."

36. Desmond, "Bottoms Up."

37. Suttles, *Social Order of the Slum.*

38. In *Paths of Neighborhood Change*, Taub, Taylor, and Dunham similarly find that interpretations of the physical environment are influenced by residents' sense that the neighborhood is improving or declining. In "A Test of the Routine Activities and Neighborhood Attachment Explanations for Bias in Disorder Perceptions," Wallace finds that neighborhood attachment and routine guardianship activities (e.g., watching a neighbor's property) influence perceptions of disorder.

Chapter Seven

1. Recent assessments of neighborhood effects research have identified the importance of examining how and why residential contexts are experienced differently by different groups of people. See, for example, Harding et al., "Unpacking Neighborhood Influences"; Sharkey and Faber, "For Whom Do Residential Contexts Matter?; Small and Feldman, "Ethnographic Evidence and Neighbourhood Effects."

2. In "Unpacking Neighborhood Influences," Harding and colleagues argue that behavioral adaptations to the challenges young people face in poor neighborhoods are a key source of neighborhood effect heterogeneity.

3. See, for example, Pattillo, *Black Picket Fences*; Small, *Villa Victoria*; Stolle, Soroka, and Johnston, "When Does Diversity Erode Trust?"

4. See, for example, Harding, *Living the Drama*; Small, *Villa Victoria*.

Chapter Eight

1. "Is River West Doomed," September 12, 2009, http://www.city-data.com/forum/milwaukee/760557-river-west-doomed.html.

2. This story is a composite of several residents' stories. It reflects patterns of block-level relationship development that emerged in my field observations.

3. Blau, "Macrosociological Theory of Social Structure."

4. In *Conflict and the Web of Group Affiliations*, theorist Georg Simmel advanced a series of propositions about the positive functions of conflict that were later rearticulated and extended by Lewis Coser in *The Functions of Social Conflict*.

5. Germain and Radice, "Cosmopolitanism by Default," 122.

6. Dovidio, Saguy, and Shnabel, "Cooperation and Conflict."

7. Aptekar, "Visions of Public Space."

8. Baumgartner, *Moral Order of a Suburb*.

9. In Maly's study of integrated neighborhoods, *Beyond Segregation*, he also finds a link between conflict and stability in the Uptown neighborhood in Chicago: "Conflict is proving functional in the sense of stabilizing the neighborhood by helping groups define the important issues, and leading to group cohesion and the formation of alliance" (85).

10. Berrey, "Divided over Diversity"; Mayorga-Gallo, *Behind the White Picket Fence*; Pattillo, *Black on the Block*; Tach, "Diversity, Inequality, and Microsegregation."

11. In "Generic Processes in the Reproduction of Inequality," Schwalbe and colleagues identify a set of interaction-based processes through which inequalities are created and reproduced in particular settings.

12. Sewell, "Concept(s) of Culture," 72.

13. Ridgeway, "Why Status Matters."

14. Fine, "Sociology of the Local," 359.

15. Amin, "Ethnicity and the Multicultural City," 970.

16. Sewell, "Concept(s) of Culture," 173.

17. Putnam, "*E Pluribus Unum*," 164.

18. Some integration scholars concur. For example, in *White Flight/Black Flight*, Woldoff finds that the concerns about disorder, incivilities, and differences in values prompt the flight of some residents. She concludes that shared values are essential for the stability of integrated communities. Woldoff suggests that engaged residents should educate newcomers about local standards and encourage them to follow a clear set of community rules.

19. Young, *Justice and Difference*.

20. Pattillo, *Black on the Block*, 285.

21. Schwalbe et al., "Generic Processes."

22. An examination of the impact of neighborhood heterogeneity in Riverwest on children who grow up in the neighborhood would provide a powerful test of these claims. It would generate an illustrative comparison with Harding's findings (reported in *Living the Drama*) about the negative impacts of cultural heterogeneity on children raised in poor and working-class neighborhoods.

23. Amin, "Ethnicity and the Multicultural City," 974.

24. In *The Ordeal of Integration*, Patterson argues, "If the integration of two groups legally and socially separated for more than 350 years does not produce friction, it is the surest sign that no meaningful change has taken place" (52).

25. Chaskin, "Integration and Exclusion"; Chaskin and Joseph, "Building 'Community'"; Oakley, Fraser, and Bazuin, "Imagined Self-Sufficient Communities"; Tach, "More Than Bricks and Mortar."

26. Ridgeway, "Why Status Matters."

27. I am less confident in the long-term maintenance of diversity in Riverwest. According to the 2010 U.S. Census, for the first time since 1960, the number of white residents in the neighborhood increased and the number of black and Latino/a residents decreased. This recent demographic shift might represent a change in the types of people choosing to move into the neighborhood. If this shift becomes a trend and those who move out are increasingly replaced by white in-movers, Riverwest will become a more racially homogeneous community (see Freeman and Braconi, "Gentrification and Displacement"). Even if the majority of those moving in are selecting Riverwest because of its racial diversity, if that group is disproportionately white, the result is the same: a whiter neighborhood. Alternatively, it may be that the local

culture is already changing in ways that more closely align with white interests or a particular set of preferences. If local culture continues to serve as a migration filter, this may decrease racial diversity by influencing who chooses to stay, who moves out, and who moves in.

Appendix

1. Public Policy Forum, *Interdistrict Chapter 220.*
2. Fine, "Sociology of the Local," 361.
3. Ellen, "How Integrated Did We Become"; Ellen, Horn, and O'Regan, "Pathways of Integration"; Fasenfest, Booza, and Metzger, "Living Together"; Lee, Iceland, and Sharp, *Diversity Goes Local.*
4. Nyden et al., "Conclusion."
5. Small, "Lost in Translation"; Small, " 'How Many Cases Do I Need?' "
6. Small, "Lost in Translation," 395.
7. Small, *Villa Victoria*, 186.
8. Gieryn, "Space for Place."
9. Corsaro, "Entering the Child's World."
10. Emerson, Fretz, and Shaw, *Writing Ethnographic Fieldnotes.*
11. Duneier, *Sidewalk*; Jacobs, *Death and Life.*
12. Weiss, *Learning from Strangers.*
13. Zukin, *Naked City*, 27.
14. Emerson, Fretz, and Shaw, *Writing Ethnographic Fieldnotes.*
15. Emerson, "Craft of Fieldwork."
16. Charmaz and Mitchell, "Grounded Theory."
17. Maxwell, *Qualitative Research Design.*
18. Fine, "When of Theory," 82.
19. Becker, "Epistemology of Qualitative Research."
20. Weiss, *Learning from Strangers.*
21. Katz, "Ethnography's Warrants."

Bibliography

Alaniz, Maria Luisa, and Chris Wilkes. "Pro-Drinking Messages and Message
Environments for Young Adults: The Case of Alcohol Industry Advertising in
African-American, Latino and Native American Communities. *Journal of Public
Health Policy* 19 (1998): 447–72.

Amin, Ash. "Ethnicity and the Multicultural City: Living with Diversity."
Environment and Planning A 34 (2002): 959–80.

———. "The Good City." *Urban Studies* 43 (2006): 1009–23.

Anderson, Elijah. *The Code of the Street: Decency, Violence, and the Moral Life of the
Inner City*. New York: W. W. Norton, 1999.

———. *Streetwise: Race, Class, and Change in an Urban Community*. Chicago:
University of Chicago Press, 1990.

———. "The White Space." *Sociology of Race and Ethnicity* 1 (2015): 10–21.

Aptekar, Sofya. "Visions of Public Space: Reproducing and Resisting Social
Hierarchies in a Community Garden." *Sociological Forum* 30 (2015): 209–27.

Baumgartner, Mary Pat. *The Moral Order of a Suburb*. New York: Oxford University
Press, 1988.

Becker, Howard S. "The Epistemology of Qualitative Research." In *Essays on
Ethnography and Human Development*, edited by Richard Jessor, Anne Colby, and
Richard A. Schweder, 53–71. Chicago: University of Chicago Press, 1966.

———. *Outsiders: Studies in the Sociology of Deviance*. New York: Free Press, 1963.

Bell, Joyce M., and Douglas Hartmann. "Diversity in Everyday Discourse: The
Cultural Ambiguities and Consequences of 'Happy Talk.' " *American Sociological
Review* 72 (2007): 895–914.

Bellair, Paul E. "Social Interaction and Community Crime: Examining the
Importance of Neighbor Networks." *Criminology* 35 (1997): 677–703.

Berkman, Lisa F., Thomas A. Glass, Ian Brissette, and Teresa E. Seeman. "From
Social Integration to Health: Durkheim in the New Millennium." *Social Science
and Medicine* 51 (2000): 843–57.

Berrey, Ellen C. "Divided over Diversity: Political Discourse in a Chicago
Neighborhood." *City and Community* 4 (2005): 143–70.

———. *The Enigma of Diversity: The Language of Race and the Limits of Racial Justice*.
Chicago: University of Chicago Press, 2015.

Black, Penny D., and Jason T. Paltzer. *The Burden of Excessive Alcohol Use in
Wisconsin*. University of Wisconsin Population Health Institute, March 2013.

Blau, Peter M. "A Macrosociological Theory of Social Structure." *American Journal
of Sociology* 83 (1977): 26–54.

Block, Richard L., and Carolyn R. Block. "Space, Place and Crime: Hot Spot Areas and Hot Places of Liquor-Related Crime." In *Crime and Place*, edited by John E. Eck and David Weisburd, 145–84. Monsey, N.Y.: Criminal Justice Press, 1995.

Bluthenthal, Ricky N., Didra Brown Taylor, Norma Guzman-Becerra, and Paul L. Robinson. "Characteristics of Malt Liquor Beer Drinkers in a Low-Income, Racial Minority Community Sample." *Alcoholism: Clinical and Experimental Research* 29 (2005): 402–9.

Bonilla-Silva, Eduardo, and David G. Embrick. "'Every Place Has a Ghetto . . .': The Significance of Whites' Social and Residential Segregation." *Journal of Symbolic Interaction* 30 (2007): 323–46.

Bonilla-Silva, Eduardo, Carla Goar, and David G. Embrick. "When Whites Flock Together: White Habitus and the Social Psychology of Whites' Social and Residential Segregation from Blacks." *Critical Sociology* 32 (2006): 229–54.

Borer, Michael Ian. "The Location of Culture: The Urban Culturalist Perspective." *City and Community* 5 (2006): 173–97.

Borowski, Greg. "Rejuvenation Resentment." *Milwaukee Journal Sentinel*, May 27, 2001, 01A.

Bourdieu, Pierre. *Distinction: A Social Critique of the Judgment of Taste*. Paris: Les Editions de Minuit, 1979. Reprint, Cambridge, Mass.: Harvard University Press, 1984.

Brekhus, Wayne H. "A Sociology of the Unmarked: Redirecting Our Focus." *Sociological Theory* 16 (1998): 34–51.

Brien, Stephanie. "Riverwest Graffiti Vandals Arrested." *University of Wisconsin–Milwaukee Post*, January 22, 2007.

Brown-Saracino, Japonica. "How Places Shape Identity: The Origins of Distinctive LBQ Identities in Four Small U.S. Cities." *American Journal of Sociology* 121 (2015): 1–63.

———. *A Neighborhood That Never Changes: Gentrification, Social Preservation, and the Search for Authenticity*. Chicago: University of Chicago Press, 2009.

———. "Social Preservationists and the Quest for Authentic Community." *City and Community* 3 (2004): 135–56.

———. "What Is Gentrification? Definitions and Key Concepts." In *The Gentrification Debates*, edited by Japonica Brown-Saracino, 11–18. New York: Routledge, 2010.

Browning, Christopher R., Seth L. Feinberg, and Robert D. Dietz. "The Paradox of Social Organization: Networks, Collective Efficacy, and Violent Crime in Urban Neighborhoods." *Social Forces* 83 (2004): 503–34.

Bushell, Vince, and Jeanne Geraci. *Riverwest Lower Eastside Neighborhood Strategic Plan, 2000–2004*. Milwaukee, Wis.: Riverwest YMCA Housing Initiative, 2000.

Carr, Patrick J. "The New Parochialism: The Implications of the Beltway Case for Arguments concerning Informal Social Control." *American Journal of Sociology* 108 (2003): 1249–91.

Charles, Camille Zubrinsky. "The Dynamics of Racial Residential Segregation." *Annual Review of Sociology* 29 (2003): 167–207.

Charmaz, Kathy, and Richard G. Mitchell. "Grounded Theory in Ethnography." In *Handbook of Ethnography*, edited by Paul Atkinson, Amanda Coffey, Sarah Delamont, John Lofland, and Lyn Lofland, 160–74. London: Sage, 2001.

Chaskin, Robert J. *Defining Community Capacity: A Framework and Implications from a Comprehensive Community Initiative.* Chicago: Chapin Hall Center for Children, 1999.

———. "Integration and Exclusion: Urban Poverty, Public Housing Reform, and the Dynamics of Neighborhood Restructuring." *Annals of the American Academy of Political and Social Science* 64 (2013): 237–67.

Chaskin, Robert J., and Mark L. Joseph. "Building 'Community' in Mixed-Income Developments: Assumptions, Approaches, and Early Experiences." *Urban Affairs Review* 45 (2010): 299–335.

Christensen, Jan. "Liminal Spaces." *Riverwest Currents*, November 2004, http://riverwestcurrents.org/2004/11/liminal-spaces.html.

Corsaro, William. "Entering the Child's World: Research Strategies for Field Entry and Data Collection in a Pre-school Setting." In *Ethnography and Language in Educational Settings*, edited by Judith L. Green and Cynthia Wallat, 117–46. Norwood, N.J.: Ablex, 1981.

Coser, Lewis. *The Functions of Social Conflict.* New York: Free Press, 1956.

Deener, Andrew. *Venice: A Contested Bohemia in Los Angeles.* Chicago: University of Chicago Press, 2012.

Desmond, Matthew. "Bottoms Up." *Contexts* 8 (2009): 69–71.

De Souza Briggs, Xavier. "'Some of My Best Friends Are . . .': Interracial Friendships, Class, and Segregation in America." *City and Community* 6 (2007): 263–90.

Dickinson, Maggie. "The Making of Space, Race and Place: New York City's War on Graffiti, 1970–the Present." *Critique of Anthropology* 28 (2008): 27–45.

Dilulio, John J., Jr. "Broken Bottles: Alcohol, Disorder, and Crime." *Brookings Review*, Spring 1996, 14–17.

Dixon, John, Mark Levine, and Rob McAuley. "Locating Impropriety: Street Drinking, Moral Order, and the Ideological Dilemma of Public Space." *Political Psychology* 27 (2006): 187–206.

Dovidio, John F., Tamar Saguy, and Nurit Shnabel. "Cooperation and Conflict within Groups: Bridging Intragroup and Intergroup Processes." *Journal of Social Issues* 65 (2009): 429–49.

Drakulich, Kevin M. "Perceptions of the Local Danger Posed by Crime: Race, Disorder, Informal Control, and the Police." *Social Science Research* 42 (2013): 611–32.

Dreier, Peter, John Mollenkopf, and Todd Swanstrom. *Place Matters: Metropolitics for the Twenty-First Century.* Lawrence: University Press of Kansas, 2004.

Du Bois, W. E. B. *The Philadelphia Negro: A Social Study.* 1899. Reprint, Philadelphia: University of Pennsylvania Press, 1996.

Duneier, Mitchell. *Sidewalk*. New York: Farrar, Strauss and Giroux, 1999.

Durkheim Émile. *The Division of Labor in Society*. 1893. Reprint, New York: Free Press, 1984.

Eder, Donna, and Stephanie Sanford. "The Development and Maintenance of Interactional Norms among Early Adolescents." In *Sociological Studies of Child Development*, vol. 1, edited by Patricia Adler and Peter Adler, 283–300. Greenwich, Conn.: JAI Press, 1986.

Eijk, Gwen van. "Good Neighbours in Bad Neighbourhoods: Narratives of Dissociation and Practices of Neighbouring in a 'Problem' Place." *Urban Studies* 49 (2012): 3006–23.

Ellen, Ingrid Gould. "How Integrated Did We Become during the 1990s?" In *Fragile Rights within Cities: Governments, Housing and Fairness*, edited by John Goering, 123–42. Lanham, Md.: Rowman and Littlefield, 2007.

———. *Sharing America's Neighborhoods: The Prospects for Stable, Racial Integration*. Cambridge, Mass.: Harvard University Press, 2000.

Ellen, Ingrid Gould, Karen Horn, and Katherine O'Regan. "Pathways of Integration: Examining Changes in the Prevalence of Racially Integrated Neighborhoods." *Cityscape* 14 (2012): 33–54.

Ellen, Ingrid Gould, and Margery Austin Turner. "Does Neighborhood Matter: Assessing Recent Evidence." *Housing Policy Debate* 8 (2001): 833–66.

Emerson, Robert M. "Four Ways to Improve the Craft of Fieldwork." *Journal of Contemporary Ethnography* 16 (1987): 69–89.

Emerson, Robert M., Rachel I. Fretz, and Linda L. Shaw. *Writing Ethnographic Fieldnotes*. Chicago: University of Chicago Press, 1995.

Fagan, Jeffrey A., and Garth Davies. "Street Stops and Broken Windows: Terry, Race, and Disorder in New York City." *Fordham Urban Law Journal* 28 (2000): 457–504.

Fagan, Jeffrey A., Amanda Geller, Garth Davies, and Valerie West. "Street Stops and Broken Windows Revisited: The Demography and Logic of Proactive Policing in a Safe and Changing City." In *Race Ethnicity and Policing: New and Essential Readings*, edited by Stephan K. Rice and Michael D. White, 309–49. New York: New York University Press, 2010.

Fasenfest, David, Jason Booza, and Kurt Metzger. "Living Together: A New Look at Racial and Ethnic Integration in Metropolitan Neighborhoods, 1990–2000." In *Redefining Urban and Suburban America: Evidence from Census 2000*, edited by Alan Berube, Bruce Katz, and Robert Lang, 93–117. Washington, D.C.: Brookings Institution, 2004.

Feagin, Joe. "Community Disorganization: Some Critical Notes." *Sociological Inquiry* 43 (1973): 123–46.

Ferrell, Jeff. "Youth, Crime, and Cultural Space." *Social Justice* 24 (1997): 21–38.

Fine, Gary Alan. "Adolescent Gossip as Social Interaction." In *Children's Worlds and Children's Language*, edited by Jenny Cook-Gumperz, William A. Corsaro, and Jürgen Streeck, 405–23. Berlin: Mouton de Gruyter, 1986.

———. "The Sociology of the Local: Action and Its Publics." *Sociological Theory* 28 (2010): 355–76.

———. "The When of Theory." In *Workshop on Scientific Foundations of Qualitative Research*, edited by Charles Ragin, Joane Nagel, and Patricia White, 81–82. Washington D.C.: National Science Foundation, 2004.

Fischer, Claude S., Gretchen Stockmayer, Jon Stiles, and Michael Hout. "Distinguishing the Geographic Levels and Social Dimensions of U.S. Metropolitan Segregation, 1960–2000." *Demography* 41 (2004): 37–59.

Freeman, Lance. *There Goes the 'Hood: Views of Gentrification from the Ground Up.* Philadelphia: Temple University Press, 2006.

Freeman, Lance, and Frank Braconi. "Gentrification and Displacement." *Journal of the American Planning Association* 70 (2004): 39–52.

Fry, Richard, and Paul Taylor. *The Rise of Residential Segregation by Income.* Washington, D.C.: Pew Research Center, 2012.

Gans, Herbert. *The Urban Villagers: Group and Class in the Life of Italian-Americans.* Glencoe, N.Y.: Free Press, 1962.

Germain, Annick, and Martha Radice. "Cosmopolitanism by Default: Public Sociability in Montréal." In *Cosmopolitan Urbanism*, edited by J. Binnie, J. Holloway, S. Millington, and C. Young, 112–30. London: Routledge, 2006.

Gieryn, Thomas F. "A Space for Place in Sociology." *Annual Review of Sociology* 26 (2000): 463–96.

Gilbert, Craig. "Democratic, Republican Voters Worlds Apart in Divided Wisconsin." *Milwaukee Journal Sentinel*, May 3, 2013, http://www.jsonline.com /news/statepolitics/democratic-republican-voters-worlds-apart-in-divided -wisconsin-b99249564z1-255883361.html.

Gould, Roger V. *Insurgent Identities: Class Community and Protest in Paris from 1848 to the Commune.* Chicago: University of Chicago Press, 1993.

Grazian, David. "Urban Nightlife, Social Capital and the Public Life of Cities." *Sociological Forum* 24 (2009): 908–17.

Greenbaum, Susan D., and Paul E. Greenbaum. "The Ecology of Social Networks in Four Urban Neighborhoods." *Social Networks* 7 (1985): 47–76.

Gregory, Steven. *Black Corona*. Princeton, N.J.: Princeton University Press, 1998.

Gruenewald, Paul J., Bridget Freisthler, Lillian Remer, Elizabeth A. Lascala, and Andrew Treno. "Ecological Models of Alcohol Outlets and Violent Assaults: Crime Potentials and Geospatial Analysis." *Addiction* 101 (2006): 666–77.

Guest, Avery M., Charis E. Kubrin, and Jane K. Cover. "Heterogeneity and Harmony: Neighboring Relationships among Whites in Ethnically-Diverse Neighborhoods in Seattle." *Urban Studies* 43 (2008): 501–26.

Gurda, John. *The Making of Milwaukee*. Milwaukee, Wis.: Milwaukee County Historical Society, 1999.

———. *Milwaukee: City of Neighborhoods*. Menomonee Falls, Wis.: Historic Milwaukee, Inc., 2015.

———. "Milwaukee's Historic South Side: Poles Then, Latinos Now." *Milwaukee Journal Sentinel*, August 2, 2013, http://www.jsonline.com/news/opinion/milwaukees -historic-south-side-poles-then-latinos-now-b9965192z1-218125601.html.

Gusfield, Joseph R. *Contested Meanings: The Construction of Alcohol Problems.* Madison: University of Wisconsin Press, 1996.

Harcourt, Bernard E. *Illusion of Order: The False Promise of Broken Windows Policing.* Cambridge, Mass.: Harvard University Press, 2001.

Harcourt, Bernard E., and Jens Ludwig. "Broken Windows: New Evidence from New York City and a Five-City Social Experiment." *University of Chicago Law Review* 73 (2006): 271–320.

Harding, David J. "Cultural Context, Sexual Behavior and Romantic Relationships in Disadvantaged Neighborhoods." *American Sociological Review* 72 (2007): 341–64.

———. *Living the Drama: Community, Conflict, and Culture among Inner-City Boys.* Chicago: University of Chicago Press, 2010.

Harding David J., Lisa Gennetian, Christopher Winship, Lisa Sanbonmatsu, and Jeffrey Kling. "Unpacking Neighborhood Influences on Education Outcomes: Setting the Stage for Future Research." In *Whither Opportunity: Rising Inequality and the Uncertain Life Chances of Low-Income Children*, edited by Greg J. Duncan and Richard J. Murnane, 277–96. New York: Russell Sage, 2011.

Harris, David R. " 'Property Values Drop When Blacks Move In, Because . . .': Racial and Socioeconomic Determinants of Neighborhood Desirability." *American Sociological Review* 64 (1999): 461–79.

———. "Why Are Whites and Blacks Averse to Black Neighbors?" *Social Science Research* 30 (2001): 100–116.

Hart, Jason. "Neighborhood Spotlight: Jeremy Prach." *Riverwest Currents*, July 2008, http://riverwestcurrents.org/2008/07/neighbor-spotlight-%E2%80%A2-july -2008-%E2%80%A2-jeremy-prach.html.

Hartigan, John, Jr. *Racial Situations: Class Predicaments of Whiteness in Detroit.* Princeton, N.J.: Princeton University Press, 1999.

Hipp, John R. "Micro-structure in Micro-neighborhoods: A New Social Distance Measure, and Its Effect on Individual and Aggregated Perceptions of Crime and Disorder." *Social Networks* 32 (2010): 148–59.

———. "Resident Perceptions of Crime: How Much Is 'Bias' and How Much Is Micro-neighborhood Effect?" *Criminology* 48 (2010): 475–508.

Hipp, John R., George E. Tita, and Robert T. Greenbaum. "Drive-Bys and Trade-Ups: Examining the Directionality of the Crime and Residential Instability Relationship." *Social Forces* 87 (2009): 1777–812.

Hubka, Thomas C., and Judith T. Kenny. "The Workers' Cottage in Milwaukee's Polish Community: Housing and the Process of Americanization, 1870–1920." *Perspectives in Vernacular Architecture* 8 (2000): 33–52.

Hunter, Albert J., and Gerald D. Suttles, ed. "The Expanding Community of Limited Liability." In *The Social Construction of Communities*, 44–80. Chicago: University of Chicago Press, 1972.

Iceland, John. *Where We Live Now: Immigration and Race in the United States.* Berkeley: University of California Press, 2009.

Iceland, John, Daniel H. Weinberg, and Erika Steinmetz. *Racial and Ethnic Residential Segregation in the United States, 1980–2000.* U.S. Census Bureau, Special Report Series, CENSR # 3, 2002.

Jacobs, Jane. *The Death and Life of Great American Cities.* New York: Random House, 1961.

James, David R. "The Racial Ghetto as a Race-Making Situation: The Effects of Residential Segregation on Racial Inequalities and Racial Identity." *Law and Social Inquiry* 19 (1994): 407–32.

Jones, Patrick D. *The Selma of the North: Civil Rights Insurgency in Milwaukee.* Cambridge, Mass.: Harvard University Press, 2010.

Kane, Eugene. "Deaths Put Riverwest on Alert." *Milwaukee Journal Sentinel,* July 26, 2009, B3.

———. "Racist Fliers Aside, Fest Could Use a Better Mix." *Milwaukee Journal Sentinel,* June 30, 2005, B1.

Kanny, Dafna, Yong Liu, and Robert D. Brewer. "Binge Drinking—United States, 2009." *Morbidity and Mortality Weekly Report* 60 (2011).

Katz, Jack. "Ethnography's Warrants." *Sociological Methods and Research* 25 (1997): 391–423.

Kefalas, Maria. *Working-Class Heroes: Protecting Home, Community, and Nation in a Chicago Neighborhood.* Berkeley: University of California Press, 2003.

Kenny, Judith T., and Jeffrey Zimmerman. "Constructing the 'Genuine American City': Neo-Traditionalism, New Urbanism and Neo-Liberalism in the Remaking of Downtown Milwaukee." *Cultural Geographies* 11 (2004): 238–58.

Kneebone, Elizabeth, Carey Nadeau, and Alan Berube. *The Re-emergence of Concentrated Poverty: Metropolitan Trends in the 2000s.* Washington D.C.: Metropolitan Policy Program, Brookings Institution, 2011.

Kornhauser, Ruth. *Social Sources of Delinquency.* Chicago: University of Chicago Press, 1978.

Krulos, Tea. "Riverwest Six-Pack Tour," Riverwest24 Blog, July 3, 2008.

Krysan, Maria, Reynolds Farley, and Mick P. Couper. "In the Eye of the Beholder: Racial Beliefs and Residential Segregation." *Du Bois Review* 5 (2008): 5–26.

Kubrin, Charis E. "Making Order of Disorder: A Call for Conceptual Clarity." *Criminology and Public Policy* 7 (2008): 203–14.

———. "Racial Heterogeneity and Crime: Measuring Static and Dynamic Effects." *Research in Community Sociology* 10 (2000): 189–218.

Lamont, Michele, and Virág Molnár. "The Study of Boundaries in Social Science." *Annual Review of Sociology* 28 (2001): 167–95.

Laurence, James. "The Effect of Ethnic Diversity and Community Disadvantage on Social Cohesion: A Multi-level Analysis of Social Capital and Interethnic Relations in UK Communities." *European Sociological Review* 27 (2011): 70–89.

Lee, Barrett A., John Iceland, and Gregory Sharp. *Racial and Ethnic Diversity Goes Local: Charting Change in American Communities over Three Decades*. US2010 Project Report Series. New York: Russell Sage Foundation, 2012.

Levine, Marc V. *The Economic State of Milwaukee's Inner City: 1970–2000*. University of Wisconsin–Milwaukee Center for Economic Development, 2002, http://www4.uwm.edu/ced/publications/innercity2002.cfm.

———. "Race and Male Employment in the Wake of the Great Recession: Black Male Employment Rates in Milwaukee and the Nation's Largest Metro Areas, 2010." Working paper, Center for Economic Development, University of Wisconsin–Milwaukee, January 2012, https://www4.uwm.edu/ced/publications .cfm.

———. *Racial Disparities, Socioeconomic Status, and Racialized Politics in Milwaukee and Wisconsin: An Analysis of Senate Factors Five and Six of the Voting Rights Act.* Expert Report Submitted on Behalf of Plaintiffs in *Frank v. Walker*, Civil Action No. 2:11-cv-01128(LA), May 18, 2012, https://www.aclu.org/sites/default/files /assets/2012.05.18_marc_levine_expert_report.pdf.

———. *Suburban Sprawl and the "Secession" of the Affluent: Metropolitan Polarization in Milwaukee: 1987–1997*. Milwaukee, Wis.: University of Wisconsin–Milwaukee Center for Economic Development, 1999, https://www4.uwm.edu/ced/publica tions.cfm.

———. *The Two Milwaukees: Separate and Unequal*. Milwaukee, Wis.: University of Wisconsin–Milwaukee Center for Economic Development, 2003, http://www4 .uwm.edu/ced/pdf/two_milwaukee.pdf.

Levine, Marc V., Lisa Heuler Williams, and Catherine Madison. *The State of Black-Owned Businesses in Milwaukee*. Milwaukee, Wis.: University of Wisconsin-Milwaukee Center for Economic Development, 2013, https://www4.uwm.edu /ced/publications.cfm.

Link, Bruce G., and Jo C. Phelan. "Labeling and Stigma." In *The Handbook of the Sociology of Mental Health*, 2nd ed., edited by Carol S. Aneshensel, Jo C. Phelan, and Alex Bierman, 525–41. Dordrecht, Netherlands: Springer, 2013.

Lofland, Lyn H. *A World of Strangers: Order and Action in Urban Public Space*. New York: Basic Books, 1973.

Logan, John R. "Ethnic Diversity Grows, Neighborhood Integration Lags Behind." State University of New York, Albany: Lewis Mumford Center, 2011.

Logan, John R., and Brian J. Stults. *The Persistence of Segregation in the Metropolis: New Findings from the 2010 Census*. US2010 Project Report, Brown University, 2011.

Logan, John R., Brian J. Stults, and Reynolds Farley. "Segregation of Minorities in the Metropolis: Two Decades of Change." *Demography* 41 (2004): 1–22.

Logan, John R., and Charles Zhang. "Global Neighborhoods: New Pathways to Diversity and Separation." *American Journal of Sociology* 115 (2010): 1069–109.

Ludwig, Jens, Jeffrey B. Liebman, Jeffrey R. Kling, Greg J. Duncan, Lawrence F. Katz, Ronald C. Kessler, and Lisa Sanbonmatsu. "What Can We Learn about

Neighborhood Effects from the Moving to Opportunity Experiment?" *American Journal of Sociology* 114 (2008): 144–88.

Maly, Michael T. *Beyond Segregation: Multiracial and Multiethnic Neighborhoods in the United States*. Philadelphia: Temple University Press, 2005.

Marti, Gerardo, and Michael O. Emerson. "The Rise of the Diversity Expert: How American Evangelicals Simultaneously Accentuate and Ignore Race." In *The New Social Engagement*, edited by Brian Steensland and Philip Goff, 179–99. Oxford: Oxford University Press, 2014.

Massey, Douglas S., and Nancy A. Denton. *American Apartheid*. Cambridge, Mass.: Harvard University Press, 1993.

Massey, Douglas S., and Mary J. Fischer. "The Geography of Inequality in the United States, 1950–2000." In *Brookings-Wharton Papers on Urban Affairs: 2003*, edited by William G. Gale and Janet Rothenberg Pack, 1–40. Washington, D.C.: Brookings Institution, 2003.

Mattson, Greggor. "Urban Ethnography's 'Saloon Problem' and Its Challenge to Public Sociology." *City and Community* 6 (2007): 75–94.

Maxwell, Joseph A. *Qualitative Research Design: An Interactive Approach*. Thousand Oaks, Calif.: Sage, 1996.

Mayorga-Gallo, Sarah. *Behind the White Picket Fence: Power and Privilege in a Multiethnic Neighborhood*. Chapel Hill: University of North Carolina Press, 2014.

Modan, Gabriella Gahlia. *Turf Wars: Discourse, Diversity, and the Politics of Place*. Maldan, Mass.: Blackwell, 2007.

Murphy, Alexandra. " 'Litterers': How Objects of Physical Disorder Are Used to Construct Subjects of Social Disorder in a Suburb." *Annals of the American Academy of Political and Social Science* 642 (2012): 210–27.

Nachmias, Chava, and J. John Palen. "Membership in Voluntary Neighborhood Associations and Urban Revitalization." *Policy Sciences* 14 (1982): 179–93.

Newman, Katherine. *No Shame in My Game: The Working Poor in the Inner City*. New York: Knopf, 1999.

Nyden, Philip, John Lukehart, Michael T. Maly, and William Peterman. "Conclusion." *Cityscape* 4 (1998): 261–69.

Oakley, Deirdre, James Fraser, and Joshua Bazuin. "The Imagined Self-Sufficient Communities of HOPE VI: Examining the Community and Social Support (CSS) Component." *Urban Affairs Review* 51 (2015): 726–46.

Oldenburg, Ray. *The Great Good Place*. New York: Paragon, 1989.

Oliver, J. Eric. *The Paradoxes of Integration: Race, Neighborhood and Civic Life in Multiethnic America*. Chicago: University of Chicago Press, 2010.

Oliver, J. Eric, and Janelle Wong. "Intergroup Prejudice in Multiethnic Settings." *American Journal of Political Science* 47 (2003): 567–82.

Patterson, Orlando. *The Ordeal of Integration: Progress and Resentment in America's Racial Crisis*. Washington D.C.: Civitas/Counterpoint, 1997.

Pattillo, Mary. *Black on the Block: The Politics of Race and Class in the City*. Chicago: University of Chicago Press, 2007.

———. *Black Picket Fences: Privilege and Peril among the Black Middle Class*. Chicago: University of Chicago Press, 1999.

———. "Sweet Mothers and Gangbangers: Managing Crime in a Black Middle-Class Neighborhood." *Social Forces* 76 (1998): 747–74.

Pawasarat, John, and Lois Quinn. *Wisconsin's Mass Incarceration of African American Males: Workforce Challenges for 2013*. Milwaukee: University of Wisconsin–Milwaukee Employment and Training Institute, 2013.

Pescosolido, Bernice A., Jack K. Martin, Annie Lang, and Sigrun Olafsdottir. "Rethinking Theoretical Approaches to Stigma: A Framework Integrating Normative Influences on Stigma (FINIS)." *Social Science and Medicine* 67 (2008): 431–40.

Petersen, Erin. "Historic Milwaukee Asks: 'What Is Riverwest?'" *Urban Milwaukee Dial*, March 28, 2011, http://urbanmilwaukeedial.com/2011/03/28/historic-mil waukee-asks-what-is-riverwest/.

Peterson, Ruth D., and Lauren J. Krivo. "Macro-structural Analyses of Race, Ethnicity and Violent Crime: Recent Lessons and New Directions for Research." *Annual Review of Sociology* 31 (2005): 331–56.

Pratt, Travis C., and Francis T. Cullen. "Assessing Macro-level Predictors and Theories of Crime: A Meta-analysis." In *Crime and Justice: A Review of Research*, edited by Michael Tonry, 373–450. Chicago: University of Chicago Press, 2006.

Public Policy Forum. *Interdistrict Chapter 220: Changing Goals and Perspectives*. January 2000, http://publicpolicyforum.org/sites/default/files/interdistrict220 .pdf.

———. *Race Relations Survey: Overview and Summary*. November 2006, http://www .publicpolicyforum.org/sites/default/files/2006RaceRelationsSurvey.pdf.

Putnam, Robert D. "*E Pluribus Unum*: Diversity and Community in the Twenty-First Century." *Scandinavian Political Studies* 30 (2007): 137–74.

Quillian, Lincoln, and Devah Pager. "Black Neighbors, Higher Crime? The Role of Racial Stereotypes in Evaluations of Neighborhood Crime." *American Journal of Sociology* 107 (2001): 717–67.

Reardon, Sean F., and Kendra Bischoff. "Growth in the Residential Segregation of Families by Income, 1970–2009." US2010 Project, Brown University, 2011.

Rich, Meghan Ashlin. "'It Depends on How You Define Integrated': Neighborhood Boundaries and Racial Integration in a Baltimore Neighborhood." *Sociological Forum* 24 (2009): 828–53.

Ridgeway, Cecilia L. "Why Status Matters for Inequality." *American Review of Sociology* 79 (2014): 1–16.

Roberts, Dorothy E. "Race, Vagueness, and the Social Meaning of Order-Maintenance Policing." *Journal of Criminal Law and Criminology* 89 (1999): 775–836.

Romell, Rick. "Drinking Deeply Ingrained in Wisconsin's Culture." *Milwaukee Journal Sentinel*, October 19, 2008, http://www.jsonline.com/news/wisconsin /31237904.html.

Roncek, Dennis W., and Pamela A. Maier. "Bars, Blocks, and Crimes Revisited: Linking the Theory of Routine Activities to the Empiricism of 'Hot Spots.'" *Criminology* 29 (1991): 725–53.

Roncek, Dennis W., and Mitchell A. Pravatiner. "Additional Evidence That Taverns Enhance Nearby Crime." *Sociology and Social Research* 73 (1989): 185–88.

Room, Robin. "Stigma, Social Inequality and Alcohol and Drug Use." *Drug and Alcohol Review* 24 (2009): 143–55.

Ross, Catherine E., and John Mirowsky. "Neighborhood Disadvantage, Disorder, and Health." *Journal of Health and Social Behavior* 42 (2001): 258–76.

Sampson, Robert J. "Collective Regulation of Adolescent Misbehavior: Validation Results from Eighty Chicago Neighborhoods." *Journal of Adolescent Research* 12 (1997): 227–44.

———. "Disparity and Diversity in the Contemporary City: Social (Dis)order Revisited." *British Journal of Sociology* 60 (2009): 1–31.

———. *Great American City: Chicago and the Enduring Neighborhood Effect.* Chicago: University of Chicago Press, 2012.

———. "Moving to Inequality: Neighborhood Effects and Experiments Meet Social Structure." *American Journal of Sociology* 114 (2008): 189–231.

———. "Organized for What? Recasting Theories of Social (Dis)Organization." In *Advances in Criminological Theory*, vol. 10, edited by Elin Waring and David Weisburd, 95–110. New Brunswick, N.J.: Transaction, 2002.

Sampson Robert J., and Dawn Jeglum Bartusch. "Legal Cynicism and (Subcultural?) Tolerance of Deviance: The Neighborhood Context of Racial Differences." *Law and Society Review* 32 (1998): 777–804.

Sampson, Robert J., and Byron W. Groves. "Community Structure and Crime: Testing Social-Disorganization Theory." *American Journal of Sociology* 94 (1989): 774–802.

Sampson, Robert J., Jeffrey D. Morenoff, and Thomas Gannon-Rowley. "Assessing Neighborhood Effects: Social Processes and New Directions in Research." *Annual Review of Sociology* 28 (2002): 443–78.

Sampson, Robert J., and Stephen Raudenbush. "Seeing Disorder: Neighborhood Stigma and the Social Construction of Broken Windows." *Social Psychology Quarterly* 67 (2004): 319–42.

———. "Systematic Social Observation of Public Spaces: A New Look at Disorder in Urban Neighborhoods." *American Journal of Sociology* 105 (1999): 603–51.

Sampson, Robert J., Stephen W. Raudenbush, and Felton Earls. "Neighborhoods and Violent Crime: A Multilevel Study of Collective Efficacy." *Science* 227 (1997): 918–24.

Sawyer, Liz. "Twelve of Twenty Drunkest Cities in America Are in Wisconsin." *Star Tribune*, May 19, 2016.

Schelling, Thomas C. "Dynamic Models of Segregation." *Journal of Mathematical Sociology* 1 (1971): 143–86.

Schmidt, Deanna H. "The Practices and Process of Neighborhood: The (Re)Production of Riverwest, Milwaukee, Wisconsin." *Urban Geography* 29 (2008): 473–95.

Schomerus, Georg, Christian Schwahn, Anita Holzinger, Patrick Corrigan, Hans Grabe, Mauro Giovanni Carta, and Matthias C. Angermeyer. "Evolution of Public Attitudes about Mental Illness: A Systematic Review and Meta-analysis." *Acta Psychiactria Scandinavia* 125 (2012): 440–52.

Schwalbe, Michael, Sandra Godwin, Daphne Holden, Douglas Schrock, Shealy Thompson, and Michelle Wolkomir. "Generic Processes in the Reproduction of Inequality: An Interactionist Analysis." *Social Forces* 79 (2000): 419–52.

Sennett, Richard. *The Uses of Disorder: Personal Identity and City Life*. New York: W. W. Norton, 1970.

Sewell, William H., Jr. "The Concept(s) of Culture." In *Beyond the Cultural Turn*, edited by Victoria E. Bonnell and Lynn Hunt, 35–61. Berkeley: University of California Press, 1999.

Sharkey, Patrick. "Residential Mobility and the Reproduction of Unequal Neighborhoods." *Cityscape* 114 (2012): 9–32.

———. *Stuck in Place: Urban Neighborhoods and the End of Progress toward Racial Equality*. Chicago: University of Chicago Press, 2013.

Sharkey, Patrick, and Jacob W. Faber. "Where, When, Why, and for Whom Do Residential Contexts Matter? Moving Away from the Dichotomous Understanding of Neighborhood Effects." *Annual Review of Sociology* 40 (2014): 559–79.

Sharkey, Patrick, and Bryan Graham. *Mobility and the Metropolis: How Communities Factor into Economic Mobility*. Washington, D.C.: Pew Charitable Trusts, 2013.

Shaw, Clifford R., and Henry D. McKay. *Juvenile Delinquency and Urban Areas*. Chicago: University of Chicago Press, 1942.

Sigelman, Lee, and Susan Welch. "The Contact Hypothesis Revisited: Interracial Contact and Positive Racial Attitudes." *Social Forces* 71 (1993): 781–95.

Simmel, Georg. *Conflict and the Web of Group Affiliations*. 1908. Reprint, Glencoe, Ill.: Free Press, 1955.

———. "The Metropolis and Mental Life." 1903. Reprinted in *Metropolis: Center and Symbol of Our Times*, edited by Philip Kasinitz, 30–45. New York: New York University Press, 1995.

Skerry, Peter. "Beyond Sushiology: Does Diversity Work?" *Brookings Review* 20 (Winter 2002): 20.

Skogan, Wesley G. *Disorder and Decline: Crime and the Spiral of Decay in American Cities*. Berkeley: University of California Press, 1990.

Small, Mario L. "Culture, Cohorts, and Social Organization Theory: Understanding Local Participation in a Latino Housing Project." *American Journal of Sociology* 108 (2002): 1–54.

———. " 'How Many Cases Do I Need?' On Science and the Logic of Case Selection in Field-Based Research." *Ethnography* 10 (2009): 5–38.

———. "Lost in Translation: How Not to Make Qualitative Research More Scientific." In *Workshop on Interdisciplinary Standards for Systematic Qualitative Research*, edited by M. Lamont and P. White, 165–71. Washington, D.C.: National Science Foundation, 2008.

————. *Villa Victoria: The Transformation of Social Capital in a Boston Barrio.* Chicago: University of Chicago Press, 2004.

Small, Mario L., and Jessica Feldman. "Ethnographic Evidence, Heterogeneity, and Neighbourhood Effects after Moving to Opportunity." In *Neighbourhood Effects Research: New Perspectives*, edited by Maarten van Ham, David Manley, Nick Bailey, Ludi Simpson, and Duncan Maclennan, 57–77. Dordrecht, Netherlands: Springer, 2012.

Small, Mario L., and Katherine Newman. "Urban Poverty after *The Truly Disadvantaged*: The Rediscovery of the Family, Neighborhood and Culture." *Annual Review of Sociology* 27 (2001): 23–45.

Smith, Allison L. "Racist Fliers Evoke Anger from Riverwest Residents; Police Investigating Source of Message." *Milwaukee Journal Sentinel*, July 13, 2003, 02B.

Social Issues Research Centre. *Social and Cultural Aspects of Drinking: A Report to the European Commission.* March 1998. http://www.sirc.org/publik/social _drinking.pdf.

Stolle, Dietland, Stuart Soroka, and Richard Johnston. "When Does Diversity Erode Trust? Neighborhood Diversity, Interpersonal Trust and the Mediating Effect of Social Interactions." *Political Studies* 56 (2008): 57–75.

Suttles, Gerald D. *The Social Construction of Communities.* Chicago: University of Chicago Press, 1972.

————. *The Social Order of the Slum: Ethnicity and Territory in the Inner City.* Chicago: University of Chicago Press, 1968.

Swanstrom, Todd, Colleen Casey, Robert Flack, and Peter Dreier. *Pulling Apart: Economic Segregation among Suburbs and Central Cities in Major Metropolitan Areas.* Washington, D.C.: Brookings Institution Center on Urban and Metropolitan Policy, 2004.

Swaroop, Sapna, and Jeffrey Morenoff. "Building Community: The Neighborhood Context of Social Organization." *Social Forces* 84 (2006): 1665–95.

Tach, Laura. "Diversity, Inequality, and Microsegregation: Dynamics of Inclusion and Exclusion in a Racially and Economically Diverse Community." *Cityscape* 16 (2014): 13–45.

————. "More Than Bricks and Mortar: Neighborhood Frames, Social Processes, and the Mixed-Income Redevelopment of a Public Housing Project." *City and Community* 8 (2009): 273–303.

Taub, Richard P., D. Garth Taylor, and Jan D. Dunham. *Paths of Neighborhood Change.* Chicago: University of Chicago Press, 1984.

Taylor, Ralph B. "Social Order and Disorder of Street Blocks and Neighborhoods: Ecology, Microecology, and the Systemic Model of Social Disorganization." *Journal of Research in Crime and Delinquency* 34 (1997): 113–55.

Taylor, Ralph B., Stephen D. Gottfredson, and Sidney Brower. "Block Crime and Fear: Defensible Space, Local Social Ties, and Territorial Functioning." *Journal of Research in Crime and Delinquency* 21 (1984): 303–31.

Tolan, Tom. *Riverwest: A Community History.* Milwaukee: Past Press, 2003.

Tönnies, Ferdinand. *Gemeinschaft und Gesellschaft*. 1887. Reprinted as *Community and Society*, translated and edited by Charles P. Loomis. New York: Harper Touchbooks, 1957.

Turner, Margery Austin, and Julie Fenderson. *Understanding Diverse Neighborhoods in an Era of Demographic Change*. Washington, D.C.: Urban Institute, 2006.

Turner, Margery Austin, and Stephen L. Ross. "How Racial Discrimination Affects the Search for Housing." In *The Geography of Opportunity*, edited by Xavier de Souza Briggs, 81–100. Washington, D.C.: Brookings Institution, 2005.

Valverde, Mariana. *Everyday Law on the Street: City Governance in an Age of Diversity*. Chicago: University of Chicago Press, 2012.

Venkatesh, Sudhir A. *American Project: The Rise and Fall of a Modern Ghetto*. Cambridge, Mass.: Harvard University Press, 2000.

Wacquant, Loïc. "Urban Desolation and Symbolic Denigration in the Hyperghetto." *Social Psychology Quarterly* 20 (2010): 1–5.

Wallace, Danielle. "A Test of the Routine Activities and Neighborhood Attachment Explanations for Bias in Disorder Perceptions." *Crime and Delinquency* 61 (2015): 587–609.

Warner, Barbara D., and Glenn L. Pierce. "Reexamining Social Disorganization Theory Using Calls to the Police as a Measure of Crime." *Criminology* 31 (1993): 493–517.

Warner, Barbara D., and Pamela Wilcox Rountree. "Local Social Ties in a Community and Crime Model: Questioning the Systemic Nature of Informal Social Control." *Social Problems* 44 (1997): 520–36.

Weber, Max. *The City*. Translated and edited by Don Martindale and Gertrud Neuwirth. 1922. Reprint, New York: Free Press, 1956.

Weiss, Robert S. 1994. *Learning from Strangers*. New York: Free Press.

Welch, Susan, Lee Sigelman, Timothy Bledsoe, and Michael Combs. *Race and Place: Race Relations in an American City*. New York: Cambridge University Press, 2001.

White, Garland F., Randy R. Gainey, and Ruth A. Triplett. "Alcohol Outlets and Neighborhood Crime: A Longitudinal Analysis." *Crime and Delinquency* 61 (2015): 851–72.

White, William L. "Long-Term Strategies to Reduce the Stigma Attached to Addiction, Treatment, and Recovery within the City of Philadelphia." Philadelphia Department of Behavioral Health and Mental Retardation Services, 2009.

Whyte, William F. *Street Corner Society*. Chicago: University of Chicago Press, 1943.

Wilson, James Q., and George L. Kelling. "Broken Windows." *Atlantic Monthly*, March 1983, 29–38.

Wilson, William Julius, and Richard P. Taub. *There Goes the Neighborhood*. New York: Alfred A. Knopf, 2006.

Wirth, Louis. "Urbanism as a Way of Life." *American Journal of Sociology* 44 (1938): 1–24.

Woldoff, Rachael A. *White Flight/Black Flight: The Dynamics of Racial Change in an American Neighborhood.* Ithaca, N.Y.: Cornell University Press, 2011.

Young, Iris Marion. *Justice and the Politics of Difference.* Princeton, N.J.: Princeton University Press, 1990.

Zeidenburg, Matthew. *Moving Outward: The Shifting Landscape of Poverty in Milwaukee.* Madison, Wisc.: Center on Wisconsin Strategy, 2004, www.cows.org/pdf/rp-conpoverty04.pdf.

Zukin, Sharon. *Naked City: The Death and Life of Authentic Urban Places.* New York: Oxford University Press, 2010.

Index

Page numbers for figures and tables are indicated by *f* and *t*.

72872821R00150